MARK N SPENCER

Ocean of Self

BENEATH THE WAVES OF OUR INDIVIDUAL SELVES

© 2019 Copyright Mark N Spencer

Mark N Spencer asserts the moral right to be identified as the author of *'Ocean of Self'*

Design and typeset by Green Avenue Design

Published by Mark N Spencer

ISBN: 978-0-9954138-1-8

All rights reserved. No part of this publication may be reproduced, stored in a retrieval system, or transmitted, in any form or by any means, electronic, mechanical, photocopying, recording or otherwise, without the prior permission of the author or publishers.

Cover photo
Surya Namaskara ("Sun Salute")

The ocean diver salutes the sun, whose rays penetrate the ocean and infuse it with life. The 'outer' sun is symbolic of our 'inner' sun – the light of life or the 'light of God' that lies within all of us. Cover design by Evan Shapiro. Original photo by Becca Saunders.

for Becca

> *"There are more things in heaven and earth, Horatio, than are dreamt of in your philosophy."*
>
> – Hamlet, William Shakespeare

CONTENTS

Overview 1

Chapter One
An Ocean of Life – Life Begins in the Sea 15

Chapter Two
Ocean mythology 33

Chapter Three
Waves 45

Chapter Four
Life Expresses More Life 55

Chapter Five
Sharks 65

Chapter Six
Manta Rays – Angels of the Sea..79

Chapter Seven
Shipwreck Exploration – the Risks and Rewards 93

Chapter Eight
The Shipwreck Experience 109

Chapter Nine
Modern science – Part one
The progress of science towards unity 121

Chapter Ten
Modern Science – Part Two
Superstring theory and cosmology: unifying the large and the small 149

Chapter Eleven
Vedic Science – Part one
Consciousness as the Universe's basic ingredient 167

Chapter Twelve
Vedic Science – Part two
Consciousness as the Universe's basic ingredient 183

Chapter Thirteen
The Maharishi Effect...201

Chapter Fourteen
Levitation and flying..229

Chapter Fifteen
Paranormal experiences in extreme environments 255

Chapter Sixteen
Diving into the Ocean of Self 271

Chapter Seventeen
God, Life and Love – An Ocean of Life 303

Postscript 327

Appendix
The Seven States of Consciousness 330

Glossary 337

Acknowledgements 339

Some chapters in this book will have references to short video presentations. Use this QR code to gain direct access to the author's YouTube channel where you will identify the relevant presentation.

Overview

Some memories pull you back again and again. It's like being drawn to certain pictures on a wall, down a corridor that represents life's journey.

In one such picture, I was 10. My grandmother had taken my younger sister and me on a ferry journey across the harbour from Circular Quay in the busy commercial hub of Sydney, to Manly on the north side. Manly was a fun place for a young boy. There were fun rides, visits to the Manly Aquarium[1] with its display of menacing-looking sharks, stingrays and turtles, the surf beach a short walk away and the busy activity of ferries, boats, swimmers and tourists on the harbour. Leaning over a stone breakwater near Manly's ferry terminal, I looked down onto the shimmering, opaque surface of Sydney Harbour, and wondered what mysteries lay hidden underneath. I knew there was another world down there out of sight and mind to most terrestrials.

A desire to know what lies hidden beneath our normal superficial view of things has prevailed throughout my life. As a boy I was always the young scientist, day-dreaming about owning a laboratory, doing important experiments and making discoveries. But I never became a scientist. Instead I pursued a career in clinical dentistry, following in the footsteps of my father and his father before him.

I did, however, plunge into the mysterious depths of the ocean as a dedicated diver. I learned to scuba dive in 1974, and pursued it with enthusiasm. My friends and I would – in the early years of diving – plunge ourselves off ocean rock platforms to enter and exit our ocean playground. Often, as an exercise – without scuba cylinders and wearing only protective wetsuits, fins and gloves – we would jump off the rocks into the heaving ocean and then allow the waves to deposit us back onto the rock platform. We would even hold hands and do this in unison. Bad timing or a bad choice of wave gave us some bruises, but it was all fun and all part of gaining confidence in the sea.

Before long I was taking a camera to record what I saw while diving and learn more about the creatures I came across. I soon acquired a taste for the adventure and discovery associated with undersea exploration, and sharing these discoveries with others through my photography became a lifelong passion and a parallel vocation with my professional life as a dental surgeon.

I would eventually see these photographs published in respected journals like those of the National Geographic and Australian Geographic societies. Photographic assignments and sponsored diving projects (mainly through the support of the Australian Geographic Society) gave my diving career extra focus and the ability to engage friends in teamwork towards a satisfying goal.

This photograph was taken from under Sydney Harbour, very near where I looked over the stone parapet as a young boy, wondering what was under the surface. From this perspective, the terrestrial world above – with Manly's Ferris wheel in view – looks more ethereal and less real than the world beneath.

As my familiarity and confidence in the ocean grew with experience, I was soon introduced to shipwreck diving, which usually meant diving to greater depths. At first, we would explore scuttled hulks or genuine wrecks using compressed air breathed from a single scuba tank. Then, as we descended further – to explore even deeper wrecks – we wore two tanks for the extra air we needed at depth, and also to allow time for the inevitable decompression stops needed to avoid the bends.

I would soon extend my skills to freshwater cave-diving, for which special training and certification was required. Flooded caves are usually pitch black with absolutely no penetration of sunlight, and the entrance is often the only safe exit. Getting lost in such an environment with a limited air supply is not an option. Cave-diving is definitely not for the claustrophobic! However, this foreboding underground world can delight the explorer with mineral sculptures that have taken Earth hundreds of thousands of years to shape. It's also a world that can re-set a diver's appreciation of the passage of time from a human scale to a much vaster one.

I placed my camera on a tall tripod for this underwater shot, and "painted" light using a flash-gun throughout this section of McCavity Cave in Wellington, NSW, Australia, capturing myself as a silhouette against the wall to the left. The large calcite decoration at centre is known as a "pendant drapery" and has been estimated to be some 200,000 years in formation during the dry period of the cave before the last ice-age.[2]

With some effort, I'm exiting the flooded McCavity Cave. The tight canal through which I am squeezing is appropriately called "The Birth Canal". I was part of a team exploratory and research project supported by Australian Geographic during 1992-1994. Photo by Rob Featonby.

The ocean, however, was where I spent most of my time underwater. Around the mid-1990s, my wreck-diving friends and I undertook training in the use of specially mixed breathing gases – helium, oxygen and air – to more safely manage deeper plunges into the ocean. Mistakes in blending or not carefully checking the gas in our breathing mixture could be fatal, and it resulted in the deaths of some friends and acquaintances.

As THE YEARS AND DECADES PASSED, I CONTINUED TO PRECARIOUSLY balance the high demands of my dental career and my passion for ocean exploration and underwater photography. But – as busy as I was with these pursuits – I found time for another discipline.

A few years after I graduated from university, I read an article in *Reader's Digest* about a meditation technique known as Transcendental Meditation (TM). I read that it had been introduced to the western world by an Indian scholar by the name of Maharishi Mahesh Yogi. I was aware that this man had been involved with The Beatles. I was intrigued by the evidence-based claims of improved self-actualisation, improved health and sense of wellbeing, greater stamina and clarity of mind.

I had been brought up a Catholic and had no wish to embrace another religion, but the article stated that Transcendental Meditation was not a religion and that it did not matter whether one was religious or non-religious – it was a secular technique for the natural resting of the mind to achieve a highly beneficial state of consciousness that came with a whole bunch of health benefits. I was intrigued.

After talking to a doctor friend of mine who practised TM, I was assured of the wisdom of learning this life skill and started in 1981. I have virtually not stopped since!

I recall once stopping my meditation practice for a number of months, perhaps a year after I learned the technique. It was my own experiment to see if it really was giving me benefits. I was reassured by this test and took it up again, disciplining myself to practise the technique twice a day for 20 minutes each time.

THE TM TEACHERS PROVIDED SOME BASIC KNOWLEDGE TO HELP NEW meditators understand what was going on when they 'transcended' – meaning to 'go beyond' or 'pass through the superficial levels of familiar wakeful consciousness'. They would speak of an 'ocean' or 'pond' of consciousness with all our busy mental activity happening at the top, just like busy ocean waves on the surface of the ocean depths. Thoughts, they said, were like incipient bubbles arising from the depths of this ocean, getting bigger as they reached the surface. Transcendence was the reversal of this process –moving deeper and deeper into the silent realms of the mind, where the bubbles of thought become less dominating. Often while 'diving' into the silent depths of my own awareness, I find myself attached to a thought again and brought to the surface. TM meditators are taught to then go back to repeating a non-sensible word that acts as a vehicle for the mind to dive back into the depths.

It was a silent, peaceful world down there in the depths of my consciousness. It reminded me of a similar silence and peace I encountered while scuba diving or free-diving. When diving into the watery ocean, I became very present – 'in the moment' – just as I did while meditating. It didn't seem to matter if I was burdened with problems on the surface. They all became irrelevant as soon as I plunged underwater. I also experienced silence, freedom, unboundedness and even a sense of unity – a sense of greater 'being' that transcended my small self. It's a sense of belonging to something larger.

The correlation captured my interest. One diving medium – the ocean – was very physical, the other more nebulous and abstract. Could the two possibly be related?

THIS BOOK HAS RESULTED FROM MY RESEARCH INTO THAT CORRELATION. The curiosity I expressed as a young boy for what lies under the surface of Sydney Harbour culminated in my becoming an underwater explorer. Little did I know then that those acquired skills in ocean exploration plus my acquisition of an effective meditation technique would equip me in dealing with my later curiosity for what lies beneath the superficial sensory-dependant levels of conscious awareness.

Just recently, I was reading a newsletter[3] of the Explorers Club to which I belong as an international fellow. The president of the club reiterated the sentiments of some prominent fellow explorers. "An essential character of any explorer is curiosity acted upon," he wrote. "The question of what makes the world tick is the universal bond that connects explorers." If we accept those criteria, then the examination of consciousness should also be considered valid exploration.

While I accept that the disciplined approach of neuroscience is making great progress in our understanding of the workings of the brain and is important research, I do not believe that the 'source' of consciousness is going to be found only "between the ears".

The special transcendent experiences I've had while diving underwater, in meditation and increasingly in ordinary day-to-day life activities, have been very real. I find it difficult to accept these experiences as mere constructs of neuronal activity in my brain. You may well have had similar experiences which you have either dismissed as irrational or simply pushed aside for lack of any satisfying explanation. My desire to understand the rationale of these experiences has made it impossible for me to simply dismiss them. The experiences suggest to me a broader foundation to the materialistic framework upon which we normally view reality – a reality that includes not only those things outside us, but that which we define as our 'self'.

This book will explore the nature of consciousness, spirituality and life itself, but not in a doctrinal or religious sense. My interest in the physical sciences has led me to a point where I can reconcile some of the amazing discoveries of modern science with the age-old descriptions and explanations resulting from the subjective exploration of consciousness. For this understanding, I have drawn on the knowledge of both Maharishi Mahesh Yogi and renowned physicist Dr John Hagelin who worked closely with Maharishi.

I believe that an intellectual and experiential understanding of the ocean of consciousness that constitutes the 'self' will allow us to see how spirituality fits in with the material world we all know. Our planet's ocean is a great metaphor to explain consciousness as I and many learned scholars see it. That is why an ocean diver is telling this story.

As far back as the early 1990s, I was giving public talks about my diving adventures, but becoming bored with simply showing nice photographs and talking about the technicalities of diving. There was a more important message I felt I had to convey – a message that I thought everyone would want to hear. So, I attempted to communicate my interpretation of the transcendent experiences associated with deep ocean diving. I even put together a three-projector slide show with programmed slide transitions and accompanying music to help my audience get in the mood. This was the era before digital photography and projection. At times I had some big audiences, such as at a major national diving congress in Sydney and a gathering of members of the Australian Geographic Society. Sadly – and at times even embarrassingly – I was unsuccessful in conveying my message to the majority. I couldn't help but notice the uncomfortable fidgeting of friends and acquaintances in the audience. It seemed to me that the very mention of words like 'consciousness', 'death', 'meditation' or 'spirituality' were still taboo subjects. My friends told me that they had come to look at my photographs and hear about our projects, not to hear about philosophy. Clearly, I had to improve my delivery of this challenging topic.

A few people did come up to me after these presentations indicating that they appreciated what I was trying to communicate and asking me if I was ever going to publish anything on these ideas. They were almost all women. I think women are generally more open to new ideas and concepts – especially those connected with feelings.

I soon discovered that I was not entirely alone in this desire to examine a deeper – even spiritual – connection with the environment around us, whether it be the ocean, the mountains, rainforests, the cosmos, or our fellow humans.

In the *Explorers Journal*[4], an article written by Sir Walter (Wally) Herbert (1934–2007) titled 'Ice Dreams' assured me I was not the only soul who desired to make a deeper connection between what was experienced in extreme environments (in my case, the deep ocean) and what we can learn about our own nature and connection with that environment.

Sir Walter was a British explorer with an incredible pedigree of achievement in polar exploration during the middle of the 20th century. He is now widely recognised as being the first man to walk to the North Pole[5], with Robert Cleary's claim in official dispute. He was also a talented artist who used pencils and scalpel, or paint, to create amazing portraits of his fellow team members, polar bears and the beautiful but harsh environment of the Arctic.

During Sir Walter's explorations, little attention was given to spiritual matters or 'connection' with nature. But in his bravely honest article, Sir Walter mentions that it was times outside his comfort zone in dangerous environments when he learned that "harmony with nature was critical to exploration. Without it, experiences were meaningless". He goes on to say that it was possibly the time he spent with the Inuit people that taught him to "tune into nature".

At the end of his article, Sir Walter issues a challenge to fellow explorers: "Perhaps the time has come for the next generation of explorers to shift their focus from the physical poles of the past toward spiritual goals. I know for a fact that the 'third pole', the mystical one, is far more elusive than the other two. So there is the challenge. Go find it!"

I had already taken up that challenge and had to agree with Sir Walter that it was indeed a difficult challenge, pursuing an elusive goal. I always believed that it could be done however, and that is what this book aims to do.

Sir Walter also wrote: "Perhaps my shift in consciousness was also influenced by Sir Laurens van der Post, who had urged me to look between the lines for what explorers so often kept to themselves – their secret sense of mission".

After I read Sir Walter's article, I couldn't wait to communicate with him myself. As a fellow member of the Explorers Club, I emailed him to enthusiastically support what he had written and to tell him I too was exploring that path of knowledge and wisdom. He emailed back saying that he had written more in that article, but that some of it had been edited out and that he would send me his unedited submission. I received a package in the mail of some other published material, but never received the unedited version of his article. Sir Walter passed away in 2007. I wish I had had the opportunity to meet this great man in person.

THAT "SECRET SENSE OF MISSION" TO WHICH HE REFERRED IS CLEARLY evident when you read or hear the stories of many explorers. Not having an intellectual or conceptual framework upon which to hang their special experiences, they use poetic expression or metaphor that hints of their perception of a broader reality or spiritual dimension. Typically they won't elaborate on their experiences – western culture has never encouraged that. The English language itself is ill-equipped to handle any description of spiritual experience. These explorers might only attempt a few words in reference to what has been called the "ineffable".

In my own attempt to draw out their perceptions, and make more concrete the possibilities their hints of a broader reality suggest, I will not only look between the lines of what other explorers say, but also of what poets, philosophers and scientists say in their own (sometimes brief) intellectual excursions beyond the confining parameters of the predominant world view.

From these poets and scientists, there are many, many such suggestions of a broader reality base to our generally agreed paradigm (or conceptual framework) of how the world works. I will therefore use quotations from poets, philosophers, scientists, saints and sages. Some of the more exquisite quotations – "a list of quotations beautiful from minds profound"[6] – I will confine to their own page. They are worth framing for study and contemplation. Poetry, like any other art form, attempts to convey the shadows and hidden agendas, the ethereal limits of our every-day perceptions and beyond. So, too, do the profound comments of wise scientists and philosophers, past and present.

I will attempt the difficult task of exploring the nature of consciousness as something more than a by-product of the brain. Through a deeper understanding of consciousness, I will explore the realm of spirituality and how spirituality actually underpins what we call the "real" world. It isn't the other way around. Please don't feel uncomfortable here. I'm not referring to religion per se, and I certainly have no religious agenda. While some commentators will have a dig at my "new age" thoughts in attempting to make a distinction between religion and spirituality, I clearly see a marked difference between the two. Sadly, religion has increasingly distanced and often discouraged personal spiritual experience, with its doctrines, rituals and Cartesian[7] attitude of separating things physical or things 'of this Earth' from 'heavenly' things. The knowledge unfolded in this book should not be seen as mere dabbling in eastern mysticism, but as a universal understanding that can and should become the foundation for the wisdom taught by the major religions.

WHY HAVE I TRIED TO TACKLE SUCH AN INTANGIBLE TOPIC? WELL, FIRST of all, I have a basic curiosity about how the world works. Since the Enlightenment, we've mostly looked at parts of the world in an analytical way[8]. I'm using a synthetic approach in looking at how we connect all the parts and examine their relationship to each other. Those parts include you and me – the observers as well as what we observe.

But there is more to my motivation than just curiosity. As long as we seek better solutions to our physical and mental health; as long as we seek workable solutions to seemingly never-ending conflict arising from political or ideological disparity; and as long as we continue questioning whether there is a spiritual dimension to our lives and if so, how it fits into our lives; then the knowledge uncovered in this book is essential.

I can assure you I am not the only one attempting to get this message across. This knowledge has been available to us for centuries. Look particularly at the wealth of knowledge and wisdom in the publications of Deepak Chopra and Neale Donald Walsch. I'm not a qualified expert in physics and I'm not an official guru or scholar in eastern mysticism. I am just bringing to you the age-old wisdom of consciousness – found in Vedic science – from the point of view of an ocean diver who meditates. I will use the ocean and my diving experiences as a metaphor to help explore and explain this knowledge.

For the scientifically curious, the book will review physics and its evolution over the last few centuries. We'll look at quantum field theory and cosmology. I've included brief overviews at the beginning of these 'modern' science chapters, but it is my hope that you gain at least some comprehension of the content, as it is relevant to the following chapters on Vedic Science.

Disciplined physicists – generally among the smartest of academics around, working in arguably the hardest and most exacting of the sciences – probably feel that their science has been hijacked by an increasing number of new-age philosophers like me. But over the past century physics has uncovered a reality that is radically different to our normal materialistic frame of reference. We're talking about a reality that is without the dimensions of time and space, without anything 'solid' or 'material' at all, and where everything is interconnected in some way. This newly described base upon which we can now interpret our world lends itself to the inclusion of the spiritual.

I will examine Einstein's proposed 'unified field' and how modern-day superstring theory supports the existence of such a field. Superstring theory is the closest thing we have to the long sought-after "theory of everything".

There are many who have successfully dived into the depths of their own consciousness and recognised it as the one "ocean of consciousness" or "ocean of self" underlying the diverse waves of our individual consciousness. It's the one ocean, expressed as individual waves. I will explore the true notion of unity – that every 'thing' and every 'one' is One!

I WILL THEN EXPAND ON THIS PREMISE, WITH THE OBVIOUS CONCLUSION that, if our individual consciousness is based in a universal consciousness – like a single wave on the one ocean of consciousness – then we should be able to access that fundamental deep level in our own awareness. If this ocean of consciousness that we can all dive into is the suspected unified field from which all material and phenomenal existence ultimately arises, then we can create and do anything and be anything we want to. Yes, we can even make miracles happen.

Does that ring a bell? Did not Jesus say that we too could do the things that he did – and more?[9] It's all physics basically. It's only 'meta-physics' as long as we don't understand or accept the science underlying it. Jesus also said: "I have still many things to say to you, but you are not able to bear them or to take them upon you or to grasp them now."[10] Knowing the level of scientific understanding at the time, Jesus would have had a difficult task talking to his disciples or the general community about the notion of unity – that we are all "One". Now, more than 2000 years later, our scientific progress has provided us a model with which we can understand the concept of unity. Our scientists are actually grasping the notion of Einstein's unified field and using current superstring theory to provide very plausible explanations for the birth of our universe and its eventual demise, and even describing the behaviour of nature beyond the existence of 'concrete' sub-atomic particles. Might Jesus – if he was here with us today and learning of our scientific discoveries – have dared to reveal to us now what he deemed too difficult for people to understand 2000 years ago?

Rigour and discipline are needed in the formal sciences to tease out fact from fiction. But the application of purely 'objective' scientific method in the study of consciousness – a 'subjective' phenomenon – may have its limitations. As physicist John Hagelin says, "Physics has walked the *Planck*"[11] to a large extent in the application of its traditional approaches to a realm (the unified field described by modern superstring theory) that is beyond space, time and therefore causality. Does that mean that any serious investigation of consciousness and spirituality is inadmissible territory? Explorers do not readily heed No Entry signs in front of unknown terrain. Direct experience can be all the evidence we need. It might be difficult to share that evidence with others, but it can be ultimately convincing at a personal level. If experience is supported by a conceivable explanation, then we have a contextual understanding that allows us to accept something as real rather than simply imagined.

The full gamut of life experience – including that thing called love – for most of us includes experiences that defy explanation by conventional science. The conceptual model explored in this book – that consciousness has its basis in a unified field of all the laws of nature (a unified field model of consciousness) – enables us to make sense of these experiences, even if we don't understand all the detail.

Knowledge and experience together consolidate our view of reality and allow us to define ourselves (our very being).

A somewhat contracted and commonly quoted interpretation of a saying by the Buddha (that I myself have edited even further) is worthy of continued reflection. Regardless of the liberality of this translation, I agree with its essential message:

Believe nothing, no matter where you read it, or who said it, no matter if I have said it, unless it agrees with your own reason based on clear understanding and life-supporting wisdom derived from personal experience.[12]

That applies to what is written in this book too!

NOTES

1. Now called *Manly Sea Life Sanctuary*
2. The story of McCavity – 'Mysterious McCavity' – was told in *Australian Geographic*, Issue 45, Jan–March 1997
3. Alan Nichols, J.D., D.S., FN'84; *The Explorers Log*, Spring 2014, Vol 46. No. 2.
4. *A periodic publication of the Explorers Club*; Vol 79, No. 4, Winter, 2001/2002, p 16–21.
5. April 6, 1969 – what a year for exploration!
6. Dorothy Parker (1893-1967), *The Little Hours*.
7. An adjectival reference to the Italian philosopher Rene Descartes, who initiated the mechanistic approach of modern science, and separated 'things extended' (of this world) from 'things of the mind' (of a spiritual domain). See also Ch.9
8. Sometimes referred to as a 'reductionist' approach, because of our traditional need to break things down to their constituent components.
9. John 14:12, *The Amplified Bible*, (Zondervan Publishing House, Michigan).
10. John, 16:12, *The Amplified Bible*, (Zondervan Publishing House, Michigan).
11. The Planck Scale or Planck Length is that smallest measurable distance at which our normal concepts of space, time and causality break down. The term honours the Nobel-prize winning German physicist Max Planck who originated Quantum Theory.
12. A very rough and commonly used interpretation (with my alterations pertaining to "reason" and "wisdom") of a comment made by the Buddha in the *Kālāma Sutta*, a collection of his sayings opposed to blind faith, dogmatism and belief spawned from specious reasoning. Part of the original saying emphasises the need for actual experience to ascertain our own truth: *"When you know for yourselves that, 'These qualities are skillful; these qualities are blameless; these qualities are praised by the wise; these qualities, when adopted and carried out, lead to welfare and to happiness' — then you should enter and remain in them."*

Chapter One

AN OCEAN OF LIFE – LIFE BEGINS IN THE SEA

"The waves thudding on a distant shore are the heartbeat of man's ancestral home. The salt solution of the sea flows in man's veins, and is it coincidence, or part of nature's master plan? – 70% of man's body is water, the same proportion as the surface of the earth."

– Jacques Yves Cousteau

All life on Earth as we know it began in the ocean, with evidence suggesting that some of the complex molecules seeding life were introduced to Earth with the bombardment of comets. Billions of years later, earthly beings are pondering their beginnings and the nature of consciousness. We have a deep genetic connection to the sea, and that connection can be seen in remnant embryological and physiological traits we all share. Our attraction to the ocean is largely explained by this evolutionary link, but does the ocean also remind us of deeper qualities within our own nature?

Earth is born

A LONG TIME AGO, JUST BEFORE THE BIRTH OF THE SUN AND PLANET Earth, the universe – at that time more than 9 billion years old – was vibrant with stars and galaxies. Life had ample opportunity to establish itself throughout the inconceivable vastness of the cosmos. Well before the Earth was conceived, it's very possible that beings more advanced than we are now – technologically and socially – inhabited distant planets in the Milky Way or in another far away galaxy.

A star much larger than the Sun had died, just as our Sun too will expire billions of years from now. The dramatic end to this big star's life came with what is known as a supernova explosion – an explosion releasing such enormous energy that iron and lighter elements already in the star fused to become heavier elements such as lead, silver, uranium and gold. A cloud of star dust and gas called a nebula was all that was left. This cloud of dust and gas would provide the building blocks for the future Sun and all its planets, including the Earth – and us!

The shock wave caused by the death and subsequent explosion of yet another nearby star is thought to have stirred and energised this nebula, causing it to whirl and stick together. The friction of condensing dust particles increased the temperature until hydrogen protons fused to form helium. With this ongoing chain of nuclear fusion, the Sun[1] was born – 4.6 billion years ago – with enough fuel to burn for 10 billion years.

And so, in a pattern we have seen throughout nature to this present day, the death of one entity enabled life for another. The death of that star also made it possible for planets to slowly arise from its ashes. The swirling gases and dust left over after the making of our sun – dust particles smaller than the eye could see – began to stick together and aggregate to form clumps. The clumps attracted more dust, which made them into large rocks. The rocks gathered more dust and grew large enough that gravity itself started to attract bigger rocks. Soon some of these rocks assumed sizes large enough to be called planets.

In the early period after the Sun was born, there were many planets surrounding the Sun – dozens! Over millions of years, collisions between these planets annihilated or augmented each other, until a more manageable number of planets took their position around the Sun. One of them was Earth, born 4.54 billion years ago. Earth, like the Sun, is also made of the stuff of that once proud star. The supernova explosion accompanying the death of that star gifted our planet with a wide-ranging pharmacopeia of chemical elements to make life possible, and a rich supply of essential ingredients for whatever Earthlings might conjure in the future.

Earth however, in its formative years, was not a place you would call 'home'.[2] The whole planet was a fiery ball of liquid rock with an endless ocean of lava. The constant bombardment of Earth with meteors – dominant in the early solar system and rich with radioactive elements – heated the Earth until it turned into a complete molten mass with a temperature of more than 1000°C (2000°F). That was enough heat to melt iron, much of which sank with other heavy elements such as nickel into the centre of the planet, forming the dense metal inner core.

These were violent times for our early solar system. Earth was just beginning to settle down, although still fiery hot, when another Mars-sized planet called Theia collided with Earth. The impact – a deep glancing blow – caused the liquefaction of much of Earth and the annihilation of Theia. The impact tore away a massive chunk of Earth's crust and mantle, which eventually molded itself into our Moon. The Moon can therefore be described as the stuff of the Earth! Some scientists think that the Pacific Basin could represent the area of Earth where Theia hit.

The impact tilted Earth 23 degrees off its axis, giving us our seasons. Scientists believe that Theia may have had a chemical composition similar to Mercury, and contributed to Earth the sulphuric compounds needed to maintain radioactivity in the Earth's core[3]. This radioactivity heats and churns the core's outer layers of molten metal, generating a magnetic field which in turn shields us from the constant bombardment of cosmic radiation. Without Theia, life as we know it would probably not have eventuated on this planet.

In these early times, the Moon was only 22,000km (14,000 miles) away[4], and the Earth was spinning four times faster than it does today – six-hour days! Around 3.9 billion years ago, another hail of meteors hit the Earth. This bombardment went on intensely for a further 20 million years. Inside the meteors were tiny salt crystals, and it's likely that inside each of these salt crystals was a drop of water. The continued barrage of meteors over millions of years contributed more H2O to the body of water that might have already existed inside Earth, brought to the surface when its molten rock began to cool.[5] With the cooling of Earth and the continued bombardment of meteors, water began to accumulate, perhaps first into puddles, then lakes and then into oceans.

The Earth was beginning to look a little more familiar, but there were only small islands – no large land masses. And it was still a dangerous place for life as we know it. The air temperature was at this point around 77°C (170°F). As a comparison, your hot cup of coffee is served to you usually at just under 60°C. With the rapid spinning of the planet and the huge tidal pull of the close Moon, the oceans looked angry and wild, with huge seas inconceivable to mariners of today. Planet Earth had transformed from a fiery red ball of molten rock to a wild, blue, tempestuous ocean planet.

The first seeds of life
EARTH 3.8 BILLION YEARS AGO WAS FAR FROM BEING A HABITABLE PLANET, and it would undergo huge climatic fluctuations as well as further assaults from meteors slamming into Earth. Comets are also likely to have brought significant amounts of water to Earth. These comets and meteors may have carried more than just water. We now know that the very dark surface of one comet[6] has engendered active photochemistry that has resulted in the formation of organic polymeric compounds. These organic compounds and possibly – in other comets – primitive amino acids (the precursors of structural proteins), are thought to have been carried to Earth with debris left over after our Sun's formation.

A rich chemical soup of introduced complex molecules along with the planet's own chemical contribution was now available for processing in Earth's ideal laboratories – the deep hydrothermal (underwater volcanic) vents spewing fire and gas from the Earth's interior.

> *"Double, double; toil and trouble; Fire burn and cauldron bubble."*
> – William Shakespeare, MacBeth

SHAKESPEARE'S MEMORABLE LINES IN *MACBETH* COULD WELL BE APPLIED to the miraculous event that transpired in the abysmal depths of the ocean those 3.8 billion years ago. In mother Earth's own cauldron – on the deep ocean floor – it is highly likely that hydrothermal vents from a more volcanically active Earth belched "fire and bubble", effectively bringing together the essential ingredients of water, gas, fire and earth to form nucleic and amino acids – the first seeds of life.

Also probably belching out from the vents were heat-soluble fats called lipids that formed spherical vesicles upon cooling. Some of these lipid vesicles may have contained just the right mix of dissolved clay particles with their burden of amino acids, nucleotides[7] and other elements that set the stage for the first life forms. The lipid vesicles might have become the cell membranes of living, reproducing simple cells – the first single-celled bacteria.[8]

For hundreds of millions of years, the only life forms on Earth were these ocean-living single-celled bacteria. These simple life forms were the precursors to the much more complicated organisms we see now, including us.

About 3.5 billion years ago, Earth still resembled a brilliant blue ball of water with very little land. Days were becoming longer – 18 hours.

Colonies of single-celled bacteria formed what are known as stromatolites, which were capable of using sunlight to turn carbon dioxide and water into food (glucose) – photosynthesis. In the process, oxygen was released into Earth's water and atmosphere. This process continued for another two billion years, with more and more oxygen entering the atmosphere with the flourishing stromatolites. Even 1.5 billion years ago, nearly all life was still underwater. There may have been patches of algae on land, but certainly no animals or plants.

Stromatolites (unique humps of single-celled cyanobacteria), Hamelin Pool, Western Australia. The bacteria organise themselves into biofilms (microbial mats) that secrete calcium carbonate, forming rock-like structures more than a metre in size. Photo by Gary Bell, Oceanwideimages.com

If we fast forward to about 700 million years ago, the great southern supercontinent known as Rodinia was breaking apart. The intense geological action associated with this caused volcanic eruptions, producing CO2 that mixed with rain to become acid rain. The acid rain was absorbed by rocks, taking the CO2 out of the atmosphere. With no more trapping of heat by CO2, the temperature plummeted. By 650 million years ago, the whole planet was covered in ice sheets up to 3km (10,000 ft) thick. Earth was covered in ice, but the Earth's core remained hot, and those resistant bacteria were still hanging around.

After 15 million years of 'Snowball Earth', volcanos again became active, the rising CO2 melted the ice and in doing so, released huge amounts of oxygen from the hydrogen peroxide (H2O2) trapped in the ice. About 600 million years ago, the atmosphere became warmer and the days increased to 22 hours long. The breakup of Rodinia opened up new oceans and caused the seabeds to rise, creating shallower seas that offered the much-needed stepping stone for animals and plants to eventually make their way onto land. Earth had lots of water and lots of oxygen – conditions perfect for life to flourish.

About 540 million years ago, primitive bacteria that hung on through the deep freeze were thriving. Plants began to make an appearance. But something else made an appearance – an armored slug (*Wiwaxia*) representing a new generation of multi-cellular organisms and the first appearance of the animal kingdom. Not much is known about this jump from multi-celled bacteria to more complex animals, but this period represents the greatest event in Earth's evolutionary history – what is known as the Cambrian Explosion[9].

The earliest animals we know of from this Cambrian period included trilobites – members of that family known as arthropods (animals with a hard external skeleton and jointed appendages). Modern-day examples of arthropods include insects and crustaceans. Trilobites were some of the most successful creatures to have inhabited this planet. They thrived as ocean floor scavengers or free-swimming creatures for more than 270 million years before their mass extinction about 250 million years ago. Because of their hard external skeleton, they left behind beautifully preserved, exquisite fossils that allow us a glimpse into this ancient world of so long ago.

A well-preserved trilobite fossil (**Koneprussia**) from Morocco that lived during the Devonian Period about 400 million years ago. Courtesy of Smithsonian Institution. Photo by C.Clark.

Two groups of animals that appeared during the Cambrian period and dominated the seas for millions of years included the nautiloids and ammonites. These earliest members of the cephalopod family (which today includes octopuses, squid and cuttlefish) were conspicuous for the exotic protective 'homes' they carried with them at all times. A living nautiloid today called the chambered nautilus allows us a glimpse into the fascinating life of nautiloids.

The chambered or emperor nautilus – ***Nautilus pompilius*** – is considered a 'living fossil' and the only survivor of an ancient group of cephalopods that emerged in the Cambrian Period, 500 million years ago – long before there were any bony fishes.

Based on what we know of the modern nautilus, they never willingly left their shell. Without their shell they would look like a squid with an over-abundance of tentacles. If threatened, they could retract into their shell and close it off with a leathery hood, or operculum.

It appears that the modern chambered nautilus relies heavily on chemical sense to find its food. Eyes are lens-less pinholes and therefore probably not very efficient – especially in deep water environments.

Nautiloids were mostly of a small size like our modern nautilus – which are usually smaller than a human hand – but some did reach great size. *Endoceras giganteum*, a nautiloid that dates back to 450 million years ago, lived inside a very long, straight shell up to 5m (15 ft) long. That would have been a challenging photographic subject, but oh to witness such a creature!

Ammonites were very similar to nautiloids and appeared about 420 million years ago. They dominated the seas for hundreds of millions of years before dying out completely 65 million years ago, during the extinction event that also took out the dinosaurs. Unlike the nautiloids, these cephalopods had excellent vision. While some may have crawled along the bottom, others may have been free-swimming, assisted by their apparent ability to extend themselves further out from their shell. The shell too, took on a bizarre array of shapes – some were closed spirals like the nautilus, but others looked like exotic wind instruments.

Age of the fishes
LIFE SPROUTED IN MANY FORMS DURING THIS PERIOD KNOWN AS THE Cambrian Explosion. One small animal – *Pikaia* – only about 4cm (1.5 inches) long, resembled a worm, but possessed a stiffening rod and a nerve cord behind it (known as a notochord) that ran up most of its length. While it would be overly ambitious to identify this creature as our direct ancestor, it is certainly the earliest known representative of the Chordata group of animals to which we belong.

The first fish appeared during this Cambrian period and were initially elongated and without jaws. Then jawed fish appeared and thrived in the Age of Fishes known as the Devonian period (419–359 million years ago). Fish are now – and have been for a long time – the dominant animals in the sea, and certainly the most diverse of all vertebrates.

A small shrimp has hitched a ride on the back of this Saddleback anemonefish, and also enjoys a protected commensal relationship with the fish and the host anemone.

It didn't take long for the cartilaginous fish to appear – around 395 million years ago. From this group sprang the sharks and rays. The cartilaginous fishes still possessed a vertebral column and were therefore still vertebrates, except that the vertebral column was made of cartilage, which is softer and less rigid than bone. Cartilage serves us well as shock absorbers in our joints, and flexible, shape-preserving stiffeners in our nose, ears and windpipe (trachea). One drawback from the point of view of palaeontologists studying cartilaginous fishes is that their cartilage often disappears before good imprints in mud or clay can form to become fossils.

Sharks' teeth are encased in enamel – the hardest, most durable substance in the body – and so they are well preserved as fossils. From these fossils we know some very large sharks existed, and some very odd-looking sharks too.

Carcharodon megalodon[10] was a fearsome predator, like a stockier, bigger version of the great white shark. Reaching 18m (60 ft) in length, it would use its array of teeth up to 15cm (6 inch) long set in a jaw that could be 2.7m (9 ft) across, to crush and tear flesh from its victims – probably mostly large baleen whales. *Megalodon* first appeared about 16 million years ago and co-existed with the great white shark until it disappeared mysteriously about 2.6 million years ago. On the evolutionary scale, that's mighty close to humankind's entry into this world! If *megalodon* was still plying our waters, I might have considered taking up another interest apart from ocean diving.

Animals crawl out of the sea
THE HISTORY OF LIFE ON EARTH HAS BEEN MOSTLY A SUBMERGED ONE. It still is, with water being the home of 90% of Earth's living things. Life remained underwater for 2.5 billion years, until a relatively short 375 million years ago, when a strange-looking fish that might have resembled (in some respects) a large mudskipper of today, left the water to spend more time on land.

It isn't known which fish first crawled out of the sea to become terrestrial. *Tiktaalik* is representative of a line of amphibious fish that ventured onto land. They probably inhabited warm shallow waters, where oxygen levels were low enough that air breathing with primitive lungs became an advantage. Perhaps the stress of marine predators also motivated the transition to a terrestrial life. *Tiktaalik* had well-developed shoulders that could support the weight of the animal out of the water on its fore fins, which were hinged with a 'wrist' that enabled it to walk and might have helped the animal hold ground underwater in strong currents.

Amphibious animals that first ventured onto land had four 'feet' and were thus known as tetrapods. The tetrapods evolved in different directions. One group evolved into mammals[11] and another group evolved into lizards, which eventually grew larger, until about 230 million years ago when they became dinosaurs and birds. Dinosaurs would become the dominant, ruling terrestrial vertebrates from the beginning of the Jurassic Period (about 201 million years ago) until their extinction around 65 million years ago.

Scientists now know that this massive extinction coincided with the impact of a huge asteroid in what is now the Gulf of Mexico. At impact the asteroid stood 10km high! The asteroid vaporised, releasing the equivalent energy of millions of nuclear weapons. Debris the size of whole city blocks circled the Earth. Earthquakes and tsunamis with kilometre-high waves followed. World-wide fires and the disappearance of much vegetation made survival for most land creatures impossible.

The mammals living underground were the terrestrial survivors of this massive global event. With the disappearance of the dinosaurs, the mammals took over. Some of these mammals took to living in and feeding from trees. Eventually this particular line of mammals became the primates. They developed proportionally larger brains than most of the other mammals, relied on stereoscopic vision more than smell, and most had opposable thumbs – useful for the dexterity needed for an arboreal life and creating tools.

There were two broad lines of primates. One line, the Prosimians, became the lemurs of today, and the other line, the Anthropoids, became the apes, monkeys and humans. While a reasonable amount is known about the early humans back to a few million years ago, not much is known about our earlier tree-living primate ancestors.

One very exciting recent discovery[12], was of a primate fossil found in the Messel Pit of Germany – a site renowned for the superb preservation of animals of the Eocene Epoch (56–40 million years ago). This was an important period for the development of early primates as oxygen levels in Earth's atmosphere doubled, allowing the development of larger energy-hungry brains. This remarkably preserved fossil of an early female juvenile primate – named *Ida* (pronounced "eeda") – could well represent an ancestor of modern humans. Calculated to have lived 47 million years ago, this young primate demonstrated distinct characteristics that place her more on the Anthropoid line of mammalian evolution than the Prosimian path. One notable finding was that Ida's pelvis (hip bone) and talus (ankle bone) were shaped and orientated for a more upright human-like posture.

Excluding the long tail, the fossil skeleton measured only 24cm (9.4 inches) long. The jury is still out as to whether Ida represents a distant parent of modern humans or a distant cousin.

Returning to the sea
Some terrestrial animals returned to the sea. Those totally committed to the sea were all mammals – the future Cetaceans (whales and dolphins) and Sirenians (manatees, dugongs and the now extinct Steller's sea cows). Others less committed to a full life in the sea kept a foot in both camps. These included the ancestors of seals (among the mammals) and sea turtles, sea snakes, crocodiles and penguins (representing the reptiles and birds).

The evolutionary story of whales and dolphins deserves special attention, because in one respect they remind us a little of us, and in another, they represent the huge success of the mammals in 'conquering' the Earth. In a relatively short space of time – only 50 million years – a land creature resembling a wolf with a long snout evolved to become a master of the sea, and a majestic, charismatic one at that.

Pakicetus looked somewhat like a dog and swam like one too. Fifty million years ago *Pakicetus* was trying to survive in a world that had become hotter and more arid. It found some replenishment at the edge of lakes and rivers, where it scavenged dead fish, but soon entered the water to attempt to capture live fish. This made it vulnerable to crocodiles, and it disappeared from the fossil record.

Pakicetus, thought to be the terrestrial mammalian ancestor to all our modern whales and dolphins. It was about 1.8 m (6 ft) in length, and weighed about 150 kgs (330 lbs). It might have had webbed paws and spent a semi-aquatic existence much like the modern day otters. Paleoartist Roman Uchytel; prehistoric-fauna.com

The lineage of *pakicetus*, or similar terrestrial creatures, is shown in whales and dolphins today. Whales and dolphins move their horizontal fins (flukes) up and down, while fish move their vertical fins (caudal fins) sideways. If you watch a dog run, its spine undulates up and down. A human swimmer using the dolphin kick underwater or the butterfly stroke, also uses an up and down undulation of the spine and legs to create power. Otters, seals and the Australian platypus are the same – mammalian spines are designed with the greatest flexibility in an up and down (dorso-ventral) direction.

It is now thought that an immediate predecessor of our modern whales and dolphins was a smaller toothed whale that grew to about 5m (16 ft) long, the *dorudon*. *Dorudons* grouped into pods to avoid predation and were capable of diving quite deeply. Unlike some of its ancestors, this stocky cetacean had a shorter, more powerful vertebral column and swam with less undulation of its spine and more with powerful oscillation of its tail and flukes, which is the propulsion method of modern whales and dolphins.

Our link to the sea
HUMANS EVOLVED FROM SINGLE-CELLED MARINE LIFE FORMS THAT became fish, amphibians, mammals and eventually primates. This evolutionary history links our species to the sea, and we have inherited some remnant biological traits that maintain that relationship.

"The waves thudding on a distant shore are the heartbeat of man's ancestral home. The salt solution of the sea flows in man's veins, and is it coincidence, or part of nature's master plan? – 70% of man's body is water, the same proportion as the surface of the earth." Jacques Yves Cousteau was an ocean explorer famous for his inspirational TV documentaries in the 1970s and '80s. Like many divers, he "felt" at some deep level this connection we all have with the ocean.

Journalist Charles Siebert once asked molecular biologist Neal Epstein to name a multi-cellular organism that does not possess a heart[13]. "A sponge," Epstein said. "A sponge is all the same cell, but it is the same cell multiplied. Now what does it use for a pump? The ocean. The ocean is the heart of the sponge. The sponge has been designed to live within a huge pump, bathing in its nutrients, washing away its waste. Now, you'll notice that the salinity of the ocean is not that different from what we're carrying around in our bodies. So somehow, when life came out of the ocean, it had figured out a way to carry around its own bathing ocean and circulate it."

Siebert continued with his own thoughts on this bewildering scenario. "Ever since, I've thought of each of us, you and me, as our own pinched-off, ambulatory seas, ones in which only our hearts keep us buoyed. When our hearts fail, we can no longer tread our own bodies of water, and we drown."

Leaving the ocean came at a price – we had to carry some of the ocean with us, our own "pinched-off ambulatory seas". When a surfer, diver or sailor tells us that the sea is "in my blood", that person is speaking almost literally.

A human embryo goes through a stage of development in which it has slits and arches in its neck like the gill slits and gill arches of fishes[14]. It is well accepted amongst anatomists and embryologists that these arches – which develop into the jaws, ears and structures in the neck – are so similar to gill structures in fish at this point in development, that humans clearly share a common ancestor with fish.

We have other physiological traits that link us to the sea. The mammalian diving reflex enables a man or woman to slow their heartbeat and metabolic rate when immersed in the sea. When a trained breath-holding human diver descends into the deep, even their brain activity can adopt the same patterns recorded in quiet, alert meditation.

Shaping our home

OUR HOME PLANET HAS BEEN PUMMELLED AND BASHED AROUND SINCE ITS inception, looking red, white and blue at different times. Now Earth is lit up at night with city lights, and it's getting brighter[15].

It's obvious there's a new force shaping our Earth – humans. Nobel prize-winning chemist Paul Crutzen and University of Michigan biologist Eugene Stoermer have called this new episode in planetary history the Anthropocene Epoch[16] – the human-dominated era.

"Humans have become a hundred times more numerous than any other large animal in history,"[17] says biologist and artist Richard Ellis. Not only are we now having an effect on the planet's climate, we are also pushing much wildlife to the edge of extinction. As Ellis comments, "the previously inconceivable question 'why do we need albatrosses (or lemurs, or sea turtles, or tigers)?' is now, sadly, considered a legitimate one to ask".[18]

Our unstoppable pursuit of technological advancement and political obsession with commercial and industrial progress at the expense of 'softer' social or environmental considerations raises huge concerns for our own long-term survival on this planet. As Ellis points out, 99.9% of all species that have ever lived on Earth have become extinct[19], and these were extinctions that did not require our help! Are humans necessarily exempt from this statistic? The fossil record would suggest 'no'.

We would do well to consider the wisdom of American Indian Chief Seattle, who, while delivering a speech to a gathering in Seattle on the concession of native lands to the settlers in 1854, said: "This we know. The earth does not belong to man. Man belongs to the earth. This we know. All things are connected like the blood which unites one family. All things are connected."

All things *are* interconnected, and this connectedness extends further than just the sharing of a common evolutionary source in ocean-dwelling bacteria. The realisation of this connection is unifying, empowering and uplifting!

Coogee Beach south of the entrance to Sydney Harbour. People have an affinity with the sea that makes us unique among the terrestrial animals. Our evolutionary link with the sea may partly explain this attraction to the ocean, but deeper existential qualities we sense in ourselves are reflected in the ocean, and these shared qualities might also be responsible for our attraction to the sea.

NOTES

1. There were 'sister' suns born too from this one nebula, although they have been scattered throughout our region of the galaxy since their inception. Scientists have already been able to identify one of them.
2. Much of this information pertaining to the formation of our solar system was derived from the excellent TV documentary *Earth: The Making of a Planet*, Yavar Abbas, National Geographic TV, 2011. There was also a follow-up documentary involving interviews with scientists, with the same title in December, 2013. As much as possible, the information has been checked with other references for currency and accuracy, and supplemented.
3. Powell, Devin; 'Earth May Have Become Magnetic After Eating a Mercury-Like Object'; Smithsonian.com, April 15, 2015.
4. Today it orbits Earth on average 384,000km (238,000 miles) away.
5. Hallis, L. J., Huss, G. R., Nagashima, K., Taylor, G. J., Halldórsson,, S. A., Hilton, D. R., Motti, M. J., and Meech, K. J. (2015) 'Evidence for primordial water in Earth's deep mantle'. *Science*, 350(6262), pp. 795–797.
6. Comet 67-P Churyumov-Gerasimenko; In November 2014, the European Space Agency successfully landed a probe (*Philae*) on this comet and analysed the chemistry of the surface. See Science Interviews, www.thenakedscientist.com, Monday, Aug 3, 2015.
7. The building blocks of nucleic acids like DNA or RNA, involved in the production of energy, the creation of proteins, cell multiplication and reproduction.
8. Ellis, Richard; *Aquagenesis*, Viking Penguin, p 13.
9. The Cambrian Explosion, which began around 540 million years ago and ended about 490 million years ago, was a relatively short period during which most of the major animal phyla appeared.
10. Megalodon meaning "great tooth".
11. Mammals differ from reptiles and birds in having hair, mammary glands, three middle-ear bones and a four-chambered heart.
12. *Uncovering Our Earliest Ancestor: The Link*; BBC, May, 2009
13. Siebert, Charles; an essay on the human heart written for The Sydney Morning Herald's *Good Weekend* magazine, May 8, 2004, referring to a conversation he had with Neal Epstein, from the National Institute of Health in Bethesda, Maryland, USA
14. Called branchial (gill) or pharyngeal arches.
15. Meredith, Peter, 'The End of Darkness', p 62–75, *Australian Geographic*, Issue 126, May/June, 2015
16. Roston, Eric, *The Sydney Morning Herald*, 12 March, 2015.
17. Ellis, Richard; *Aquagenesis*, Viking Penguin, 2001, p8.
18. Ellis, Richard; *Aquagenesis*, Viking Penguin, 2001, p8
19. Ellis, Richard; *Aquagenesis*, Viking Penguin, 2001, p8

Chapter Two

OCEAN MYTHOLOGY

"Most people talk about fear of the unknown. If there's anything to fear, it's the known. The known is the rigid patterns of past conditioning. The unknown is the field of infinite possibilities, that field of infinite choices, into which we can step every moment of our life when we go beyond the camouflage of our past memories, our past conditioning."

— Deepak Chopra

Mankind has developed many myths and fables to fill gaps in our knowledge of the world around us. This is particularly so with the ocean. Humans have projected their fear of the unknown depths of their own mind into the unknown depths of the sea. In most cases, the creatures invented are to be feared. The reality so far uncovered in our explorations of the ocean has been of a world far more friendly and inviting than once thought – certainly one not to fear. The same can be said of those depths in the ocean of our own awareness. Far from being a scary place, it is a realm of bliss, peace, love and ultimate empowerment.

I HAVE A POSSIBLE EXPLANATION FOR THE MERMAID LEGEND. An incident or encounter often initiates a myth, and my first-hand encounter with an amorous dugong in Vanuatu – one of the tropical South Pacific islands north of Australia – suggests behaviour that just might have started the fable.

Dugongs (in the south-east Pacific) and their close relatives the manatees (Florida, Amazon Basin and West Africa) are mammals. They have terrestrial predecessors that took their first steps into the sea to eventually become fully adapted to an aquatic life. The mammalian forerunner of dugongs and manatees was a hoofed animal that also gave rise to our modern elephant and hippopotamus.

Dugongs are generally shy animals. They're good swimmers with a powerful tail that closely resembles the forked flukes of a whale[1], but they lack a dorsal fin and have a head and face that is more like a walrus without the long tusks. Because they're shy, it can be difficult to get good photographs of them, but my wife Becca and I had heard of a particularly friendly male dugong called Dudley that visited a shallow lagoon near a village in Tanna Island, Vanuatu.

Becca and I took a trip to Tanna Island in 1994 to see if Dudley lived up to his reputation[2]. After being driven to the village alongside Dudley's favorite haunt, we put on our diving gear and watched one of the local boys 'call' Dudley. He did this by heavily driving his cupped hands through the surface of the water to create a deep gulping sound for about 30 seconds. Within just a few minutes, Dudley appeared.

Dudley was big – about 300kg and some 2.5m long. We entered the water timidly with underwater cameras in hand, only to find Dudley barreling down on us with a mission.

Dudley you see, had an erection, and it was obvious that he was pleased to see us. Nor did he have any concern for introduction or foreplay. It's just as well we were wearing wetsuits! To have 300kg of sheer passion trying to embrace us was a scary experience.

Dudley played rough, trying to hold us down under the water with his front fins and head-butting us with his coarsely whiskered face. I know of one person who had a rib broken as a result of this.

It wasn't easy, but we got some photos, in less than ideal water conditions. We both spent most of our time evading the affectionate approaches of Dudley.

DUGONGS AND MANATEES BELONG TO THE ORDER SIRENIA, WHICH REFERS to the mythological Greek "sirens" that lured poor sailors into the sea. Dudley certainly fits the amorous criterion of the sirens of Homer's *Odyssey*. I'm not sure though that anyone would call Dudley's face "beautiful", at least in the classical sense. It's possible, however, that – from a distance – dugongs or manatees somehow triggered the imaginations of sailors long separated from their wives or girlfriends. It's also possible that someone had an in-water experience like we did!

The local villagers 'call in' Dudley the dugong by slapping the water heavily. Dudley's outline can be seen in the middle of the picture.

Homer's epic poem the *Odyssey*, written about 700BC, tells of the maritime adventures of Odysseus, a Greek hero who took 10 years to find his way home from the Trojan war. Ulysses (as he was known in the Roman legends) is warned by the goddess Circe to avoid the deadly lure of the sirens as he passes their island, because all who surrender to the calls of the sirens have drowned. She suggests he plug the ears of his crew with wax and, if he wants to hear their sounds, get them to tightly bind him to the ship's mast, and to command his men to ignore any orders or pleas he makes while passing the island. The sweet songs emanating from the sirens' island proves irresistible to Ulysses. He begs his crew to untie him, but the crew abide by his original command and keep Ulysses tied up until they safely pass the island.

Dudley the friendly dugong from Tanna Island in Vanuatu.

I'm escaping the approach of Dudley, so Becca (taking this photo) is now the focus of Dudley's intentions.

Dudley has reached his target. Becca took this photo unintentionally by reflex. I contend that I'm swimming towards Becca to help her.

Jayne Jenkins - a friend of ours - tries to crawl out of the water while Dudley tries to convince her otherwise. Photo by Barry Andrewartha.

Were dugongs responsible for the mermaid legend? We can't really answer that with any certainty. It seems unlikely to me that dugongs or manatees could ever have been mistaken for a fish–human hybrid (or chimera), but maybe it doesn't take much to start some legends.

Quite possibly, the legend of a human–fish chimera reflects a yearning to connect in some way with the ocean.

Many of these fables centered round a supernatural humanoid being or god that clearly didn't have the best interests of humans at heart. Triton, the son of Poseidon, was a merman with a human torso and a fish tail. In old engravings, he's seen blowing his conch shell and stirring up the waves. This was the power of the gods, understood at that time, over the elements of nature.[3] Poseidon, better known by his Roman name Neptune, had a petulant personality that was clearly reflected in the unpredictable behaviour of the sea.[4]

Creatures of the sea were also endowed with malevolent abilities. One of the most enduring images of sea lore is the picture of a giant squid encircling a ship with its arms and creating havoc. Homer refers to the monster Skylla in his *Odyssey*, which is very likely an octopus or squid of enormous size. When Odysseus sails his ship near the rocks where Skylla concealed herself, "each of her six slavering maws grabbed a sailor and wolfed him down". Circe warned Odysseus about Skylla, but he had little choice other than to sail by her domain.

This legend has never been put to rest. One of the Hollywood productions of *Pirates of the Caribbean* with star Johnny Depp depicts the attack of the pirate ship by an enormous squid.

Giant squid have been seen dead and floating on the surface by fishermen and also washed up onto beaches. They've been measured up to 13m (43 ft) in length[5]. Their natural habitat is deep in the sea, and it is very rare to find one near the surface. Sperm whales dive very deeply to battle with giant squid, which are the whale's natural prey. It would be understandable that early mariners might envisage one of these squid attacking a small ship, but such a situation would have almost certainly never occurred.

Humans have left open some other maritime mysteries to keep us on edge. The Bermuda Triangle covers an area bounded by Bermuda, the southern coast of Florida and Puerto Rico. Official records confirm that over 100 boats, ships and planes and more than 1000 sailors and airmen have disappeared within the region. The disappearance of Flight 19 in 1945 secured the Triangle's reputation. On a routine training mission, five Avenger torpedo bombers, as well as a Martin Mariner rescue plane, disappeared. UFOs, space-time warps, demonic forces, crystals from the sunken city of Atlantis and giant gas bubbles have all been blamed for the mysterious disappearances.[6] There is undoubtedly a natural explanation for these events, but the Bermuda Triangle is a prime example of the sea's influence on our imagination and the prevailing fear of the unknown.

Ships in the Bermuda Triangle have mysteriously disappeared, but some ships make a mysterious reappearance – ships that have been long gone. The most famous of these ships is the so-called *Flying Dutchman*.

Legend has it that a sailing ship belonging to the Dutch East India Company in the 17th century was commanded by a rather rebellious and stubborn Captain van der Decken, who is actually the 'Flying Dutchman'. According to one version of the story, while returning home to Holland via the Cape of Good Hope, he encountered stormy weather and was determined to battle through anything that God or nature might throw at him, and apparently said as much in very defiant terms. As soon as he openly defied God, his ship hit rocks and foundered, taking everyone down with the ship. According to another equally fanciful version, during the storm he cut down the ringleader of a group of passengers and crew demanding he take down sail and keep well away from land. At that moment, the clouds parted and an apparition appeared, laying a curse on the captain, condemning him to sail the oceans for eternity "with a ghostly crew of dead men, bringing death to all who sight your spectral ship, and to never make port or know a moment's peace".[7]

The first recorded sighting of this phantom ship was by a handful of crew on the British ship HMS *Bacchante* in 1881. Apparently the spectral ship approached them, surrounded by its own storm. It approached so close that some aboard the British ship feared it would collide with them, but it disappeared at the last moment. Among the witnesses was a young midshipman who would later become King George V. He recalled, "A strange red light as of a phantom ship all aglow, in the midst of which light the mast, spars and sails of a brig 200 yards (183 m) distant stood out in strong relief".

The *Flying Dutchman* was reportedly seen a few more times over the decades, once off the coast of South Africa by swimmers and people on shore, and another time by crew from a German U-boat off Cape Town during WWII.

How can one rationally explain these sightings? I don't pretend to have all the answers, but let me recount some experiences I have had while staring into the blue-green void of the ocean during my long decompression stops. These stops are typically made during my ascent from a deep shipwreck, to avoid decompression sickness, commonly called "the bends".

In my boredom, I sometimes stare into the void and – at times – I almost convince myself I have seen a big shark cruising like a menacing phantom through the edge of my visibility. Light does amazing things when it diffracts, reflects and bounces around the top 10m of the ocean. The waves at the surface, jellyfish and plankton all contribute to density variations in the water that create changing shapes and shadows. Think hard enough about a particular shape – especially something you might fear – and there is a very good possibility you can project that form onto the accommodating blank screen of changing light and shade around you. It's a little bit like seeing shapes in clouds.

Conditions just above the surface of the ocean may not be that different, especially if you add sea mist or fog to the picture. It's possible that similar light diffraction and reflection might create shapes that could readily be perceived as something that looks like a particular object.

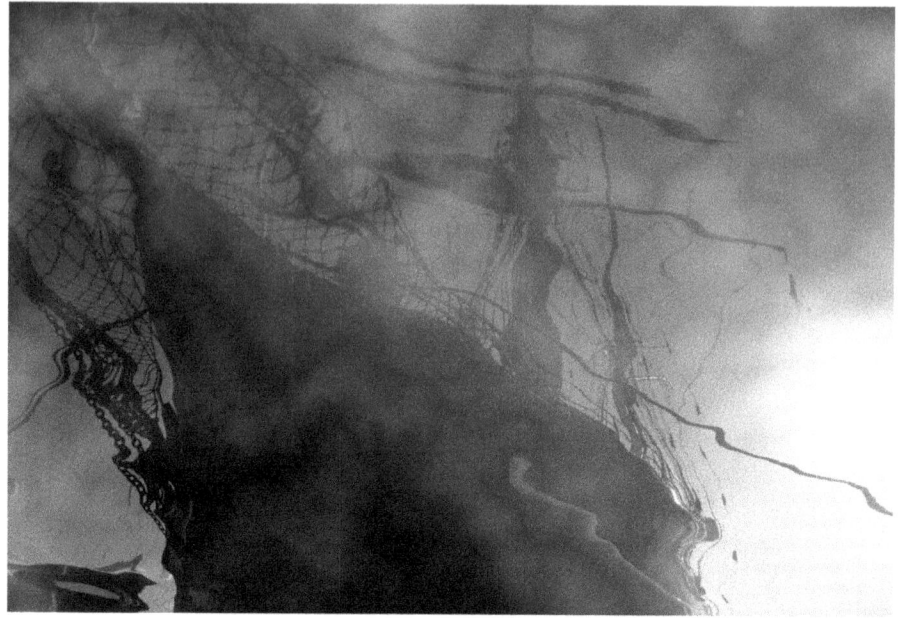

A phantom ship? Or the ghostly reflection of another vessel on smooth water? Add some mist, and then light and shadow can take on some eerie appearances. This was an old sailing ship reflected on the surface of Sydney's Darling Harbour.

The vast depths of the ocean remain to this day largely unknown. Humans have never been good at leaving mysteries unexplained, and are therefore inclined to fill the gaps in their knowledge with imagination. Humans have projected into ocean lore the fears and unresolved mysteries they have fabricated from the unfamiliar depths of their own minds. We have effectively filled the gaps in our knowledge with inventions of the mind that don't actually exist. Modern humans now have the technology to better explore the ocean depths, and what we have come up with so far is far from frightening.

"We shouldn't fear the unknown", says endocrinologist and Vedic science expert Deepak Chopra.[8] "If there's anything to fear, it's the known." The 'known', according to Deepak, includes "the rigid patterns of past conditioning", and the many assumptions shared throughout society and certain cultures – perpetuated over hundreds or even thousands of years. This includes myths that have been long established but are in fact just products of our vivid imaginations.

Before a deep dive or a dive into unknown waters, my mind can conjure up all sorts of fearful scenarios that could prevent me from going ahead with the dive. In all cases I can recall, the reality has been very different to the fears I imagined. The real ocean is not a fearful place and I have always felt 'in the moment', alert, responsive and respectful, but not fearful when I'm actually undertaking the dive.

The unknown depths of the mind can also be explored. To dive into this "ocean of consciousness", we don't have to don heavy breathing equipment. All we need is an effective and proven technique of quietening the mind – meditation. The results – like diving into the watery ocean – are far from fear-provoking. The opposite, in fact, awaits – the discovery of a realm of our own nature that is peaceful, silent, alert, encompassing, integrating, beyond any notion of time, and promising of all possibilities. We don't fear what we learn through direct experience, as opposed to what we learn second hand or what we conjecture.

NOTES

1. The manatees on the other hand have a very different looking paddle-shaped tail.
2. That was 21 years ago. We have heard from reliable sources that Dudley has now passed on.
3. Fisher, Mariea, 'Secrets of the Sea-Gods and Sirens', *Signals – Quarterly Magazine of the Australian National Maritime Museum*, Number 50, p6, March–May, 2000.
4. Fisher, Mariea, 'Secrets of the Sea-Gods and Sirens', *Signals – Quarterly Magazine of the Australian National Maritime Museum*, Number 50, March–May, 2000.
5. 'Ocean Portal' – Smithsonian Museum of Natural History; http://ocean.si.edu/giant-squid
6. Sedgwick, Susan, 'Secrets of the Sea – Mysteries and More' *Signals – Quarterly Magazine of the Australian National Maritime Museum*, Number 50, p7, March–May, 2000.
7. Konstam, Angus; *Ghost Ships – Tales of Abandoned, Doomed, and Haunted Vessels*, p 62, Lyons Press
8. Chopra, Deepak; *The Higher Self – the magic of inner and outer fulfillment*; audio-book, Nightingale-Conant Corp., Chicago, Illinois

Chapter Three

WAVES

"In this playhouse of infinite forms I have had my play and here have I caught sight of him who is formless."

– Rabindranath Tagore, Gitanjali

All physical particles and the forces of nature are nothing – ultimately – but waves of energy. The birth and death of individual waves on the surface of the ocean give the ocean its vitality – its 'aliveness'. This metaphor can be used to explore how we too cannot die from the perspective of personal experience, because I will argue that our notion of "self", that core sense of awareness (consciousness) we all possess, relates more to a deeper immortal 'ocean of self' underlying all the individual transient 'waves' of self. Our senses are generally attached to an individual wave of self, unaware of the larger ocean of self beneath. I propose that our attraction to the ocean waves is largely because of this unacknowledged comparison to a broader aspect of our own existence.

A powerful wave – strong, proud, magnificent, unique – and transient. Photo by Russell Ord, russellordphoto.com

THE SUN ENABLES ALL LIFE ON PLANET EARTH. THE SUN BATHES THE Earth with much-needed heat and light in the form of electro-magnetic radiation. This energy propagates in a wave-like fashion and energises the atmosphere. Transferred to the atmosphere, the sun's energy generates the wind, which in turn generates the ocean's waves.

Waves represent the "playhouse of infinite forms" referred to at the beginning of this chapter. They give the ocean its huge variety of character and flavour. There are gentle waves, waves in harmony, angry waves, huge waves, tiny waves. The variety of different waves on the one 'unchanging' ocean provides the context by which we can experience the ocean in so many different ways.

All things, material and phenomenal, in this universe are made of waves – oscillating, vibrating packets of energy. Even objects that are 'hard' are basically waves of energy.

Drew Kampion has been an editor of several surfing magazines and the author of a beautiful coffee-table book on waves. He has a deep fascination for the phenomenon of ocean waves.

> *"Indeed we are all at sea in this life, borne on an infinite network of complex oscillations. No part of our life is free of waves. We are all surfers, are we not?"* [1]

IN THE *UPANISHADS* – A COLLECTION OF ANCIENT INDIAN PHILOSOPHICAL texts concerned with the nature of ultimate reality – it is said, "As is the microcosm, so is the macrocosm".[2] So many times what we 'sense' and are drawn to reflects what is going on at scales far beyond (in the macrocosm sense) or finer (microcosm) than our physical senses are capable of detecting. We may have a feeling about or even a memory of a broader reality of which our consciousness is also a part.

The statement from the *Upanishads* reflects a symmetry we notice at many different levels of nature. Physicists have identified many such symmetries operating at both the sub-atomic and cosmic levels of the Universe. These symmetries are the correlations that will hopefully be apparent to you throughout this book. By "correlations" I refer to the comparisons, the similarities and reflections we identify in the world around us that trigger some awareness of a deeper reality to which we are connected. One such example covered in the first chapter on evolution is the comparison of the ocean as our source in the biological sense and a broader ocean of consciousness – or ocean of self – which is also our source in a more existential sense.

We might see these correlations in the matching patterns in the expression of life at many different levels. We also might notice correlations presenting as the similar messages built into the comments of different poets or scientists. In the absence of experimental or observational evidence (empirical evidence) – easy enough to obtain in the relatively gross material world – we rely on correlations, reproducibility and personal first-hand experience to support a concept. We may then derive a model of understanding to lend further support to that concept.

In this book, we will look at the concept of individual waves of consciousness on one ocean of consciousness. These 'waves' of individual consciousness will be equated with the notion of 'waves of being' or 'waves of self' (you and me) on one 'Ocean of Being' or 'Ocean of Self'. We will explore the very satisfying and fulfilling concept of a Unity that ties and connects all diversity together as One. In the absence of classical experimental proof, we can consider this concept a hypothesis.

The ocean and its waves provide an excellent metaphor to help us understand this important concept.

A big-wave surfer will tell you that every wave is different. Every wave can be appreciated for its uniqueness. Each wave lives a relatively short time though. It arises from the sea, it expresses itself as the unique version of wave that it is, and it melts back into the sea. In dying, the wave's essence has never been lost or even diminished, because its essence is the ocean. We – as waves of individual 'being'– define our essence (or 'self') as our consciousness, and we will explore the concept of that essence of consciousness being one Ocean of Consciousness (Ocean of Being, Ocean of Self or Ocean of Spirit) underlying and giving rise to all our individual consciousness. Our essence – like the ocean underlying and expressing the waves – cannot die!

From a distance we don't see the birth and death of waves. We see only the one un-changing ocean. Without the existence of waves, the power and magnificence of the ocean is not made manifest. The very vitality of the ocean – its 'aliveness' – is surely dependent on this expression of multitudinous but temporary wave forms. Here we see a paradox – the ocean is seen and felt to be 'alive' because of the birth and death of many varied waves. The grandeur of Life is felt and experienced on the basis of its ever-changing expressions.

"How the water sports and sings! (surely it is alive!)"[3]
– Walt Whitman

At the time of our death, we will experience more life, intense life, quintessential life, than ever! That is because we will relate more to the ocean of our existence than the mere wave of our existence at that time. This is a lot to take in at this present time, and we will revisit this concept in further chapters.

We can learn much by observing in life around us the subtle messages inherent in life. But to look more deeply into life around us, we must look more deeply into ourselves. What we see within, we will see also without (and vice-versa).

When we look at the ocean, we can see the essence of ourselves reflected in the ocean and its waves. The multiplicity of temporary forms arising from one unchanging entity fascinates us. It keeps us in wonder, awe and contemplation.

> "These ocean waves are perhaps the most incredible things on the planet…I have never gotten tired of watching them. It's almost as if they're trying to tell me something. Or that they are telling me something, and I'm trying hard to hear it."
>
> – Drew Kampion[4]

What might the waves be trying to tell us? It could be a number of things, and the biggest message to me is what I have just discussed – that the appearance and disappearance of multiple but unique waves is what accounts for the creative and ever-renewing expression of life. Furthermore, this life is not separate from us, but is our very essence – that which we define as our sense of 'self'.

You might have your own interpretations. Another message may be that the ocean waves are individual expressions or manifestations of the one formless ocean beneath. In this way, ocean waves are representative of the oneness or unity of all life.

> "Like echoes of the heartbeat of the absolute being, waves give expression to the divine will. They give form to the universe."
>
> – Drew Kampion, *The Book of Waves – Form and Beauty on the Ocean*

The mesmerising beauty and awe inherent in an ocean wave as captured by photographer Russell Ord, russellordphoto.com.

The surfer "feels" and identifies with the power and magnificence of the whole ocean when riding a big wave. He or she feels the quality and "specialness" of that unique wave, but relates more so with the enormous ocean that expresses the wave. The surfer – even momentarily – feels "one with the ocean".

> *"I love the sea as I do my own soul."*
> *– Heinrich Heine (1797–1856)*

I wonder what craziness impels a terrestrial creature – ill-equipped for mobility or extended periods in the sea – to ride a monstrous ocean wave? "How likely is it that any conceivable evolution would have taken man down a critical path that would lead him eventually (and in our time) into the hollow pocket of a 30-foot wave…to ride in the belly of the beast… to slide through the maelstrom of a collapsing cathedral of water with the composure of a matador, with the exhilaration of a wild-haired youth, with the primitive awe of an elemental man," says Drew Kampion.[5]

Just how critical is this drive for a connection to a primordial source – a source that goes even deeper than our phylogenetic link to the sea? We will examine the nature of that source, and we will see it as the very cradle of life and our ultimate 'home'.

When we, like the ocean surfer, see and feel the one ocean of life – ocean of consciousness or the big 'Self' – as the essence of our own individual wave of self (we'll call it the small 'self'), and that one ocean as also the essence of the individual waves of other selves, and that one ocean as the essence of seemingly separate waves of all material things, then we are truly 'awake'. We become accomplished surfers on the Ocean of Life. We are Self-realised. We are enlightened. We feel our small selves expanding to encompass all of 'Life' – the big 'Self'. It's a glorious feeling.

"To me the sea is a continual miracle,
The fishes that swim – the rocks
The motion of the waves
The ships with men in them
What stranger miracles are there?"

– Walt Whitman

Riding a heavy 10m (30-foot) wave with "the composure of a matador, with the exhilaration of a wild-haired youth, with the primitive awe of an elemental man…" (Drew Kampion – *The Book of Waves*). Picture by Russell Ord, russellordphoto.com.

*"The bleat, the bark, bellow, and roar
Are waves that beat on Heaven's shore."*

– William Blake

NOTES

1. Kampion, Drew, *The Book of Waves – Form and Beauty on the Ocean*, p 26
2. See p 12, Chapter Twelve.
3. Whitman, Walt, 'Song at Sunset', *Leaves of Grass: A Textual Variorum of the Printed Poems, 1860–1867*.
4. Kampion, Drew, *The Book of Waves – Form and Beauty on the Ocean*, p 29
5. Kampion, Drew, *The Book of Waves – Form and Beauty on the Ocean*, p 27

LIFE EXPRESSES MORE LIFE

*Flowers turned to stone! Not all the botany
Of Joseph Banks, hung pensive in a porthole,
Could find the Latin for this loveliness,*

– Kenneth Slessor, Five Visions of Captain Cook

Life is constantly ensuring that life continues. Coral reproduction is fascinating because the individual coral animals cannot move about and meet other coral animals. Nature has invented a clever mechanism to overcome this restriction. Coral spawning can remind us that life is all there is.

THE EVER-CREATIVE, EXUBERANT NATURE OF LIFE ALWAYS PUSHES MORE life out of itself. Reproduction is very much part of the miracle of life. Perhaps nowhere is the idea of life begetting more life better illustrated than the dramatic annual event of coral spawning.

In late November 1996, Becca and I joined scientist friend Russell Kelley to document coral spawning on Australia's Great Barrier Reef. We headed out to sea in Russell's yacht – mostly under sail – to arrive at Myrmidon Reef in the outer, central section of the Great Barrier Reef just north of Townsville.

Russell has a great knowledge of just when certain species of hard or soft coral will spawn. As it turned out, other invertebrates such as giant sea clams and sea cucumbers were also reproducing when we were there. We anchored in a quiet part of the reef, did some surveillance dives to acquaint ourselves with the area, and then planned our working dives, which were usually night dives often ending near midnight. Although a lot of work, the effort was well worth it, as we were witnesses to some extraordinary, rarely seen events.

MANY ANIMALS IN THE SEA ARE UNABLE TO MOVE AROUND. THEY'RE labelled 'sessile' rather than motile. Food and basically everything they need comes to them in the ocean. All they need to do is perch themselves in such a way that they can maximise their access to sunlight (especially in the case of hard corals), and food carried in the moving water. Because of this sessile character, they are sometimes mistaken for flowers or plants rather than animals.

Eminent Australian diver and TV documentary producer Valerie Taylor has used the imaginative description "posy" – as in a bunch of flowers – in reference to the colourful assemblage of animals perched on a black-coral whip. Becca and I have ever since referred to these collections of invertebrate animals as "posies", even though we are well aware that they animals and not plants.

Hard and soft corals are collections of very small individual animals, called polyps, that look like sea anemones. Each polyp has a central mouth surrounded by stinging tentacles. These stinging tentacles grab plankton drifting by in the water, and draw the tiny animals into the gut. From a distance, all we see are pretty coloured and attractively shaped gardens that resemble plants, with lots of little fish swimming in and around the corals for protection.

Australian poet Kenneth Slessor beautifully described the hard corals of the Great Barrier Reef as Captain James Cook might have seen and appreciated them:

> *Flowers turned to stone! Not all the botany*
> *Of Joseph Banks, hung pensive in a porthole,*
> *Could find the Latin for this loveliness,*
> *Could put the Barrier Reef in a glass box*
> *Tagged by the horrid Gorgon squint*
> *Of horticulture. Stone turned to flowers....*[1]

– Kenneth Slessor

A 'posy' of marine invertebrates that include ascidians, encrusting sponges and colonial anemones (or zoanthids) – all complex animals that live a sessile existence with food and oxygen brought to them in the ocean currents. A certain amount of exposure to sunlight is also useful, especially for the zoanthids.

To reproduce, corals and other sessile organisms must shed their reproductive cells (gametes) into water in a process called spawning and hope that the complementary male and female cells meet. There's a clever strategy associated with this seemingly haphazard method of reproducing.

Just a few nights every year during late spring or early summer, when the water temperature has been warm enough for a long enough period, and the tide is at the right level, corals of many species along the Great Barrier Reef release their gametes – be they eggs or sperm or both – into the water at the same time. The cue is provided by the moon, with spawning commencing in the nights following the full moon, and activity greatest on the fourth, fifth or sixth night.[2]

Many corals are hermaphrodite[3], which means they are both male and female and thus release sperm and eggs in one package typically referred to as a gamete bundle. Each polyp rolls gametes into a bundle in the hours before release, collecting them near the mouth of the coral polyp. Inside this bundle might be hundreds of eggs, with the testes (containing the sperm) wrapped around them.

Watching this sudden release of gametes is simply amazing. Little balls of perhaps two or more millimetres in diameter (typically pink but sometimes red, orange, blue or green) are released from the coral polyps over a few minutes. The scene has been described as "an upside-down snowstorm"[4], with the little brightly coloured spherical packages gently floating toward the sea surface. This "upside-down snowstorm" effect was beautifully captured by a video-cameraman working with us at Queensland's Magnetic Island, where we also went to document the spawning in glass aquaria. As he panned his camera very slowly upwards (faster than the ascent of the gametes), it appeared that the gamete bundles were falling like snowflakes. It looked cosmic, and since this book explores the universal connections and interplay of life, I can hopefully be excused for using such a romantic word. Certainly we see a connection that can be legitimately described as "out of this world", with the moon and sun providing the cues for the simultaneous release of gametes.

Some corals are gender-specific and release only sperm or eggs into the water. For the male corals, this 'nocturnal emission' of sperm is timed to match the release of eggs by female corals of the same species. The mass release of sperm appears more like the release of smoke, as the sperm cells are much smaller than the larger (millimetre scale) egg-sperm bundles.

The elegance inherent in nature is further illustrated by another clever orchestration of events. All gamete bundles and individual eggs and sperm make their way to the surface of the sea, disperse, and then begin their search for the appropriate gamete partner of the same species. The egg-sperm bundles break up at the surface to enable the eggs and sperm a chance to find a partner from another colony of the same species. The two-dimensional space of the surface greatly increases the chances of egg and sperm finding each other.

Once fertilisation has taken place, cells multiply quickly to form small coral larvae, which live in the ocean currents for a period before settling on a hard surface. These larvae, called planulae, have tiny hair-like cilia that they use to crawl around on the seafloor before metamorphosing and cloning into a new colony of polyps – a new coral.

We saw many predators feasting on this massive release of reproductive cells. In the days following the spawning, the tiny larvae that develop must also escape an ocean full of hungry fish and jellies. This is another reason that such a massive release of gametes is made at the same time. The sheer number of gametes overwhelms these predators, assuring a new generation "sets sail on the high seas".

Becca examines a large red soft-coral tree in the Coral Sea, representing the outer reaches of Australia's Great Barrier Reef

A hard coral (bottlebrush coral – Acropora longicyanthus) spawns during the night at Myrmidon Reef in the GBR. Photo by Becca Saunders

A hard coral with its gamete bundles (2.5mm diameter) at various stages of release.

When we look closely at this image of gametes filling the black screen of the ocean at night, the word 'cosmic' comes to mind again. They look like stars in the night sky. In the previous chapter, author Drew Kampion mentioned the effect ocean waves had on him. "It's almost as if they're trying to tell me something. Or that they are telling me something, and I'm trying hard to hear it," he said.[5] This image of coral reproductive cells filling the void tells me something. My conclusion is not too dissimilar to what I inferred from ocean waves in the last chapter – that the waves represent the creative and ever-renewing expression of life – the vibrancy of life.

The gamete bundles floating in such large numbers to the surface also represent life in all its creative expression and potential. The background represents space – the whole space/time arena upon which life acts out its myriad roles. In this underwater scene of gametes against the night ocean backdrop, all that appears to exist is life. There is nothing but life.

The messages of nature are forever 'ringing' in the world, and it is up to us to refine our ability to detect and understand those messages.

Kampion was aware of the voice of the ocean waves "trying to tell [him] something". Should we ignore subtle perceptions because we find them too whispery, intangible, and unreliable? Or, like tuning a radio dial, can we better 'tune' our reception into the messages of nature? I propose that it is possible to fine-tune our perception by going beyond our reliance on the five physical senses. In this way, we eliminate the 'radio static' or 'noise' that smothers our awareness of the ever-present connection we have with all aspects of nature.

I believe 'life' is everything expressed in our universe – be it material or phenomenal, organic or mineral. This concept of life is a big jump for the discriminating mind to embrace, but as we develop arguments for the existence of a more comprehensive model of consciousness through the following chapters, this broader view of life just might make sense. It's a concept that must be felt. It's a concept that will ultimately be realised rather than just reasoned – that life is all there is.

> *"Life is a miracle……… Life is a miracle".*
> – Maharishi Mahesh Yogi

NOTES

1. Slessor, Kenneth (1901–1971), *Five Visions of Captain Cook,* Selected Poems (A&R Poetry Classics), permission to reproduce text by HarperCollins Publishers.
2. *Readers Digest Book of the Great Barrier Reef,* 1984. Corals, Sexual Reproduction, p 112.
3. Derived from the Greek god Hermes and the goddess Aphrodite.
4. *Readers Digest Book of the Great Barrier Reef,* 1984. Corals, Sexual Reproduction, p 112
5. Kampion. Drew, *The Book of Waves – Form and Beauty on the Ocean*, p 29.

SHARKS

"What is man without the beasts? If all the beasts were gone, men would die from great loneliness of spirit. For what happens to the beasts soon happens to man. All things are interconnected."

– Chief Seattle, 1854

Even predatory sharks do not act purely on instinct. Displays of curiosity and playfulness – even verging on friendliness – have been observed in sharks, demonstrating a richness of character and a depth of expressed consciousness we have not usually attributed to them. An explanation lies in the concept of a common ocean of consciousness underlying the sharks' and our consciousness.

A Caribbean reef shark (*Carcharhinus perezii*), fairly typical of the whaler group of sharks and similar to the dusky shark in Pacific waters.

SHARKS REPRESENT PERHAPS THE MOST-FEARED CREATURES ON THIS planet. The very thought of a shadowy, ghost-like predator gliding stealthily towards a hapless human elicits a primal fear in most of us.

Only a small minority of shark species are dangerous to humans. The species that get the most publicity in this regard include the great white and whaler sharks such as the tiger and the bull shark. Some of the oceanic species of whalers can also be very dangerous to humans, but fortunately, they inhabit deeper offshore ocean environment where humans are less likely to be swimming or diving. These sharks are important apex predators in the ocean's food chain and have an important role in keeping the ocean's eco-system in balance.

Over more than four decades I've completed thousands of ocean dives. Sharks are low on the list of risks I assume with my diving, although I never discount the risk altogether. I've seen two tiger sharks in my diving career – one very large one off the Socorro Islands in the Pacific Ocean off Mexico[3], and the other while we were diving in the open ocean in the Coral Sea. Neither presented a direct threat to us, although we chose to leave the water. I've also dived (without cages) with oceanic white-tips and oceanic blue sharks, although all were fairly small specimens. The oceanic white-tips (not to be confused with reef white-tips) definitely had to be watched constantly, and I consider these as perhaps the most aggressive and dangerous of the whaler sharks – and perhaps of any shark species.

I've seen great white sharks only on one expedition in South Australia, where they were deliberately attracted with bait to allow us to take photos from inside the safety of a cage. I know five divers (four of them based where I live in the north coast of NSW) who have seen great whites in the normal course of their diving activities. Three of them were free-diving (breath-hold or snorkel diving) and spearing fish. In all cases, the shark approached the diver out of curiosity then turned away two or three metres from the diver and wasn't seen again. Anecdotally therefore, I believe that a diver who sees a great white shark is not likely to be attacked by that shark. All these friends of mine have wisely exited the water though. There is still a significant risk that a large great white will attack if the diver just ignores the shark.

Eye contact between shark and human seems – with my limited observations – to suppress the element of surprise that sharks prefer in attacking prey. This is why surfers and swimmers – generally ignorant of what is beneath them – are more vulnerable to shark attack, especially in murky water.

Whaler sharks are generally smaller than great whites and are usually not a danger when they are solitary (with the exception of tiger and bull sharks). Whalers become more daring when they congregate in numbers of six or more and can behave like a pack of wolves.

By nature, sharks are cautious and usually take their time swimming around humans suspended on a line. They can lose interest and move on, but sometimes their circling tightens to ever-decreasing distances from the divers.

This happened on one occasion many years ago, when a school of dusky sharks[4] circled closer and closer to me. My dive buddies had completed their decompression commitments before me, and left me alone in the water.

Fortunately, I didn't have too much deco time remaining, so I decided to exit the water.[5]

A SIMILAR SITUATION TO THIS OCCURRED ONE MORE TIME WHEN WE WERE decompressing after a dive on a wreck off Sydney. The dusky sharks this time appeared more curious than menacing, and did not approach too closely, enabling us to safely complete our decompression commitments.

Another couple of friends had a more scary experience while decompressing after a deep dive on a shipwreck on the central coast of NSW. In their case, they still had some 30 minutes of scheduled decompression ahead of them, when circling bronze whalers[6] started to physically bump them. Clearly the sharks were becoming bolder, and this couple had no choice but to quickly leave the water. One of the pair subsequently presented decompression sickness symptoms and needed treatment in a recompression chamber.

Since these incidents, on deep dives where decompression is required, we use a Shark Shield[7] – an electronic device that emits an electro-magnetic signal unpleasant to the sensitive ampullae of Lorenzini found on the snouts of all sharks. These sense organs detect electromagnetic fields emitted by muscle contractions in other animals. We have been told that the electronic repellants will probably not stop a committed, determined shark attack, but are likely to deter most sharks in their cautionary approach to divers. With ascents from deep wrecks taking as long as three or more hours, we find these Shark Shields comforting additions to our armamentarium.

WHEN I WAS A YOUNG SCHOOLBOY, I REMEMBER BEING TAUGHT THAT animals do not have souls, and act purely on instinct. In other words, they are 'programmed' to act by an inherited pre-determined wiring of their primitive brains, and are not conscious to the extent that they can choose whether to behave one way or another. Those of you who own pets might question this teaching. My observations of marine animals, including sharks, and the observations others have made over the years, has definitely steered my opinion of all animals away from this very human-centric way of thinking.

A great white shark off the South Australian coast. (Photo by Brett Vercoe, Liquid Focus)

Australian journalist Paul Raffaele wrote an informative article for *Smithsonian Magazine* in June, 2008, examining the behaviour of great white sharks[8]. Reliable accounts by shark researchers tell of divers who were grabbed lightly by their hands by great white sharks and towed a short distance before being released with minimal injury. In giving their human guests a little 'tour', the sharks had no option but to use their sharp pointy teeth to gently 'hold hands' with the diver. Another incident observed was a white shark gently taking a floating bird in its mouth and then swimming around the observers' boat. "A few seconds later, the bird resurfaced and flew off, hardly the worse for wear," Paul writes. Could we infer an element of playfulness here?

Mike Rutzen and his family run a shark cage-diving business in South Africa. Rutzen is famous for diving with great white sharks outside of a cage. In the Smithsonian article, Rutzen recounted his first open-water encounter with a female great white. "I was right by the boat and she came close to me," he reported. "I nervously prodded her away with a spear gun. She swam away a few yards, turned and surged back at me. She thrust her face at mine and opened wide her enormous mouth to show me her teeth, and swam away. She was saying, 'Don't do that again'."

These stories, and the stories I will shortly relate of other members of the shark family, suggest a depth of consciousness underlying the behaviour of these animals rather than the automatic, instinctive responses we have been taught about.

Since moving to the north coast of nsw in Australia 10 years ago, Becca and I have done many dives on the nearby Solitary Islands, which are situated at the interface of warm currents from the tropical north and the cooler currents coming up the coast from the temperate south. This assures us of an interesting mixture of tropical and temperate-water marine animals. There are healthy numbers of grey nurse sharks[9] inhabiting the rocky gutters alongside these islands, and I never tire of swimming with them and taking photographs of them.

Years ago, a friend of mine told me that he undertook an experiment while diving. When he was close to a blue groper (wrasse), he thought about the fish as food on his plate for dinner. My friend reported that the fish immediately swam away, as if picking up on his thoughts. I was sceptical as to whether the fish did indeed pick up his thoughts, but never dismissed the idea as complete "hog-wash".

Years later, while diving on the Solitary Islands, I noticed a few grey nurse sharks swimming in broad circles that took them along a shallow rocky gutter alongside which was a beautiful yellow soft coral tree. As most sharks are various shades of grey, I was after something colourful to include in a photograph of one of these sharks. I swam down to the coral tree and positioned myself in such a way that I could photograph both the coral and the shark as it swam down the gutter. One of the sharks swam away and one of the others paused at the end of the gutter, as if deciding whether it should also make a detour or continue on its original path, having to negotiate the strange-looking creature with the big camera. Instead of thinking of fish on my dinner plate, I tried to project loving, caring thoughts of this beautiful animal. I actually did have those thoughts – and they were genuine! Immediately, the shark swam down the gully along its habitual path and almost over my left shoulder. Whether or not it had picked up my thoughts (which I know could never be proven), it had obviously decided that I was harmless and swam the path I hoped it would, allowing me to get the photo!

The grey nurse shark that hesitated before swimming along the rocky gully. With its slightly deflected pectoral fins, it still appears mildly cautious.

I don't blame you at all if you reject such a story as wishful thinking on my part. But I dare to mention the story because I believe that animals may be more highly tuned – or at least equally tuned – to the dispositions of other animals than we are. Without verbal communication, such awareness – even if it is 'extra-sensory' – might be an important survival skill to develop.

IN APRIL 1994 I SPENT A WEEK DIVING WITH WHALE SHARKS[10] OFF Ningaloo Reef in Western Australia. The migration of whale sharks down the west coast of Australia is an annual phenomenon and one that attracts divers and snorkellers from around the world. These huge creatures are the largest fish in the world and are genuine sharks – not whales. They can reach 10–12m and possibly longer – equivalent to many whales. They are essentially plankton eaters (including schools of very small fish) and are incapable of swallowing a human. So they, like whales, can be considered gentle giants of the sea.

Ningaloo Reef is one of the few places in the world where divers can reliably encounter one of these huge animals, without travelling too far to sea. Their appearance – usually between March and August/September – coincides with the coral spawning event, which usually happens around March and April. The whale sharks feed on the plentiful small creatures that feast on the coral gametes.

A commercial dive-charter boat will usually cooperate with an aircraft pilot who spots the sharks and relays the information and location of the sharks to the skipper. Just a few swimmers are allowed to enter the water ahead of the sharks to give them the best chance for an encounter and picture-taking opportunity. It's usually possible to keep up with the sharks for a short while, as they only swim slowly, and 5–10 minutes is a typical time for each encounter before the next group takes their turn.

Whale sharks can grow to 12.5m (41 feet). They sift plankton and very small fish through filter pads as they expel water through the gills.

On my trip, there was one young whale shark we later called 'Herbie' who showed particular interest in me. We were told not to touch the animals, but it kept swimming towards me – head on! I evaded its path a couple of times and then decided to swim back to the dive boat. Herbie followed right behind me till we all arrived back to the platform at the stern of the boat. There, Herbie placed his mouth almost out of the water up against the platform and stayed there for 20 seconds of more. At this stage, the people on board began patting Herbie, and I – still in the water beside Herbie – decided to join in. Herbie then took a slow swim alongside the boat and disappeared. We were all quite amazed at this shark behaviour, as it clearly demonstrated curiosity, friendliness, trust and even possibly playfulness.

Herbie turned directly towards me when I tried to swim away from his approach.

One diver I've met, Joe Sciberras was out fishing in his boat off the city of Wollongong, just south of Sydney. He and his two friends were visited by a large whale shark that parked itself with its mouth almost against the stern of their boat and just stayed there. Curious about this strange behaviour, Joe entered the water with his mask and snorkel to get a better look at a magnificent animal rarely seen that far south.

He quickly discovered that the shark had a huge rope – which he likened to a ship's mooring rope, about 100mm thick – bound tightly around its girth just in front of its pectoral fins, cutting into its flesh. It was quite apparent to Joe that the shark was seeking help from the humans. He returned to the boat and asked his companions for a knife. They only had fish filleting knives, which are not the most efficient at cutting through thick rope covered in barnacles. Joe spent the good part of 20 minutes kneeling on the back of the compliant shark in the water, using all five filleting knives aboard the boat to cut the rope. Once he completed the task, the shark slowly swam forward just to the left side of the boat and disappeared. Joe was left with bleeding knees from the sandpaper-like skin possessed by all sharks and rays.

Joe just happened to have a new video camera aboard his boat, so that one of his friends was able to record the whole event, and I later produced a three and a half minute narrated video segment for YouTube.[11] At the end of the clip I ask the question "How did it know?" meaning "how did the shark know that there was help available by approaching the floating object?" I can surmise only two possibilities:

1. The shark is more intelligent that we normally assume and was somehow able to deduce from previous experience or observation that boats are associated with humans, and possibly therefore they are able to assist.
2. There are other mechanisms operating, of which the exact detail is unknown, but which fall into a broader framework of understanding. This broader paradigm sees consciousness as one ocean underlying individual waves of consciousness. These individual waves of consciousness include the consciousness of the shark and the consciousness of each of the three men on the fishing boat.

The first possibility – that the shark intelligently deduced that humans could help it – seems unlikely to me. The second possibility, while outside our normally accepted paradigm for understanding consciousness, is actually more acceptable to me. A view that we share a common underlying field of consciousness, which expresses itself through different nervous systems, allows for a common 'medium' through which we are all connected – humans with humans, animals with animals and humans with animals. Communication at this deeper shared level seems possible, even if such communication is not acknowledged or experienced at the superficial level of awareness, which is normally occupied with the five senses.

I believe that this one 'ocean of consciousness' is also a level of nature that transcends time and space. All possibilities – past, present and future – are contained in this ocean of awareness. With access to all possibilities, there is presumably access to all solutions as well.

Any acceptance of this model of consciousness represents a big leap of faith. It represents a huge paradigm shift in the way we see life and ourselves. But perhaps it is a paradigm 'expansion' rather than 'shift', since it does not necessarily substitute our current way of thinking about consciousness and life generally, but expands on it.

To acknowledge the existence of this ocean of consciousness, we ultimately have to experience it first-hand. To do this, we need to become virtual divers in this ocean within. There are many who caution us against exploring the depths of our mind. They fear that, like the watery ocean that occupies two thirds of our Earth, there are 'sharks' down there – "bad spirits", demons, possession and the like. Such an attitude reminds me of the fear early mariners projected into the unknown depths of the ocean. The reality was found to be very different when we became explorers of the ocean depths.

Just as we have hopefully gained a less fearful view of sharks and other denizens of the deep, we should have no fear of exploring and becoming familiar with those depths to the ocean of consciousness that underlies all living things. A very different, welcoming, loving world awaits us – the world of your own essential Self.

NOTES

3   This was on the trip where we dived with the large manta rays off San Benedicto Island, near the Socorros group. See next chapter on manta rays.
4   *Carcharhinus obscurus*
5   We were diving on the wreck of the SS *Catterthun* off Seal Rocks, NSW, Australia
6   *Carcharhinus brachyurus*
7   Mine is a Mariner Shark Shield – www.sharkshield.com
8   Raffaele, Paul; 'Forget Jaws, Now it's ... Brains!' *Smithsonian Magazine*, June, 2008.
9   *Carcharias taurus*. The very similar looking sand tiger shark is *Odontaspis ferox*.
10   *Rhincodon typus*
11   See : https://www.youtube.com/watch?v=dpvB5qouSMM or search for "whale shark seeks help". There is also a link to a radio interview, where you can hear Joe relate his story.

MANTA RAYS – ANGELS OF THE SEA

*I mount! I fly!
O grave! Where is thy victory?
O death! Where is thy sting?*[1]

— Alexander Pope

Manta rays – sometimes referred to as "devilfish" by fishers because of their black colouration and furled cephalic lobes which resemble horns – are in fact curious, trusting and playful creatures that will readily approach and interact with divers.

MANTA RAYS ARE THE LARGEST OF THE RAYS, BUT – UNLIKE STINGRAYS – do not possess a stinging barb on their tail and swim about in the open ocean rather than scavenging on the bottom. As with all rays, they are members of the shark family, and therefore have a cartilaginous skeleton and small tooth-like denticles on their skin.

Peter Benchley, author of *Jaws* – a story about a great white shark with a distinct taste for humans – wrote another novel in which the predator was man, threatening the balance and harmony of an underwater seamount rich with vibrant, diversified sea life. His book *The Girl of the Sea of Cortez* is a fable about the unique relationship of a young islander girl Paloma and the creatures belonging to the seamount and her heroic efforts to protect these creatures, including a giant manta ray.

When I first read this book, I was dubious of the existence and behaviour of mantas like the huge one that Paloma befriended, complete with its 7m wing span. My excursion with Becca to the remote island of San Benedicto in the Pacific Ocean off Mexico some years later[2] softened my scepticism of Benchley's manta ray and has left both Becca and me with a sense of wonder, awe and huge respect for these charismatic sea creatures.

The journey from Australia to San Benedicto is a long one. We flew from Los Angeles down to Cabo San Lucas at the tip of Mexico's Baja Peninsula. We then boarded the live-aboard dive boat *Ambar 3*, and steamed for a day and a half south and westward into the Pacific Ocean. Our destination was the volcanic island called San Benedicto, an un-inhabitable cone of solidified magma that sticks out of the deep blue ocean. It's worth having a look at Google Earth to see the island from above. The island's tallest peak, Bárcena, is a typical volcano that rises about 310m high near the southern part of the island. It last erupted violently in 1952, which in geological terms makes it 'active'.

San Benedicto Island, a volcanic island that juts out of the sea west of Mexico.

A couple of hundred metres from the main island is a completely submerged seamount known as The Boiler. It is a protrusion of solidified magma with a flat top and nearly vertical sides that was once the core of a smaller volcano. Geologists refer to these as volcanic plugs. Its base is probably 80m or more deep and it stretches up to within 6m of the surface.

This seamount is the haunt of huge Pacific manta rays (*Manta birostris*). Like whale sharks, manta rays filter-feed, straining plankton and small fish through their gills. While it is true that manta rays can reach 7m from wing tip to wing tip, the mantas we saw reached up to about 5m across the wings – which is still pretty big!

On our first day of diving, the mantas were curious, but remained a cautious distance away. We had all agreed to a diving etiquette that allowed the mantas to control the nature of any interaction with us.

On the second day, the mantas manoeuvred themselves beneath us and slowed right down. Body language speaks volumes, and it was clear to us that we were being invited to hop on their backs and go for a ride. I recall gently introducing myself by touching the back (dorsum) of the manta ray with the flat palm of my hand, to which I would sometimes get what appeared to be a short sensuous, quivering muscle response. I would then slide my hand over the cartilaginous ridge of the upper part of its mouth (rostrum) for stability and gently lower my knees down on either side of the manta's spine.

With broad sweeps of its huge wings, whoosh! We were away!

The manta carried me for a long lazy circle around the top of the seamount and then hovered again almost exactly where I got on.

The overall experience was like riding on the back of a bird. Where else on Earth could we possibly come even close to this? What we were experiencing was normally the stuff of fantasy, mythology and dreams.

We were two creatures alien to each other and more different in physiology and anatomy than I could ever imagine, yet we were bonded by a common trust, curiosity, friendliness and even playfulness. We were sharing more in common than I would have possibly conceived before this event.

In this silent realm beneath the sea, my physical senses were acutely alert. Being truly in the moment, any normal sense of time had slipped away. I felt calm and tranquil in the silence of this huge ocean realm. There was a harmony here – both with the creature and the unbounded ocean around me. This was freedom at its exhilarating best.

For the next few days, we all rode mantas. I'd be on one manta, and then look across to see Becca on another manta. The situation was almost surreal.

WHILE WE ALL MOSTLY WORE SCUBA GEAR[3], I ALSO ENJOYED THE simplicity of free diving (breath-hold diving) and within a few days I was able to ride a manta ray for 90 seconds or more on a single breath, enjoying a tour over the seamount. The mantas generally swam quite slowly, which provided a comfortable journey for their human friends.

Such an intimate encounter with a little known animal certainly provides a feel for their anatomy and behavior. The strong, bunched muscle where the wing attaches to the torso of the manta contrasted with the almost trampoline-like nature of the skin as it stretched from this muscle to the spine. The backwards orientation of the denticles on the manta's skin (so designed for hydro-dynamic efficiency in moving through the water) meant that it felt smooth in the head-to-tail direction, but rough like sandpaper in the opposite direction.

I watched the wing tips beat up and down either side of me. The wings were thick nearest the torso and muscular – certainly not as fine or as long as one would expect on a similarly sized bird (the water medium is much denser than air).

During my journeys, I noticed that I wasn't the only passenger. One or two *remoras* or suckerfish – about 60cm (2 ft) long – were also hitching a ride, generally behind the cephalic lobes (the curled-up fins either side of the mouth and above the manta's eyes). These quite large fish often remained stubbornly attached to the manta while we were sharing the ride. Some divers even held onto the remora tails to hitch their ride on the mantas. A closer inspection of the remoras revealed smaller parasitic crustaceans or worm-like critters on them – riders on riders.

Often, the remoras would move to the underside (ventral) surface of the manta ray while we secured ourselves on the top (dorsum). We speculated that this could be one reason why the mantas actively engaged with us. As far as we know, the remoras provide no benefit for the mantas and we saw skin lesions resulting from their long-term attachment. Perhaps the mantas thought of us as giant cleaning fish capable of removing the annoying remoras, which get a free ride with minimal energy expenditure.

Could there be other reasons why the manta rays didn't mind us riding them? It's possible that the combination of human and manta makes for a larger, more powerful looking animal than the manta alone. Size in the ocean is an advantage. It just might deter their main enemy – the tiger shark – which we did see while diving on this trip. It's also possible that we could be the sacrificial victim that would be left stationary and alone if the manta decided to make a run for it in a threatened situation – and believe me, with a violent twist, mantas could easily eject their human passenger if they wished.

There may be many other reasons why the mantas allowed such intimate contact with their terrestrial guests, but we can't entirely discount the possibility that the rays genuinely enjoyed the interaction. In the last chapter I drew attention to a broader range of behaviours demonstrated by some sharks – even the great white shark. Behavioural qualities such as friendliness, playfulness, curiosity, trust and even intelligence may not strictly be the prerogative of humans.

How do we explain the antics of the mantas as they swam around us in circles, seemingly encouraged to continue as we mimicked them? We were worn out before they were. On one occasion I was photographing some small fish on the top of the seamount when I became aware of a big stationary shadow beside me. It was one of the larger mantas pausing to see what I was up to and possibly wondering what interest I could have in such small critters.

Stories I've heard about mantas keeping human riders near the surface if their breath-holding abilities are limited were proven when two mantas did just that with the *Ambar*'s skipper and me. While we were swimming with just snorkels, the mantas allowed us to ride on their backs and kept us near the surface so we could breathe through our snorkels at the same time.

On one dive, Becca and our American friend Tom became caught in a strong current that swept them away from the seamount and the boat. They tried for several minutes to fight the current and get back to the boat, but eventually they ran out of air and had to surface. Fortunately, we knew of their predicament and came to the rescue with a powered inflatable craft. Becca said that during the whole episode a manta accompanied them, and she feels confident that the manta would have taken one or even both of them back to the seamount if they had hitched a ride.

My description of manta ray behavior could again be seen as an imaginative interpretation of events for which there is no real evidence one way or the other. However, we were all affected in a very positive way, and all those who have dived with these wonderful animals have come away feeling more respect and a heightened sense of wonder and intrigue for this enigmatic creature of the sea.

I SHOULD POINT OUT THAT MOST ANIMALS IN THE SEA – INCLUDING manta rays – do not wish to be touched, let alone ridden. Many manta encounters I have had in the Great Barrier Reef and here off Coffs Harbour in Australia have been with much smaller animals. Any attempt to hold onto one of these rays will almost certainly scare them away. On the other hand, if any animal takes the initiative and makes it apparent that such a physical relationship is welcome, then I feel it is up to the diver to determine how to act. We saw no evidence whatsoever that we were having any negative effects on these mantas, although I accept that a possible negative consequence of regular interactions of this nature might lead to a loss of healthy fear of humans and the boats that carry them. Sadly, manta rays are hunted by some commercial fishing operations in that part of the world.

> *"The voice of the sea speaks to the soul. The touch of the sea is sensuous, enfolding the body in its soft, close embrace."* Kate Chopin (1851-1904), from *"The Awakening"*.

IN 2002, I WAS COMMISSIONED AS THE PHOTOGRAPHER FOR A DETAILED *Australian Geographic* feature on manta rays.[4] Almost as soon as it was published I received a phone call from a good friend who was a scientist working in cancer research at the Sydney Children's Hospital. She and her partner had befriended a 12-year-old patient at the hospital – Rhys Jarratt[5] – who was dying of a rare form of incurable leukaemia.

Our friends were also divers and had told Rhys about the many ocean creatures they have seen, including manta rays. For some reason, Rhys became fixated with manta rays in the last two weeks of his life. He absorbed every piece of information in the *Australian Geographic* article and any other article that was found for him.

I was asked to visit Rhys in his hospital ward and show him my photographs of mantas and share my experiences with him.

It was more than a week before I managed to visit Rhys. When I entered his private room, he was surrounded by a few doctors and his mother, father and younger brother. I couldn't help but notice the manta ray paraphernalia that surrounded Rhys – manta posters, models and even a manta blanket (actually it was a stingray blanket – but close enough).

Rhys asked many questions about mantas during my projected slide presentation, and while he did look very ill (I clearly didn't appreciate just how ill he was), he appeared to be alert and fully focused on the subject of his devotion. At the end of the presentation, after we exchanged goodbyes and I had left, Rhys said to his father, "I'm ready for a big manta to take me away from this misery"[6]. He died the next morning.

Rhys stated very clearly to us during my presentation that he wished to have a swim with mantas at Lady Elliot Island in tropical Queensland. While the rest of us were busy deciding how we might be able to make this happen, the acting nurse told us flatly (in private) that there was no way Rhys could even get onto an aircraft and survive the flight. We were jolted back into reality when we heard this, but I like to think that Rhys finally fulfilled his wish and got his magic ride on a manta ray – probably a more glorious and intimate ride than any of us could imagine or for that matter experience on this earth.

WHAT WAS THE NATURE OF RHYS'S ATTRACTION TO MANTA RAYS? I'M SURE Rhys had his own personal reasons, but I also have some theories. One very significant thing the head nurse told me in private was that young children facing death very often adopt an animal or even an inanimate object such as a tricycle "as a vehicle into the next life". This is clearly not a behaviour that has been indoctrinated into a child, but rather appears as an innocent and very spontaneous interest in the days or weeks before death. Rhys's simple but highly charged comment to his father – that he was ready for a big manta to take him away – would appear to support this observation.

I have touched on the symbolic nature of the ocean and how the qualities of the ocean depths experienced by a diver reflect those qualities experienced in the depths of the diver's own awareness – that realm I have referred to as an 'ocean of consciousness'. We can also refer to this ocean of consciousness as a field of pure consciousness or 'universal consciousness'. Pure consciousness is that ocean of consciousness that underlies and gives rise to our individual consciousness – like waves (individual consciousness) on the one ocean (pure consciousness).

The qualities that can be experienced by the diver include unboundedness, freedom, endless wonder, timelessness, all possibilities, unity amidst diversity, harmony, silence and peacefulness. The ocean realm of the manta ray represents these qualities. If we add to this list the qualities of character demonstrated by the manta ray itself – friendliness, curiosity, playfulness and trust – then we have an even more complete package that I believe also represents the qualities (or at least tendencies) of pure consciousness.

Because this one ocean of consciousness connects and unifies all the individual expressed waves of consciousness, we could infer that its nature is to attract rather than repel, to provide a *uni*fied basis to all the di*verse* forms that arise from it. This one field of consciousness is truly "*uni-versal*". This binding or attractive quality of pure consciousness is why love is also one of its universal features. The attractive, binding quality of love is associated with friendliness, curiosity, playfulness and trust. These are qualities we have seen expressed to some degree with manta rays and perhaps even with some of the more traditional sharks in the whole shark family. The ocean of consciousness – 'pure' consciousness – represents that which binds all creatures and all things.

We can take this further and equate this one ocean of pure consciousness to a unified field originally proposed by Albert Einstein, which now quite likely is the field described by modern physicists in superstring theory. Einstein was convinced that the discoveries of modern physics were becoming progressively unified and were heading inexorably towards a single field of nature's functioning from which all the diverse laws of nature – including the fields and particles that make up our physical world – emanate. If the realm of pure consciousness – the ocean of consciousness sometimes referred to as the 'absolute' – is indeed this hypothesised unified field, then this one ocean of consciousness can be seen as the very source of life itself.

From here on I will refer to this concept of consciousness as the unified field model of consciousness. I propose that pure consciousness

– being also a unified field, and therefore the source of all material and phenomenal existence – is life itself!

If you think about it from your own life experience, those episodes when you have felt these qualities of pure consciousness (unboundedness, peace, wonder, connectedness and love of everything) – the so-called 'peak experiences', whether they be from under the ocean or the top of a mountain, looking into the night sky or enjoying the beauty of a sunset – are also those that make you feel more 'alive' than ever. I am proposing that the essence of life is pure consciousness, equated with a unified field underlying the laws of nature. We have referred to pure consciousness as an ocean of consciousness, ocean of self, ocean of being, ocean of spirit…and now we can add 'ocean of life'. In eastern philosophy pure consciousness (the proposed unified field) is called Ātmā – the essence not only of human consciousness, but of all reality.

Rhys then, was embracing the very essence of life itself (symbolised by the manta rays in the ocean) at the time of bodily death. I did not see this as a panicky, desperate embrace, but rather a welcoming and surrendering embrace. This would appear to be a paradox to most readers. At the time of someone's death, could that person possibly embrace the very essence of life – more life? Rather than anticipating the end of it all, or some form of ultimate blackout, we just might experience more intense life than ever at the time of our 'death'. Maybe – from a first-person experiential point of view – there is nothing but life; at all times and forever. Perhaps, awaiting us is the biggest paradox of our lives!

Becca introduces herself to a large manta ray at San Benedicto Island, Mexico

Becca rides on the back of a trusting manta ray at San Benedicto Island, Mexico

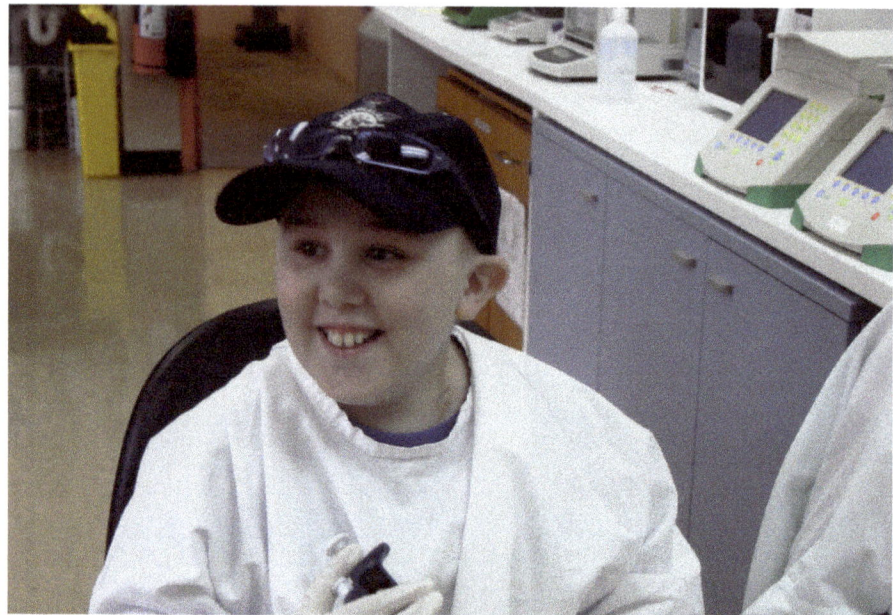

Rhys Jarratt (13-06-1990 to 16-04-2002) loved all creatures, but enjoyed a special relationship with manta rays in the last weeks of his life

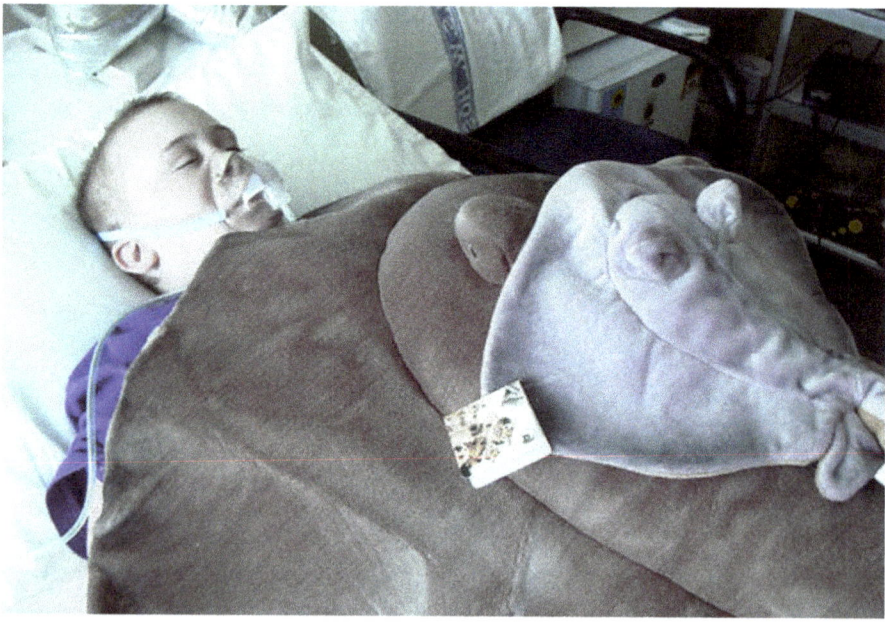

Rhys with 'manta ray' blankets

NOTES

1. Alexander Pope, 1688–1744, British poet, 'The Dying Christian to his Soul'; Words most likely borrowed from *The Bible*, Corinthians; 15:55 – "O Death, where is your victory? O death, where is your sting?"
2. December, 1995
3. Scuba stands for "self contained underwater breathing apparatus" – usually comprising a tank filled with compressed air and a breathing "regulator".
4. *The Journal of the Australian Geographic Society* – Issue 66; April–June 2002, "Manta Ray", pages 40-59.
5. Rhys's parents have given the author their approval of the use of Rhys's name and his remarkable story.
6. Rhys's father had confirmed this statement of Rhys's with me at a later meeting.

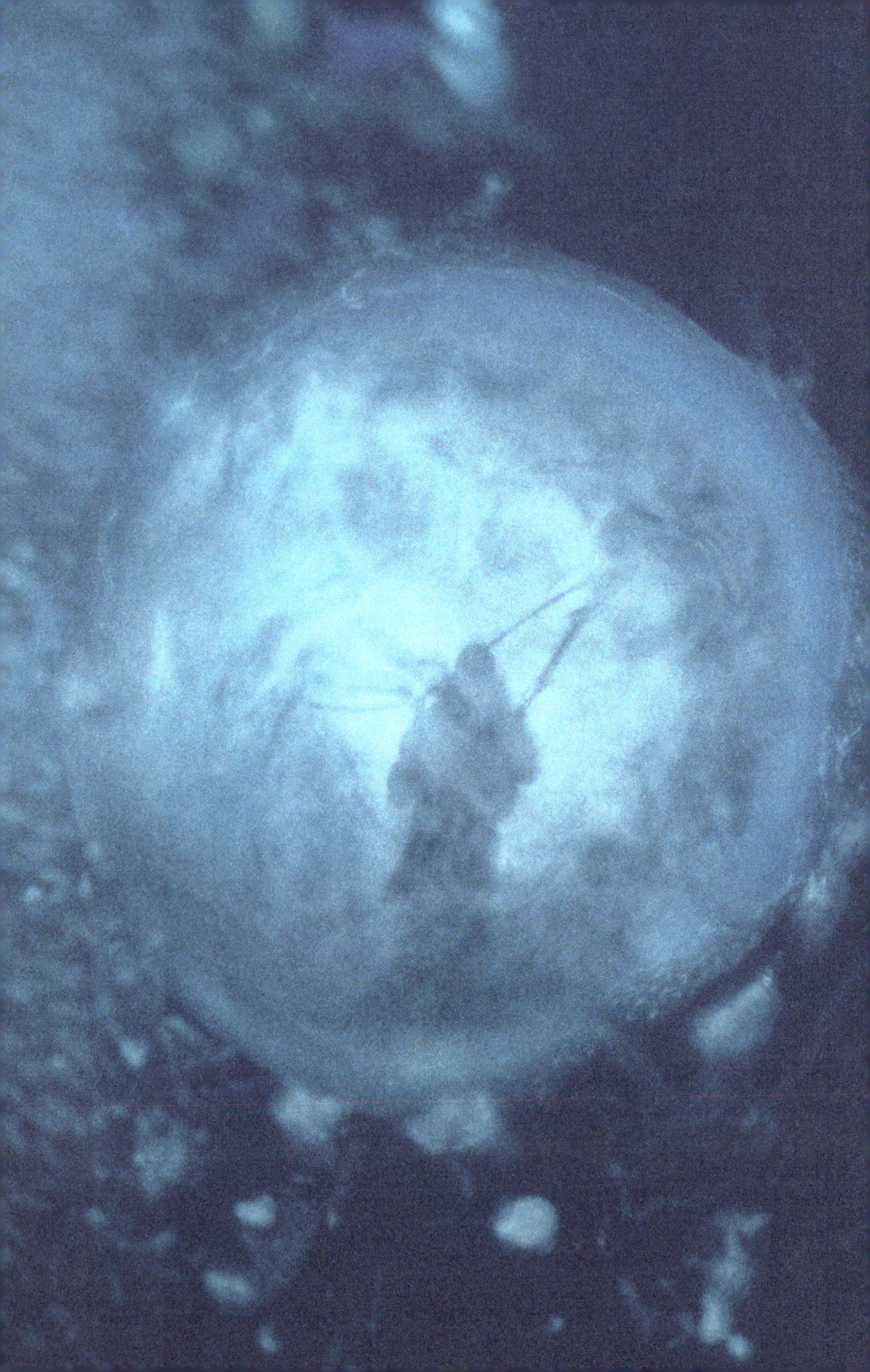

SHIPWRECK EXPLORATION – THE RISKS AND REWARDS

*"But doth suffer a sea-change
Into something rich and strange"*

– Shakespeare, The Tempest, 1610

Diving on deep shipwrecks has many attractions and many risks. This chapter looks at the practical aspects of shipwreck exploration so that the reader might appreciate the difficulties and efforts spent in bringing back images of these relics.

SHIPWRECKS ARE MUSEUMS UNDER THE SEA. THEY REPRESENT A PERIOD OF life typically 100-plus years ago when people dressed differently, spoke differently, held different values to our modern societies and lived without the medical and technological comforts many of us enjoy now. When divers explore a wreck, they can see evidence of everyday items from that era. The wreck makes history very 'real' and tangible. With little else down there to contrast the wreck with our present human world, it is easier to imagine ourselves transported back in time. In fact, the out-of-place appearance in the natural world below of something that represented the best in technology and engineering at its time reminds us that humans have rarely 'mastered' nature.

In the late 1970s and 1980s, it was deemed acceptable to recover items from wrecks and display them at home. Most divers openly shared and discussed their findings with other divers or those interested in maritime history. As a photographer pre-occupied with a bulky camera, my sampling opportunities were limited, but I was often impressed with the discoveries and recoveries undertaken by my friends.

In the 1980s, maritime archaeologists appointed to the NSW State Government heritage departments in Australia began a very effective education program encouraging divers to document what they saw, but leave wreck items where they were found for the enjoyment of future divers and to conserve the contextual information of the item's location in a particular part of the wreck. In other words, more information might later be gleaned from a wreck if items are left where they are found. Also, without specialised and sometimes expensive conservation efforts, many recovered items exposed to air do not last as long as they would if left in situ. Underwater photographers therefore have an important role in sharing the historical significance of shipwrecks with the general public. Shipwrecks also attract a significant amount of sea life, which is part of the enjoyment of exploring and photographing wrecks.

Many shipwrecks lie on the sea floor well off the coast and so are in deep water. Deep ocean diving poses many risks that the diver must be trained to manage. To balance these risks, the diver should identify their motives for diving deep or penetrating wrecks. Are the rewards worth the risks involved? That's a pretty good question to ask in many of life's undertakings.

Let's look at some of the risks of deep diving and penetrating shipwrecks.

Too much of a good thing
A GIVEN VOLUME OF WATER IS MUCH HEAVIER THAN THE SAME VOLUME OF air. Underwater, we have to worry about the pressure caused by water, and the deeper we go, the more pressure water exerts on our bodies. The feeling of this water pressure is not like the feeling we get supporting a heavy object on our shoulders. That's because we're made up mostly of water too and the pressure is distributed evenly and in all directions through us. It is only the air spaces within our body that need to 'equalise' with the increased water pressure. Those spaces are our lungs, ear cavities and sinuses.

If we breathe normal air (approximately 80% nitrogen and 20% oxygen) at depth, the pressure of water is such that it compresses more closely together molecules of all the gases we breathe so that, with every inhalation, we breathe in more molecules of any gas component. Increased exposure to oxygen is okay to a certain extent because our bodies metabolise that gas quite readily. Too much nitrogen, on the other hand, leaves us feeling like we had too many martinis. We can be rendered 'drunk' and can experience positive sensations (euphoria) or unpleasant sensations (dysphoria). This is called *nitrogen narcosis* (or classically 'raptures of the deep'). I've felt both euphoric and dysphoric feelings when diving deep while breathing air.

Typically, for the average diver, nitrogen narcosis can start to be felt around 30–40m under the surface. With familiarity and practice, the diver can deal with this narcosis. With experience and a more relaxed attitude to the effect, the diver can perform fairly safely even at 50–60m.

Too much nitrogen, however, causes unconsciousness, and even a moderate level of narcosis results in impaired decision-making and slow reaction times. This is dangerous when deep under the ocean. The diver might panic, which can result in irrational decisions that can be life-threatening, such as surfacing too quickly, which can result in 'the bends'.

I recall one of my very early deep air dives off the northern beaches of Sydney on the wreck of the *Birchgrove Park*, at 51m, when I felt a sudden, inexplicable urge to panic. It was like a wave of panic had come over me. Fortunately, I was capable of realising that giving into panic would very likely result in my death or serious decompression injury. I kept the wave of panic in check through sheer mental discipline and it soon disappeared. Such mind control to manage difficult situations is an important skill acquired by most divers over the years.

ONE OF THE SADDEST AND MOST TRAUMATIC LIFE EVENTS FOR ME AS A young man was losing a very good friend to a diving accident on this very wreck. We were both aged 31 years at the time – a prime period of our lives.

My friend was a martial arts expert and very fit. He was a very talented man and a good, dear friend. On this particular day he was diving on the wreck with a couple of other mutual friends. When the other two divers returned to the anchor line to begin their ascent, they assumed our friend had already begun his ascent. He never surfaced. Having already spent so much time at this considerable depth, they were unable to go back down to look for him immediately. They would need to wait many hours before it would be safe to dive that deep again, and by then, it would be too dark.

I returned with the two divers the following day to try to recover his body, with the permission of the water police, who were present before we commenced our dive. When we found our friend, there was still air in his tanks and his mask was still attached to his face. My best guess was that he was heavily affected by nitrogen narcosis. Perhaps he couldn't find the anchor line and began what we call a "free ascent". Without a line to hold onto while ascending, divers have no point of reference to gauge whether they are indeed ascending. It is important in these occasions to refer to a depth gauge. Perhaps he didn't and found himself kicking for some time, thinking he was ascending but in fact barely off the sandy bottom. On discovering that he was still on the bottom, anxiety would have increased, breathing rate increased and narcosis enhanced. Most likely a black-out followed, and he drowned.

While lifting our deceased friend out of the water into our small boat, I was hit with the distinct feeling that this wasn't my friend. He was no longer there. This was just the body he used, but it wasn't him. On the night of the following day, I went outside for a walk, feeling the sense of loss and heaviness associated with the events of the previous couple of days. He used to place an arm around my shoulders sometimes when we walked – his way of demonstrating true friendship. In the silence of that night, I again subtly felt an arm around my shoulders with an accompanying wave of feeling – maybe a faint communication – that "everything is alright!" *This* was my friend.

His death was most likely caused by too much nitrogen. We can also get too much oxygen. On the surface, after breathing pure (100%) oxygen for about seven hours, our lungs will start to complain and become inflamed. It's basically because we're providing our body with too much rich 'fuel' for our metabolic furnaces.

AT AN OCEAN DEPTH OF 60M, EVERY BREATH WE TAKE OF NORMAL AIR from our scuba tanks exposes us to many more oxygen molecules than we would take with a breath of pure (100%) oxygen at the surface. Most healthy divers can handle this extra exposure to oxygen for a certain period, but continual exposure to breathing oxygen under pressure poses the distinct risk of acute oxygen toxicity. At this point, the lungs aren't the main problem – the nervous system goes into overdrive and the diver can convulse and quickly become unconscious. Again, this is very bad when deep under the sea!

Sixty metres, therefore, is about the depth limit for scuba diving on normal air. I recall another diving trip in my earlier years, when I was quite ignorant about the depth limits for oxygen toxicity. We were diving with compressed air on a wreck off Sydney called HMAS *Encounter*, an Australian WWI cruiser that was scuttled in 1932 to a depth of 74m (about 240 ft). The oxygen pressure in the air we breathed at this depth was at a dangerous level – not that I knew that at the time.

On one dive I felt very heavily affected by nitrogen narcosis, with symptoms of tunnel vision. I was almost certainly being affected by oxygen toxicity, which can be exacerbated by nitrogen narcosis. My way of solving this at the time was to ascend about 10–15m until the symptoms abated, then go down again. But the problem with oxygen toxicity is that it can cause unconsciousness with little or no warning. Dumb? In hindsight, yes.

When we add helium to our breathing gas, we can reduce the pressure contribution[1] from each of the other gases. Helium is a light and fairly inert gas in so far that it has little effect on our physiologies until we get to 200–300m deep. For this reason, 300m ocean depth is about the limit for humans diving in flexible suits. Submersibles, submarines or rigid suits that maintain the interior pressure at one atmosphere are needed for deeper exploration. Helium and nitrogen get absorbed into our body's tissues and are not metabolised to any extent. Therefore, both gases have to come out of our system when we ascend towards the surface. We have to let these gases come out slowly, or they form bubbles in our blood and/or tissues, and we can suffer what is known as the bends – which can cause great pain in the joints and lead to paralysis or death.

The trick to avoiding the bends is to minimise the amount of nitrogen and helium we breathe by determining the maximum amount of oxygen we can safely breathe at our deepest depth. I then determine how much nitrogen load I want. I will typically allow a nitrogen exposure equivalent to diving on air to about 30m. What is left over is helium. Fairly simple math calculations or computer programs are then used to determine the amount of each gas we fill our tanks with. When filling scuba cylinders, I start with helium, then add oxygen, then complete the fill with air. The mixture of three gases – oxygen, nitrogen and helium is called Trimix.

It took serious deep water recreational divers until the early 1990s to adopt this technology, which commercial divers had been using for decades. It just required additional training. It wasn't until 1996 that my regular diving friends and I incorporated this technology to explore deeper wrecks.

The bends

THIS IS PERHAPS THE BIGGEST AND MOST SERIOUS RISK ALWAYS PRESENT for the deep diver. It can be managed and largely prevented, but never with 100 per cent guarantee.

Absorbed nitrogen and any helium we have breathed in under pressure must slowly come out of our bodies during ascent, otherwise the gases will come out in the form of bubbles large enough to block finer blood vessels. These blockages create what is called ischaemia – starving a tissue or organ of oxygen, with damage and eventual death to that tissue or organ. It can be felt as acute pain in (typically) joints such as the shoulder, or can cause cells to die in the brain or spinal cord. Our return from depth therefore must be controlled and calculated.

One experienced diving friend battled constant pain and dysfunction for years following a spinal cord bend after surfacing from a moderately deep wreck (less than 50m deep). And just a couple of months before I wrote this chapter I received the sad news that another friend had died while diving a 100m deep wreck off the north coast of NSW. Some malfunction or error in the operation of his equipment caused him to make a rapid ascent to the surface with no stops after spending more than 20 minutes on the wreck at 100m. He would have died before he even reached the surface.

Personally, I have experienced shoulder pain twice on ascent from deep wreck dives. One incident was when I was in my late 20s. The pain subsided the following day. The other incident (at about the age of 50) was on ascent from a 100m deep wreck called the *Cumberland*. In both cases, I was working too hard on the bottom or ascended to my first scheduled stop too quickly. On the *Cumberland* dive (around 2004), as I made my ascent from the 9m decompression stop to the 6m stop, I felt acute pain in my left shoulder. When I descended back to the 9m stop, the pain largely went away. When I tried again ascending slowly to 6m, the pain returned. I completed my decompression as per the decompression tables, but going no shallower than 6m, then surfaced briefly, asked for an oxygen bottle, then went down to 12m to begin another slow ascent over about 45 minutes or so. My shoulder was still reasonably sore for a day, but improved quickly.

Divers wear wrist computers that tell us what stops to take on the way up and for how long. As a redundant (or back-up) source of information, we also calculate our decompression requirements using computer programs. We then print out decompression tables for that particular dive onto waterproof paper and refer to these underwater if our computers malfunction. The printed tables also give us an idea ahead of time of our decompression commitment. For example, a 20-minute dive to 100m might require 2.5–3 hours of ascent time. It can get very boring, but that is the price we pay for visiting these deep treasures.

Strong ocean currents
SOMETIMES, THE OCEAN CURRENTS ARE JUST TOO STRONG TO ENABLE A safe and enjoyable dive. Many times we have struggled and strained to get to the bottom, fighting against the strong movement of water. Sometimes it's worth it, but it can be a fine line between deciding whether to proceed or abort. Equally relevant is the long ascent time. I have held tightly to an ascent line on many a dive, sometimes for more than two hours, virtually waving in the 'breeze' like a flag in the wind. It isn't fun. Mostly, once everyone has returned to the anchor line, we release the anchor from the bottom so that we drift with the current. The line is attached to a large coloured buoy on the surface, which can be seen by the boat skipper, or our smaller boats remain attached to the anchored line. Sometimes though, the anchor re-grabs something on the bottom. If this happens, we cannot go down again to release the anchor and we are stuck finishing a long decompression hanging on tight to this line in a raging current.[2]

On one occasion I was diving with some friends on a 125m (412 ft) deep wreck off the south coast of NSW. I had travelled some 1000km by road to get to this part of the coast. I was the first into the water and there was no discernible current at the surface. It looked like it was going to be a comfortable dive. I was using a diver propulsion vehicle[3] or dive scooter, with the intention of getting to the best part of the wreck quickly for photography. At these depths, there is very little time on the bottom if you want to avoid more than three hours of decompression.

After only about 10m of descent I noticed I was being pulled away from the line. There was a current affecting my descent. After about 40m, I noticed I was holding onto the line more firmly but still at this stage effectively using my scooter to help me descend the line. The current was clearly increasing as I descended. After about 70m I had to pull against the line with one hand while trying to direct the scooter downwards to assist my descent against the current. I was working quite hard at this point. After 90 metres, the scooter would 'catch' the current and swing wildly to the side, causing me to pull it back into the right direction, at the same time pulling hard on the line with my left arm to make just a few centimetres of descent. The current was now almost impossible to work against. But I was so close to the wreck!

At this point, I stopped and thought carefully about my situation. I looked at my computer gauge. I had already spent nearly 10 minutes getting this far. It would be probably some 3–4 minutes more before I reached the wreck, taking up most of my planned time on the bottom. What could I possibly achieve in that short remaining time? To reach my goal and say that I successfully reached the wreck was not really fulfilling my goal to bring back good photographs of it. I would have hours of decompression before surfacing again and – if my friends decided to abandon the dive – they would not be happy that they had to sit and wait for so long in the boat. I abandoned my descent and began the slow ascent to the surface, with more than an hour of decompression. As it turned out, my friends had made the same decision.

I had travelled 1000km and spent many hundreds of dollars to get to probably 20m from my goal without ever seeing it! Despite all the planning and effort associated with deep wreck diving, divers learn to accept this kind of disappointment. And it was still a great weekend catching up with friends.

Silt-out
A SILT-OUT – THE SUDDEN CLOUDING OF WATER WITH DISTURBED MUD OR silt – can be a nightmare. In my late 20s, I was diving with two friends on one of the scuttled hulks off Sydney in about 45m of water. These old, decommissioned vessels were deliberately sunk to act as artificial reefs for fishermen and never intended as divers' playgrounds.

I followed one friend into the interior of one of these hulks. We floated down a set of stairs and both moved into a room which had storm-lights above (heavy glass ceiling windows – like portholes - hinged to open and close). We both stood to examine the room, at which time I looked behind where we had just come and saw absolutely nothing but a thick black wall of mud! We had kicked up silt from the bottom, causing zero visibility behind us and we were soon to become encased inside black soup. Within just a few seconds there would be no way we could navigate out of the wreck. We would be flailing and very likely panicking.

In the seconds that I was sensing the gravity of our situation, the third member of our team – who sensibly remained outside the wreck – opened one of the storm-lights (the grease was obviously still working on the hinges) and we swam out through the aperture. Why did he think of opening this storm-light at that critical time? I still shudder when I think of this incident. Many a sport diver has died this way, entombed inside steel walls, as good as totally blind inside a black soup where any sense of direction or even up or down quickly disappears.

IN LATER YEARS, I WOULD LEARN THE SKILLS NEEDED FOR TERRESTRIAL cave diving. It's an activity that also has a reputation for fatalities. All cave divers carry reeled nylon lines that are essential to safely navigate flooded caves. They lay out a line as they explore a cave and retrace the line to safely return to their starting point. Caves silt up very easily and quickly, so the cave diver constantly maintains contact with the line.

These reeled lines are also essential in safely penetrating most shipwrecks. In 2011 my friend Samir Alhafith and I were asked by an Australian national television news network to help them obtain some underwater video footage of a significant WWII Australian shipwreck – the HMAS *Perth* – sunk by enemy fire off Java, Indonesia, in 1942. Of the ship's complement of 681 persons, 353 died as a result of the attack and sinking of the ship. As well as the usual shots of the exterior of the wreck, the producer wanted some interior footage, and ideally footage of the engine room – which to our knowledge had never been taken.

The wreck lies on its starboard side at a depth of 35m. Being in tropical latitudes, the water was beautifully warm so we only wore thin wetsuits to protect us from abrasion and cuts. However, visibility was limited to only 2–3m and there was a very strong current. Both Samir and I were using rebreathers[4], which enabled us to spend long periods underwater without the concern of running out of air. The rebreathers could also supply us a constant ideal amount of oxygen at any depth past the first few metres, which minimised our decompression commitments.

Because the prime goal of the diving was good video footage for TV, and because I'm primarily a stills photographer, I agreed to leave my camera behind and operate the reeled line for safe navigation through the wreck into the engine room. Samir would follow me on the line and take video. We both wore helmets with attached lights.

The wreck is on its side and collapsing. What were once rooms and corridors are now twisted, distorted spaces allowing practically no sense of orientation. Bits of wire and sharp metal edges protruded everywhere. The minimal water movement inside a wreck usually presents the diver with better visibility than outside, but this was not the case with this dive. There seemed to be a lot of suspended sediment inside.

After one failed attempt, I took another direction on a separate dive and we appeared to be making progress. When spooling out the nylon cord on the way in, I carefully tied the line to objects to avoid what in cave diving is known as a "line trap". This is where the loose line works its way under a ledge or something through which we ourselves could not fit on the way back. I've experienced this situation in a cave. It's concerning to say the least!

Cave diving at Jenolan Caves, NSW, is almost identical to the highly silted conditions we encountered inside the HMAS Perth. The only difference might have been the darker rust-coloured sediment inside the wreck. There is total dependence on the guide line to safely explore and exit these environments.

As we penetrated deeper into this dark wreck, there appeared to be more pipes, cylinders and gauges, suggesting we were close to the engine room. I would occasionally pause to allow Samir time to capture some video and also for me to survey the path ahead. I looked up and saw a large black rectangular space. Such big, black unexplored spaces beckon divers, so I decided to explore. But as soon as I entered the space I was immediately caught in a strong current – not something I was used to inside a wreck. It was pitch black inside the huge room and I could see nothing with my headlight. In fear of being carried away into this darkness, I firmly kicked my way back to the rectangular opening.

I'm guessing the room was the main engine room and, while there was no ambient light whatsoever, the outside current was obviously finding its way through one end and coming out another. While that might indicate there were holes or apertures at both ends, it's possible too that water could fit through those holes but not me. I wasn't about to explore that possibility. I had come within metres of our goal and still didn't get to see it.

We decided to turn back, this time with Samir in front following the line and me behind him reeling the line back onto its spool. Even though we'd been careful, our movements through the wreck had disturbed the ever-present silt. The trip back was as good as a journey through soup, with visibility only centimetres and no sense of orientation. Our lives depended very much on that orange nylon line. I practically bumped into some of the tie-off points before I saw them. Samir paused ahead of me. I could tell he was probably caught up on something and was working to untangle himself. There was nothing I could do to help him without making matters worse and possibly coming off the line. Until he sorted out his predicament, I was stuck behind him. I waited, knowing that he was experienced and highly unlikely to panic. The beauty of using rebreathers was that we had ample time to solve problems without the fear of running out of air.

He solved the problem and we eventually exited the wreck. "That was intense diving," Samir would later say, to which I replied, "Yes it was!"

Is it worth it?
I CERTAINLY DON'T WISH TO DAMPEN THE ENTHUSIASM OF NEW OR potential deep wreck explorers. Like all extreme sports however, the diver needs an adequate level of training and preparation for this type of activity.

Other risks the diver must consider when exploring shipwrecks include cold temperatures, equipment failure, carbon dioxide build-up (especially using rebreathers) and entanglement in fishing line or net. I didn't mention sharks, admittedly low on the risk-list statistically, but still of concern when diving for long periods in deep water off the Australian coast.

With all adventurous activities, there is risk, but there are also rewards and satisfaction. I've had great pleasure in documenting things that are otherwise out of sight and mind to most people. With my photographs I'm able to make these relics of our past 'real' and relevant. You could say that I've worked to materialise what is otherwise ethereal and hidden.

Wreck-diving seems comparable to my efforts to materialise the larger, more encompassing depths of an ocean of consciousness that supports and underlies our individual waves of consciousness. This one ocean of consciousness supports and gives rise to the familiar material world we take for granted – the surface realm of change and transience. It is this surface realm, with its changing waves of material existence, that our senses would have us believe is the only reality.

A two-masted sailing vessel called Severance that sank off Lady Elliot Island in the Great Barrier Reef in 1998, and lies at a depth of 20m.

A barge used by the Australians and New Zealanders to bring back wounded and dying soldiers from shore to the hospital ships during the Gallipoli Peninsula landings of 1915. It sits at a depth of 54m off Anzac Cove in Turkey.

An artist's painting of myself in 'open-circuit' scuba gear, decompressing after diving on a wreck at 100m depth. Illustration courtesy of Australian Geographic.

A shallow wreck from WWI at North Beach, Gallipoli, Turkey at sun-set. "At the going down of the sun, we will remember them." (Laurence Binyon, 1914)

NOTES

1. We refer to this as "partial" pressure.
2. Readers who are technical divers will be aware that buoyed cross-over lines can also be released from the anchored descent line making continued ascent and decompression much more comfortable in a current. The author employs this method when there is sufficient assistance available on the boat.
3. A battery-powered propeller-driven device that the diver holds onto to assist his/her passage through the water.
4. A rebreather is an apparatus that allows the diver to re-breathe exhaled gases, so that no breathing gas is wasted (some is lost during ascent). A chemical scrubber removes the accumulating carbon dioxide, and oxygen is also admitted to the breathing "loop" to make up for oxygen that is metabolised by the body. Unlike usual scuba apparatus (open-circuit scuba) exhaled air or gas is not dumped into the water, but re-used.

THE SHIPWRECK EXPERIENCE

*"Had you such leisure in the time of death
To gaze upon the secrets of the deep?"*

– Shakespeare, Richard III

A shipwreck is like a body without the soul, in the sense that the ship was only ever a vehicle and the passengers and crew gave the ship its life. Some wreck divers and explorers hint at this understanding that our bodies too are just vehicles for our real essence. An added dimension to this experience is that wrecks are located in the depths of the ocean, symbolic of that universal consciousness that gives rise to all individual consciousness and indeed – as the proposed unified field – to all material and phenomenal existence.

THERE IS SOMETHING ALLURING AND SEDUCTIVE ABOUT EXPLORING A sunken shipwreck. But it is hard to define. Perhaps half the wrecks I have explored were accompanied by loss of life when they sank. Therefore, there is a clear juxtaposition of events – the silence, peace and tranquility often experienced while exploring a wreck, and the terror and confusion that prevailed in the wrecking process. Divers must make a special effort to reconcile these.

Shipwreck explorers I've met tend to be very pragmatic down-to-earth people. Many are adrenaline-seeking males. Yet, I have heard even the least philosophical of individuals refer to that elusive "something special" about diving on shipwrecks.

For many years I was aware of this "something special" but – like most – found it intangible and certainly difficult to communicate. It was a subtle quality of experience that lay in the depth of my awareness. I knew it had some sort of unfathomable significance, some relevance to my life.

Shortly after oceanographer Dr Robert Ballard found the wreck of the *Titanic* in 1985 – arguably the most exciting wreck discovery of the past century – I read his book *The Discovery of the Titanic*[1]. In it, he recounted a comment made by one of his colleagues: "The wreck reminds me of my own mortality"[2].

Instantly, like a light that was suddenly turned on in my head, I knew that this was the shared experience that so many wreck divers could relate to, but could not – or would not – articulate in words. When it comes to shipwreck explorers, we certainly need to "read between the lines"[3] in what they report. This is a classic example. Why did the wreck remind this explorer of his mortality?

Ballard's colleague continued with the following comment in a TV documentary[4]: "It's kind of a giant symbol of the passing of all of our lives, and how temporary life is". That's true, but I think there is even more depth of meaning in the original statement. The wreck is symbolic of death, and as a symbol, the shipwreck and the experience of diving on a shipwreck can be used to gain more insight into the nature of death. It helps if we can analyze these wreck-diving experiences using the unified field model of consciousness as a framework for our understanding.

What defined the ship, when it was afloat as a working vessel, were the working parts of the ship and even more importantly, the human crew and passengers who gave it 'life'. When a diver explores a wreck at the bottom of the sea, he or she sees an empty vehicle. The human element is no longer there. What gave the vessel its life has gone. This can be compared to the human body in death where its life essence – or soul – has also left.

The human body was only ever a vehicle for the immortal soul. I believe that some divers can relate to this existential fact when they explore a wreck. It is not an overt awareness that they can define enough to communicate with their friends, but it is still, nevertheless, a faint 'knowing' that exists deep down in their psyche. Knowledge or memory, deeply imbedded in their awareness, resonates at some level with the strong symbolism represented by a wreck. I believe it is a memory of a broader, more comprehensive existence than we normally acknowledge in our day-to-day affairs.

THERE IS ANOTHER ASPECT TO THE EXPERIENCE OF EXPLORING A WRECK. The wreck is located at the bottom of the ocean. As I have already established, the ocean can be symbolic of universal or pure consciousness. Our individual expressions of consciousness are like the waves on top of the ocean. The surface is the region we typically inhabit, one wave of consciousness living the illusion that it is separate and quite different from each and every other wave of consciousness around it. If we examine the base of our wave though – just underneath the wave – the distinction of one wave from another is not so defined.

The depth of this ocean of consciousness is 'pure' consciousness[5]. Pure consciousness is actually unlimited – unbounded. It is described as blissful by nature, fully content with itself. It is considered self-referral (it has only itself to relate to), unmanifest (formless and non-material, yet possessing infinite creativity and potential), invincible and all-knowing. It is that which underlies, is fundamental to and indeed is the source of our individual consciousness. And because it is fundamental to our individual consciousness, we have access to it. It is the vast aspect of you and me that we share in common. It is the ultimate essence of you and me. When we transcend the notion of 'you' and 'me', we are no longer separate. We are all one, just as the waves are all one ocean. This field of purely self-referral consciousness, being unmanifest of anything material or phenomenal, has been referred to as a field of the 'absolute'.

Getting back to our shipwreck analogy, the diver, experiencing the wreck as symbolic of death and more specifically the body as merely a vehicle for the soul, also relates to the location of this symbol of death in the depths of the ocean of consciousness. This is the field of pure consciousness. The diver is aware of the beautiful silence, peace and tranquility in this realm. These are the qualities of the field of pure consciousness. The diver experiences this silence, yet is fully awake and alert. The diver feels free, unbounded, a sense of timelessness, unshackled of all 'earthly' concerns and troubles – a sense of oneness and very much at peace. This is the field of ultimate freedom, infinite wonder, unboundedness, timelessness and all possibilities.

Could this be the quality of experience that awaits us at the time of our own 'death'? I believe that this experience that divers have in the exploration of shipwrecks is the tweaking of some memory or 'knowing' that lies within all of us of a broader, more comprehensive existence.

I WOULD NOT NORMALLY ENTERTAIN TOO MUCH THOUGHT OF WHAT WE might call "negative" spirituality – evil, demons, hell and related scary things. However, in the last chapter on shipwreck exploration, I mentioned that a large dark space representing the engine room of one of the wrecks beckoned me to explore it. The darkness in the heart of this wreck also beckons me to interpret it symbolically, as it can be compared to a heart of darkness sometimes apparent in man. Let me interpret it then to the best of my ability using the unified field model of consciousness.

The wreck, remember, is symbolic of the body without the soul. It has no life, as its life essence – represented by the crew or passengers – has long gone. The darkness in the heart of this wreck merely emphasises and reinforces the fact that the 'light' – the life essence – has gone. We all know though that darkness sits in the hearts of some individuals living on this Earth – individuals with a soul.

In Vedic science, there is a word called *Pragyaparada*, which means 'the mistaken intellect'. When the soul occupies a body in birth, its goal is to experience itself "anew in the next grandest version of the greatest vision ever it held about Who It Is"[6]. To experience something, we use a nervous system and its five senses. We also need to have a contextual background. For example, to experience cold, we need to have heat; to experience love, we need to have hate; to experience forgiveness, we need to have physical and mental suffering in our environment, or, if not our immediate environment, then we need to be able to relate to it somehow and somewhere. This material world with which we are familiar can be referred to as a field of the 'relative', implying that experience usually involves one thing compared to another.

This 'world' of duality, multiplicity and difference then sets up a situation where the individual – absorbed in the physical senses – loses the memory of who they truly are.

The ego is defined as our sense of self. That 'self' can be the small self – that is, the individual – or it can be the 'Big Self', the 'Cosmic Self', the entire ocean of self or the proposed unified field. Awareness of the small individual self can expand to the big Self. All too often however, the ego assumes the status of the small self. Distracted from its real cosmic nature, the ego sees itself as independent and separate from everything else. The wave on the ocean of being lives the illusion that it is not the ocean and is separate from all the other waves. In this state of disconnectedness, harming another is definitely not seen as harming oneself. Evil can thrive and persist in this illusionary and all too common human perspective on life.

It has been proposed that the soul – after death of the body – soon enough (although perhaps not immediately)[7] realises it is not the body, and also realises its true interconnected nature, its oneness with everything else. The evil is no longer with the essence of that individual we call the soul, but the memory of the previous behaviour does come with the soul and will influence the character and life events of the new individual that will again be born. In this way, good or bad actions performed by that individual will have their 'reactions' – consequences – at some stage, if not in that current lifetime, then another. Perhaps St Paul was referring to this karmic law with his comment, basically saying "as you sow, so shall you reap".

> *"[Remember] this: he who sows sparingly and grudgingly will also reap sparingly and grudgingly, and he who sows generously [that blessings may come to someone] will also reap generously and with blessings."*[8]
>
> – 11 Corinthians, 9.6

The darkness inside the engine room of the shipwreck will disappear when the wreck fully disintegrates. So, too, with humans, any darkness is restrained to this earthly life and disappears in the same way that the body also disappears without the life-giving soul occupying it. The darkness is not taken into what we call the "after-life". The memory of that darkness however does come with the soul, along with the memory of all actions in this life, and influences the karmic[9] results of later lives. Through all this, the soul itself remains pure. This is somewhat comparable to my earlier description of the life cycle of large stars that turn into black holes. Modern superstring theory predicts that when a star collapses to a black hole there is no loss of information about qualities of the star. All information is remembered in the singularity, then reprocessed and regurgitated. Again we see the relevance in the verse from the *Upanishads*:

> *"As is the human body, so is the cosmic body*
> *As is the human mind, so is the cosmic mind."*
> – Katha Upanishad, Part 111

EVIL IS MORE 'REAL' AND MANIFEST IN THIS MATERIAL EARTHLY LIFE AND becomes less real, less manifest and eventually non-existent as we transcend the 'relative' levels of existence and enter the larger, more unified, fundamental levels of our existence – our spiritual existence. This is contrary to what is taught in most religions. It is 'negativity' that disappears as we approach the broader spiritual realm, and 'positivity' – all that represents the essence of life itself – that increases and becomes more real as we immerse ourselves in the spiritual realm.

We are in essence 'spiritual' beings, as was beautifully expressed by philosopher and Jesuit priest Pierre Teilhard de Chardin:

> *"We are not human beings having a spiritual experience; we are spiritual beings having a human experience."*[10]
> – Pierre Teilhard De Chardin

ALL THIS IS TO EMPHASISE THAT EVIL IS SOMETHING WE SEE AND WITNESS in this Earthly life, not in the afterlife. Evil does not have its source in the 'spiritual realm'. I do not believe there is an eternal, real place called Hell into which bad souls suffer for eternity. Likewise, I do not believe in the absolute existence of demons and devils and the like. There is no 'ultimate' dark being, entity or place. We do a good enough job of creating 'hell' on this Earth.

Let me qualify these comments with an acknowledgment that evil does exist and it also appears possible for some people to experience or even see 'bad spirits'. These dark spiritual entities are possibly entities in transit from their corporeal (or bodily) attachment to a full realisation of their spiritual nature. They're going through an early but transient phase of death and have still not realised that they are not the body. They also might believe that they are not deserving of bliss and happiness and so have not yet come to the realisation that they are in control of this state of their being. Such is the power of individual consciousness. Soon enough, they too will experience who they really are – bliss, love and glorious unique expressions of life.

There is also the possibility that dark spirits are our own creations. They are the creations – not of God – but of the power of individual or collective (shared) human consciousness. We could possibly experience these dark (human) creations in our Earthly lives or immediately after death. Consciousness 'creates', but these constructs of human consciousness are not ultimately real, invincible and perpetual entities. They can be transcended in this life and they can be transcended in the next. At some stage after death, we simply come to a decision that these negative entities no longer serve us nor are relevant to who we really are, and they vanish.[11] Since they represent our constructs, they should have no control over us unless we let them. The fact that they are of little relevance or trouble to the vast majority of the population is testimony to this. We shouldn't entertain negative spiritual entities. Again, they're not 'real' in the ultimate sense.

The ultimate reality is that field of pure consciousness, the 'absolute', *Ātmā* or the unified field originally proposed by Einstein and supported by the mathematics of superstring theory. Everything in the universe – seen and unseen – is therefore pure consciousness in essence.

There are many symbols or events in our life experience that can remind us of a broader existence to which we are intimately connected. It's just that in most cases, we dismiss those memories or feelings. We've most likely been taught to ignore them, because they're 'irrational'.

Have you ever experienced the love for one other person suddenly and inexplicitly expand into universal love – a beautiful, unconditional, pure love for all persons and things? What is going on here? It means that focused love is nothing more than concentrated universal love – a wave of love in the one ocean of love.

Have you ever gazed into the starry heavens at night and wondered where it all ends? And if there is an end to the universe, what lies beyond that? We may not understand the concept of infinity, but there may be times when we can 'identify' with the concept at some subtle level. We take such experiences for granted – or simply dismiss them – when all along they hint of our connection to a broader existence.

The experience of diving on a shipwreck is not what it might appear to most landlubbers. Rather than being a morbid activity where one might see the wreck as symbolic of death and decay, the experience – at least for me much of the time and I suspect for others – is the opposite.

This is all good news! If our experience at the time of death is one filled with bliss, ultimate love, unboundedness and total freedom, then it doesn't sound too bad. It could be that we experience coming home – a 'home' that we have long forgotten, like a weary traveller who has been away for a lifetime.[12] And remember too, far from being removed from 'life', in death we will return to the very essence of life – life itself. In this respect, from the point of view of the person dying, death truly is an illusion.

In the Shakespearian drama *Richard III*, Clarence recounts a dream that prophesies his imminent death:

> *"Methought I saw a thousand fearful wrecks;*
> *A thousand men that fishes gnaw'd upon;*
> *Wedges of gold, great anchors, heaps of pearl,*
> *Inestimable stones, unvalued jewels,*
> *All scattered on the bottom of the sea."*

To which Brakenbury replies:

> *"Had you such leisure in the time of death*
> *To gaze upon the secrets of the deep?"*

– William Shakespeare, Richard 111
(see https://youtu.be/jNc-OK_iGRRA for an audiovisual interpretation)

Shakespeare, too, saw the shipwreck as symbolic of death, and there at the bottom of the sea, lie those secrets attainable to us at the time of death.

The secrets of the deep lie, as they always have, in the depth of our awareness – in the depth of the ocean of self. The 'secrets of the deep' are those qualities of this ocean of consciousness with which we are now familiar – unboundedness, all possibilities, ultimate freedom, endless wonder, invincibility, infinite silence yet infinite dynamism, timelessness, bliss, fully self-referral nature and self-sufficiency.

In death we are released from our sense attachment and the secrets of the deep become more obvious to us, but we do not have to physically die to access these secrets. We merely have to 'die' to our senses through the process of meditation or any other means whereby we can transcend the noise in the mind brought about by the physical senses. We need to learn to be divers in the ocean of consciousness.

> *"I protest by your rejoicing which I have in Christ Jesus our Lord, I die daily"*[13]
>
> – 1 Corinthians, 15.31

In this statement from the Bible, the Apostle Paul is of course not referring to literally dying every day. Instead, I think he is referring to dying to the small self, the individual self.

Do 'bad' people experience this same bliss and freedom at the time of their death? I firmly believe so. That does not mean that there are no consequences for the actions we perform in a lifetime. Beyond my assertion that life will continue for all of us, I am not equipped with the knowledge or insight to answer many questions pertaining to death. Personally, I have been very satisfied with the description of what happens after death proposed by author Neale Donald Walsch in his series of books *Conversations with God*, and in particular his book *Home with God – in a Life that Never Ends*.

Divers inspect an old admiralty-style anchor on the wreck of the Kelloe, off Sydney, at a depth of 51 metres

NOTES

1. Ballard, Robert D; *The Discovery of the Titanic*, 1987
2. Steven Lowe (MIR 2 Submersible)
3. In reference to explorer Sir Laurens Van Der-Post's comment, Introduction
4. *Titanic – Treasure of the Deep*, An Al Giddings Production.
5. We also identify pure consciousness or 'universal' consciousness with the conjectured unified field of all the laws of nature.
6. Walsch, Neale Donald, *Friendship with God – An Uncommon Dialogue*, p 174.
7. Neale Donald Walsch, *Home With God – In a Life that Never Ends*, Hodder & Stoughton.
8. II Corinthians, 9:6; *The Amplified Bible*, Zondervan.
9. Karma is a Sanskrit term literally meaning action, work or deed, but also refers to the principle of causality where the actions of an individual influence the future of that individual, in this lifetime or another.
10. Pierre Teilhard de Chardin was a French philosopher and Jesuit priest who trained as a palaeontologist and geologist. He took part in the discovery of Peking Man and Piltdown Man.
11. Much of this knowledge has been absorbed from Neale Donald Walsch's *Conversations with God* books.
12. I refer to this personal experience of being 'home' in the last chapter.
13. 1 Corinthians 15:31.

MODERN SCIENCE – PART ONE
THE PROGRESS OF SCIENCE TOWARDS UNITY

"There are no dancers, there is only the dance."

– Fritzof Capra

As it has developed over the past 400 years, modern science has reached a point where it has identified the 'superstring' field as a possibility for the one unified field that gives rise to the complexity of life. The view of matter as discrete, inert and 'dead' needs to be replaced with a more abstract concept of matter as a dynamic, interacting web of relationships that transcends time and space.

I HAVE ALREADY INTRODUCED THE CONCEPT OF A UNIFIED FIELD (AS originally hypothesised by Albert Einstein) and suggested that it might be a field of consciousness – an ocean of consciousness – underlying and giving rise to the waves of our individual consciousness. I have referred to this concept as the unified field model of consciousness. I will now take a closer look at the gradual development of unified field theory (culminating in contemporary superstring theory) over the past hundred years.

To be able to accept the possibility that our consciousness is based in a unified field that also gives rise to all material existence, it will be helpful to understand just what this field is and how the concept of such a field came about. I therefore need to go into some depth with this challenging topic and it is my hope that you will not find these chapters a stumbling block and miss the concluding chapters of the book. A grasp of some of the discoveries of physics and cosmology is necessary to compare the similar discoveries resulting from the subjective, inward path of knowledge associated with expanded states of consciousness. This subjective path to knowledge has been recorded in Vedic literature and comes to light in the world today through the cognitive experiences of individuals.

THE DISCOVERIES IN THE DISCIPLINED FIELD OF PHYSICS OVER THE PAST century are truly astounding and disturbing at the same time, because they shake our conventional and comfortable view of the world. The past 400 years have been considered the scientifically enlightened years coincident with the so-called industrial era. In this period, to understand the physical world, mankind largely turned to objective, analytical mathematics and scientific observation, and in doing so, relied less on the edicts and doctrines dispensed by religious.

The Italian scientist Rene Descartes set some of the modern scientific wheels rolling in the first half of the 1600s, and will be forever remembered with his famous line: "I think therefore I am" ("Cogito ergo sum"). Descartes' approach to understanding the world around us was to doubt all assumptions. He decided to ignore all existing knowledge, the impressions of his senses and even the fact that he had a body until he was left with the only thing he could not doubt – the existence of himself as a thinker.[3]

Strangely, according to Descartes' thinking, our basic consciousness is the most certain self-evident 'fact' of existence, but has remained even today a subject that most disciplined scientists feel uncomfortable talking about, let alone studying.

Descartes then proposed an analytical method of study where the subjects of study are broken up into their constituent parts and better understood from the perspective of how these parts are arranged. So began the reductionist approach to understanding nature that has been with us to this day. To understand how the human body works for example, we must break it down like a machine and study its smallest components. In current times, that's the job of medical scientists, who take that form of analysis as far as the molecular (biochemical) level. Anything smaller than that is not generally considered to be relevant to the expression of disease and falls back to the attention of chemists and physicists.

Clock-making had attained a high degree of perfection in Descartes' time, and it is interesting that Descartes compared the workings of nature with a clock. "I do not recognise any difference between the machines made by craftsmen and the various bodies that nature alone composes,"[4] he wrote. Descartes had initiated the reductionist, mechanical view of life that still permeates most of our scientific disciplines to this day. He saw the whole universe around us operating like a machine and obeying exact mathematical laws. If we could learn to break down the machines into their constituent parts, then we could understand how they work.

Descartes saw nothing spiritual in the material world. There was no life or spirit in matter. However, he did not entirely dismiss the spiritual dimension of life. He saw God as the creator of things material and of the mind, but both were separate realms having nothing to do with each other.[5] Descartes referred to the realm of the mind as "res cogitans" or "thinking thing". Disciplined science would concern itself with material things – "res extensa" (the "extended thing"). Res cogitans presumably – in Descartes' time – belonged to the realm of religion.

Does all this sound familiar? The separation of material things from consciousness, with the emphasis on 'objectivity' has been the assumed modus-operandi for formal science ever since. Even in our life sciences – and especially in the field of medicine – great effort has traditionally been made to separate those matters that belong to the mind and those that pertain to the body.

"All science is certain, evident knowledge," he wrote. "We reject all knowledge which is merely probable and judge that only those things should be believed which are perfectly known and about which there can be no doubts."[6]

This belief in the certainty of scientific knowledge is still prevalent today. Yet it is here – in the light of modern scientific discovery – that Descartes was wrong. There is no absolute truth in science. At best, our theories and concepts are approximate.

DESCARTES PROPOSED THE MECHANISTIC AND MATHEMATICALLY BASED foundation for all scientific enquiry to this day, but did little to develop mathematical theory to a level that was useful in explaining the everyday world. The man who perpetuated the 'Cartesian' approach (an adjectival reference to Descartes) and fast-tracked the Scientific Revolution was English-born Isaac Newton (1642–1727). Newton was a mathematical genius and is quite clearly the hero of many respected scientists to this day. Even Einstein would later remark that Newton contributed to the world "perhaps the greatest advance in thought that a single individual was ever privileged to make".[7]

Newton invented differential calculus to describe moving bodies, such as the Earth circling the Sun or the Moon circling the Earth. He singly brought precision and predictability to scientific enquiry. Much of the technology we enjoy in our current lifetime owes its success to Newton's development of scientific method and the disciplined mathematical descriptions of nature's processes.

Newton saw all things material, including ourselves, as being made up of small, indivisible indestructible particles called atoms. In Newton's view, God made these atoms and the forces that acted on them, so no further examination of their nature was possible or desirable. This fear of probing too close to God's domain is still with us today, and reflects the prevalent separation paradigm by which we see the world and our relationship with God. Stephen Hawking reported[8] that at a conference on Cosmology at the Vatican in 1985, Pope John Paul II declared that it was okay to study the Universe after it began, but that scientists should not inquire into the beginning itself, because that was the moment of creation and the work of God.

Newton perpetuated the Cartesian rift of things material and things of the mind. In Newton's way of thinking the material world of substance and phenomena could be studied with mathematical precision by an independent observer. Because the 'observer' was 'of the mind', the nature of mind itself would never be the subject of study and no consideration was ever given to the possible relationship of the observer and what was being studied by the observer. The physics of today tells us that it is impossible, at least when studying the finest levels of nature, for an observer to be fully 'independent' from that which is being examined.

The Laws of Motion were devised by Newton, and again, these laws depended on a very mechanistic model of the universe, one which saw all things as being the construct of basic, similar atoms packed together in different ways to result in the different properties of material substance. Newton saw all physical phenomena as taking place in the three-dimensional space of classical Euclidean geometry (the ancient Greek basis for geometry taught today in schools). Space, therefore, was an absolute entity, like an empty container in which all physical phenomena moved about independently. In Newton's own words, "Absolute space, in its own nature, without regard to anything external, remains always similar and immovable". Likewise, time was another absolute quality that moved smoothly from past, through the present, to the future. "Absolute, true and mathematical time of itself and of its own nature, flows uniformly, without regard to anything external,"[9] declared Newton. Here again, he would be proved wrong.

The predominant scientific view – still mostly with us today – of material and phenomenal nature was that it was comprised of fundamental building blocks called atoms and that nature behaved in a consistent way that could be mathematically described and predicted if we analysed it sufficiently. If we broke down the thing we were studying into its essential components, then we were in a position to fully understand it. This scientific paradigm views life as a machine operating on the assemblage of tiny lifeless components called atoms and that these atoms were viewed essentially as being like tiny billiard balls. They were hard substance things and their behaviour could be predicted once we identified them. Furthermore, space and time were considered to be absolute, unchangeable phenomena. Space and time were like a stage upon which the drama of life was played. The scenes can change and move about, but the stage stays the same.

You're thinking, "well, isn't that the way it is? Haven't Newton's laws of motion and scientific method brought us successfully to where we are today? Could we have landed on the Moon without this scientific framework?" The Cartesian-Newtonian model of scientific thought and method has worked extremely well in describing the largely tangible, macroscopic world around us. But when we delve deeply into finer subatomic levels of nature or explore the enormous dimensions of galaxies in the field of astronomy, we've had no choice but to accept a vastly different model of 'seeing' and understanding these otherwise hidden, but very real dimensions of our universe. This new model – while very different – can encompass and then expand on the old mechanistic model to create a more comprehensive understanding of reality.

The Cartesian paradigm of seeing the world has permeated every aspect of our lives. It remains the fundamental conceptual framework underpinning nearly all other sciences or fields of knowledge such as economics, medicine, psychology, education, sociology, conflict resolution and even religion, and has therefore shaped our day-to-day interpretation of all we experience. In short, this Cartesian paradigm, so ingrained into our very notion of what is real, sees the world around us as consisting of a multitude of diverse expressions of material existence – some of it 'alive' and some of it 'inert'. The diversity of this material world is seen as separate and largely independent entities. Mind – or the ability to 'think' – is considered an epiphenomenon of the brain and therefore the result of the complex interaction of billions of nerve cells (neurons) which we can see under the microscope. Time and space are also absolute qualities and considered to be like a blank canvas upon which the drama of life is painted. God may or may not exist – depending on one's beliefs. If 'He' exists, then He is typically seen as an entity separate from the rest of us, and ruling over us and His kingdom – still a Cartesian way of thinking. We are content to see God and religion as one area of our lives and the material world in which we live as another very different, but 'more real' aspect of our life. Those who do not believe in a god are content that their grasp of what is real can be determined by what they interpret with their senses and/or understand through the analytical probing of modern science.

A deeper layer: quantum mechanics
Deeper subatomic layers have been uncovered by the rigorous discipline of science over the past 100 years. As physicist John Hagelin said, "Everything we knew relevant to macroscopic[10] physics was just the classical tip of an immense quantum mechanical iceberg with layers upon layers within it – worlds within worlds, within worlds." The past 100 years have seen a most remarkable advance in our understanding of deeper layers of existence beyond the 'billiard ball' mechanics of atoms. It is a true testimony to human endeavour that we have come so far in our understanding of the fundamental workings of nature.

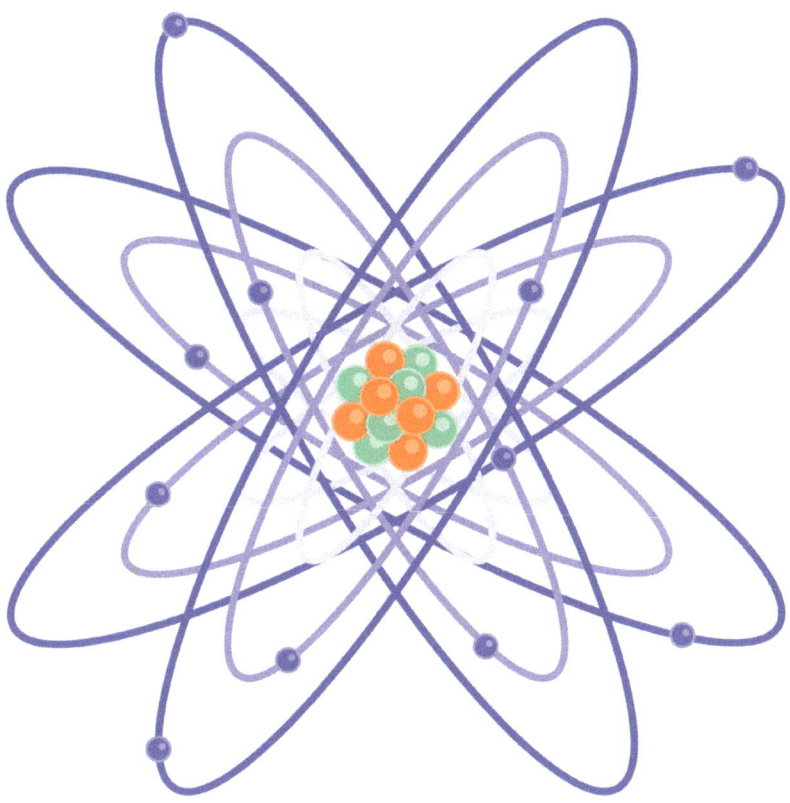

Artistic attempts fail to accurately portray the 'look' of an atom

Let's imagine we could shrink ourselves down to the size of a simple atom. We'll look at hydrogen, because it's the simplest and most abundant atom and the first one off the production line after the Big Bang some 13.8 billion years ago[11]. Hydrogen is simply one proton with one electron circling it[12]. To get a feeling of its size, it would take almost 20 million hydrogen atoms to make a line as long as this hyphen: – .

Even if we could shrink ourselves down to the size of an atom, we would be unlikely to 'see' an atom or any part of it. Our eyes require photons of light to activate the receptor cells in our retinas. Photons are similar packages of energy to electrons – both belonging to the electromagnetic spectrum – so we wouldn't have much luck in getting a photon to bounce off an electron without interfering with the electron. But if we could somehow see what's going on at this level, we would see basically empty space – not a hard, billiard-ball-like entity. That's because the electron orbits very far from the nucleus. To gain a sense of scale, if we were to imagine a proton at about one centimetre (a third of an inch) in diameter, the electron would actually be spinning about 500m (about a quarter of a mile) away from the nucleus. Another peculiarity of this tiny world pertains to the particles themselves. Protons and neutrons behave like small particles, so we can visualise them as looking vaguely like tiny billiard balls – perhaps fuzzy, ill-defined balls. The electron however, has a wave-like nature to it. In other words, the electron is more similar to a beam of light than it is to a billiard ball. Representing an electron as a small particle spinning around a nucleus like a planet around the sun is misleading. The electron is actually a wave that surrounds the nucleus of an atom like a cloud. What we can try to visualise therefore – if we were shrunk to the size of an atom – is a hazy, glowing cloud surrounding a tiny proton a long distance away. The atom – the so-called "building block" of hard, solid material things – is a very different entity to what our eyes perceive and what we can feel of the gross object. Already, even at the relatively gross scale of an atom, the vision we normally hold of reality is breaking down.

At the sub-atomic scale, it is necessary for us to largely let go of our visceral 'common sense' understanding of reality. As British geneticist J.B.S. (Jack) Haldane (1892–1964) wrote: "My own suspicion is that the universe is not only queerer than we suppose, but queerer than we *can* suppose".[13]

As we delve deeper into these fundamental layers of material and phenomenal existence we find nature less and less material and more abstract. Physicist Fritzof Capra wrote[14], "Quantum Theory has shown that subatomic particles are not isolated grains of matter but are probability patterns, interconnections in an inseparable cosmic web that includes the human observer and her consciousness". We simply need to let go of our usual concept of solid material particles. As Capra also wrote rather poetically, "There are no dancers, there is only the dance".

Even as far back as 1930, physicists were letting go of the materialistic and mechanical model of reality of which Descartes and Newton were so certain. English physicist Sir James Jeans said, "The stream of human knowledge is impartially heading towards a non-mechanical reality"[15]. And rather prophetically for this early period in quantum theory he continued, "The universe begins to look more like a great thought than a great machine. Mind no longer appears to be an accidental intruder into the realm of matter. We are beginning to suspect that we ought rather to hail it as the creator and governor of this realm".

Henry Stapp is an American physicist working in quantum mechanics at the University of California. Stapp has long maintained an interest in the connections of quantum mechanics with consciousness. He wrote: "An elementary particle is not an independently existing unanalysable entity. It is, in essence, a set of relationships that reach outwards to other things".[16]

In the 19th century, Scottish physicist and mathematician James Maxwell was probably the first to introduce concepts that would severely limit Newtonian physics as the ultimate paradigm of scientific thought. Maxwell began what would be an ongoing process of unification of the laws of physics. He discovered that what were once considered to be two separate forces of nature – electricity and magnetism – were really one and the same thing. Both these phenomena are referred to as electromagnetism.

Maxwell demonstrated that electromagnetic phenomena such as light, X-rays and radio acted in a wave-like manner. At first, these 'waves' were seen as a movement of some particulate 'ether' connecting material things. Einstein would soon demonstrate that this wave-like energy did not have to move through a substance – it was independent of the nature of the medium through which it moved. So what exactly were these waves made of? Where was their beginning and end? Maxwell also introduced the concept that electromagnetic phenomena were like a force field. Instead of the isolated, solid particulate view of matter and forces, we now had to think in terms of waves of some kind of underlying energy.

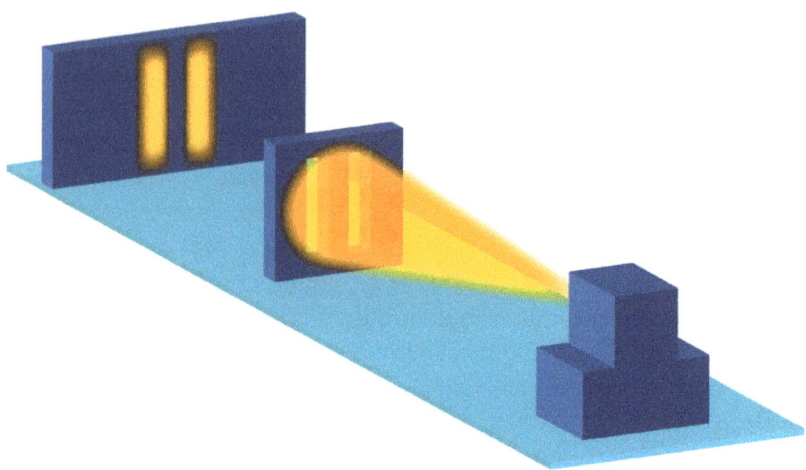

A particle view of light would have the beam split into two after passing through two slits.

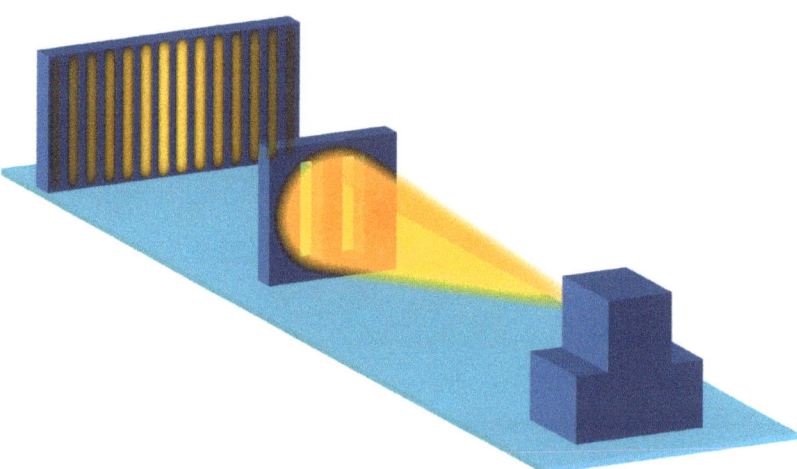

Water waves passing through two slits will reinforce or interfere with each other in such a way as to create banding.

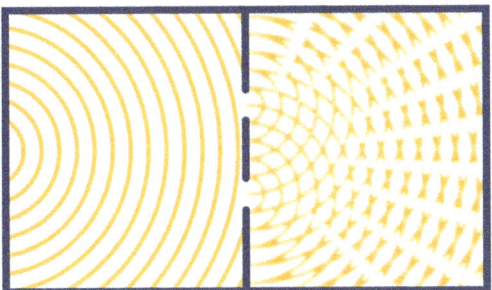

A beam of light behaves in a similar manner to liquid waves passing through two slits, creating a banding effect on a wall or screen.

When I was a young school student, I was taught in science class that light – as one example of an electromagnetic phenomenon – behaved both as a collection of isolated solid particles and a collection of waves. I could never get my mind around that. I felt that something was missing in the full understanding of this natural phenomenon. It is now clear that particles (like protons and electrons) and forces (like magnetism and gravity) are nothing but the excitation of underlying quantum fields. These fields are an unbounded, unconfined expanse of energy. When this energy is excited, it behaves in a wave-like fashion – much like what happens to the calm surface of the ocean. Just like an ocean wave, an energy wave has a distinct amplitude (wave height) and wave length (see diagram).

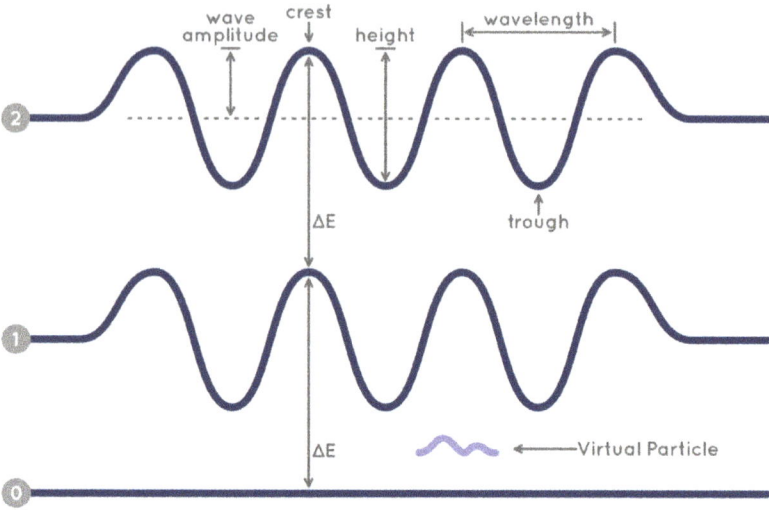

Particles are packages of waves representing excitation of an underlying quantum field. Discrete waves representing discrete whole units of energy are interpreted as 'particles'. Twitches of the underlying field which can be of any wave height and are not stable are interpreted as 'forces' or 'virtual particles'.

THE TERM 'QUANTUM' MEANS 'DISCRETE' AND 'DEFINED'. THE AMOUNT OF energy inherent in any quantum field is expressed as one unit of energy, two units of energy, three units, etc. This "quantisation" of energy refers to discrete packages of energy levels that will propagate a stable wave (see diagram). One unit of energy will create a one-particle state with that wave having one unit of height. Two units of energy will result in a wave having exactly twice the amplitude of the former. It is known as a two-particle state. This quantisation (or discreteness) of wave amplitude lends itself to an interpretation of separation and isolation. It gives that wave expression a discrete 'grainy' quality that can be interpreted as a 'particle'. When we speak of a particle at the sub-atomic level of nature therefore, we are actually referring to a discrete package of energy concentration that appears ultimately to the senses as a solid, discrete, 'marble-like' entity.

Material substance is nothing, ultimately, but the discrete and finite excitation of an underlying field of energy (a so-called "quantum field").

Einstein's famous equation "$E = MC^2$" equates energy (E) with mass (M) and the speed of light (C).

What then is the difference between a particle and a force? A particle is – in the classical sense – easy to comprehend: it's something very concrete and familiar to our physical senses of sight and touch. A force is something we interpret as more abstract, yet we know it exists because we witness it daily. We know gravity for example, because it keeps our feet firmly on the ground. It is harder to comprehend the nature of a force. Scientists have discovered that a force is also an excitation of an underlying quantum field, into a temporary wave. A force wave does not have a stable propagating character like a matter wave. Being of a more tenuous nature, it does not have to obey the discrete levels of a particle wave function, but can be of any wave height – although typically of much lower amplitude. A force represents a spasm or twitch of the underlying field which is inherently unstable and does not last for long. The apparent perpetuity of force fields like gravity would be explained by continual and repetitive twitches in the underlying quantum field.

With this model in mind, we now understand that a particle can sometimes behave as a force and a force can behave like a particle. It all depends on the level of excitation of the same underlying quantum field. So close are the natures of the two entities of force and particle, that force fields are sometimes referred to as 'virtual particles'. Light – a collection of photons – is an electromagnetic force and can be referred to as a collection of virtual particles.

Quantum mechanics provides a framework to understand that 'particle' and 'force' are really one and the same thing. For the past hundred years, science has led us towards unification of these diverse aspects of material existence.

> *"Indeed we are all at sea in this life, borne on an infinite network of complex oscillations. No part of our life is free of waves. We are all surfers, are we not?"*
>
> – Drew Kampion, The Book of Waves – Form and Beauty on the Ocean

"A rock is an example of a particle; an ocean wave is an example of a wave. Now someone's telling you a rock is like an ocean wave. What?!"

– Leonard Susskind, Physicist[17]

Albert Einstein shakes our notion of common sense

WE HAVE NOW SEEN THAT MATERIAL 'THINGS' – THOSE THINGS WE CAN touch and feel, including our own bodies – are none other than discrete waves of energy, and that those force 'fields' we refer to such as radio waves or gravity, are also waves of energy.

For decades, quantum physics studying the very small and cosmology or astrophysics studying the very large were two separate areas of study, never really sharing much in common. In the past 20 years however, the two disciplines have come together as the laws of nature have been found to be progressively unified.

Einstein singularly turned Newtonian science and the Cartesian way of seeing the world on its head. In the early 1900s his discoveries created a chasm between the respected field of physics and the common person's ability to view the world. No wonder caricatures of mad scientists depicted Einstein's shaggy, unkempt hair in his older years!

Despite a century passing since Einstein's remarkable discovery most people still believe that space and time are immutable constants, absolute values upon which or through all this material world works. Einstein proved that time and space were not absolute entities at all, but rather 'relative' concepts that had no real meaning or innate existence except in terms of comparing one thing to another. This was Einstein's Special Theory of Relativity.

Einstein unified space and time in a four-dimensional continuum – the three familiar dimensions of space plus the extra dimension of time. Both space and time could be bent and twisted like a piece of fabric, hence the common term "space-time fabric". While Newton was the first to describe some mathematical behavioural characteristics of gravity, Newton was never able to describe exactly what gravity was. Einstein succeeded to some extent, describing gravity in a way it had never been appreciated before. He described gravity as a warping of the space-time continuum which effectively held the moon to the Earth and the Earth to the Sun and so forth. Graphically, this warping of space and time was best appreciated by the comparison to a flat trampoline with the Sun at the centre depressing the trampoline (representing the space-time continuum) and causing the Earth to circle it like a marble propelled around the trampoline. This description of gravity as a warping of space-time was called the General Theory of Relativity.

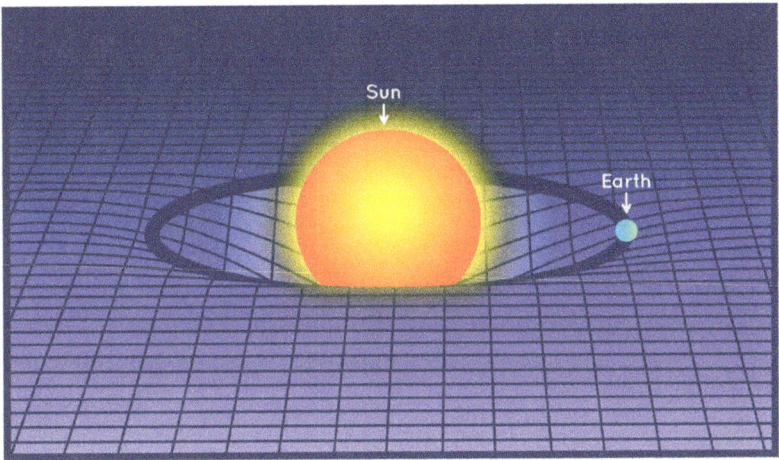

Einstein described gravity as a bending of space-time in such a way that nearby objects take the shortest path and are effectively attracted to the larger object, circling it like a marble around a round bowl.

Scientists recently confirmed the existence of gravitational waves, adding further proof of Einstein's General Theory of Relativity. A cataclysmic event involving colliding black holes, dying stars or the birth of our universe involves such high energies that waves are created in the space-time fabric of our whole universe. Visualise the above trampoline diagram having something very heavy dropped onto it. Waves of space-time are generated – like vibrations on the trampoline – representing a rhythmic stretching and shrinking of space-time. As astrophysicist Katie Mack said, "In fact you are awash in waves of space-time that periodically stretch you and squeeze you this way and that".[18] We're talking about dimensional changes however of such a miniscule scale, that you would never see or feel them.

It gets weirder the deeper we go into nature's functioning. Scientists have made some discoveries that defy all common sense, very often escaping their own ability to comprehend their findings. Our ability to reason anything is very dependent on what we perceive with our five senses.

Einstein discovered that the speed of light was a kind of cosmic speed limit – nothing can travel faster than the speed of light – even gravity. This assertion was the subject of criticism from fellow scientists steeped in the Newtonian view. If the Sun suddenly disappeared, they asked, wouldn't the Earth immediately be flung out into the heavens on a straight trajectory? It certainly makes sense to you or me, but Einstein asserted that even gravity would take 8.5 minutes – the same time that light takes to reach the Earth – to sever its hold on the Earth once the Sun disappeared. The constancy of the speed of light would even explain why, if one travels away from the Earth at near the speed of light for a period of, say, 24 hours by the traveller's watch, then upon returning, the traveller will be surprised to find that a much longer period of time has passed according to those back on Earth. Any relative motion will in fact change the relative rate at which time passes. Our instruments are not sensitive enough to measure any discrepancies between reference frames unless something is traveling many thousands of kilometres per hour.

Yes, we're talking about time travel here, although only time travel into the future. A good explanation of the phenomenon can be seen in Brian Green's book *The Elegant Universe*. Einstein's discovery of the relative nature of time and space (his special theory of relativity) and the ability of objects with mass to bend and warp space (his general theory of relativity) and the speed of light as an ultimate speed limit in nature have been proven by astronomical observation and are now indisputable. Note also here that we are continuing the process of unification of the different aspects of nature – in this case, the concept of space and time are interlinked and ultimately seen to be one and the same thing.

Back to the small: the atom
IN THE PREVIOUS CHAPTERS, I HAVE ALLUDED TO THE CONCEPT OF consciousness as an ocean underlying waves of individual consciousness. Through a few analogies and life stories I have also hinted that this deeper field of universal consciousness has attributes that have been described in terms such as unboundedness, timelessness and interconnectedness (or unity).

Already, we can correlate some attributes or qualities of human experience with qualities derived from our careful scientific study of the natural world. For example, the relativity of time and space infers their non-existence as absolute entities. Time and space only exist in reference to one another. Therefore, as we probe into ever more subtle levels of nature, time and space are eventually transcended – they no longer exist. There truly exists a level of timelessness and unboundedness.

Likewise, we are already seeing the progressive unification of the various laws of nature we have described over the past hundreds of years. Our ability to perceive a connectedness of all things in nature and of ourselves to nature should already hint that our consciousness is intimately linked with those most subtle, fundamental levels of nature. This link of consciousness with the most fundamental laws of nature will hopefully become even more apparent as you read on.

Let's return to the subatomic scale. In the 1920s, scientists were looking even closer at the make-up of atoms and discovering that the existing Newtonian view and even Maxwell's theories could not explain the behaviour of nature at these tiny levels. Niels Bohr, a Danish physicist, found that atoms were made up of even smaller particles. Up to that time, atoms were thought to be the tiniest constituents of matter and indivisible – the building blocks of nature. This reductionist concept fitted very well with the prevailing Cartesian viewpoint of the universe. As scientists studied atoms at the subatomic level, they found that gravity – at this scale of nature – was too weak a force and electromagnetism inadequate to explain what was going on.

In the late 1920s quantum mechanics developed as a serious discipline. As I have discussed, the term refers to the behaviour of subatomic elementary particles as wave-like expressions of an underlying field of undefined energy. This field actually becomes more dynamic at more subtle, fundamental levels and, along with this increasing dynamism or frenzy is more uncertainty about the particle's position and momentum. Scientists were making the uncomfortable conclusions that nature no longer behaves in an orderly, predictable fashion at this level of existence. Uncertainly rules at this level and we can only calculate the odds that things will turn out one way or the other. Nature at this subatomic level behaves in a seemingly chaotic and random fashion.

You might ask – if this level of nature gives rise to the more gross aspects of nature that we are familiar with, and these more gross levels are mathematically predictable, then how can this disparity exist? What we witness at the gross level is simply a mathematical probability that nature will perform a certain way. Physicist Brian Greene reminds us that, while normal reasoning suggests you cannot walk through a brick wall or that it would be impossible for an apple to fall up instead of down from a tree, quantum physics allows these possibilities. It might take a time span of near infinity however for these things to happen!

At this stage, many physicists were beginning to doubt their own sanity. Physics – always considered the science that does not have to deal with qualitative considerations – was uncovering an uncomfortable picture of how the universe works. One of the foremost scientists in the early development of quantum theory, Werner Heisenberg said, "I remember discussions with Bohr which went through many hours till very late at night and ended almost in despair; and when at the end of the discussion I went alone for a walk in the neighbouring park I repeated to myself again and again the question: Can nature possibly be as absurd as it seemed to us in these atomic experiments?".[19] Feynman was more accepting: "Quantum mechanics describes nature as absurd from the point of view of common sense. And it fully agrees with experiment. So I hope you can accept nature as She is – absurd".[20]

Despite his radical discoveries that initiated the departure from the strictly Newtonian path of science, Einstein did not welcome this new way of seeing nature. "God does not throw dice," he said. Yet, quantum mechanics was backing its assertions with experiment after experiment. ('Mechanics' is actually a strange name for a science that departs from the conventional way of studying machines.) "There has never been a prediction made using quantum mechanics that has contradicted an observation – never!" said MIT professor of physics Edward Farhi.

By the 1930s, the quest by Einstein for unification of the laws of nature was floundering. Neither was anyone else pursuing this quest with any vigour or success. Most physicists were seduced by the fascinating discoveries in quantum mechanics. Two new forces were discovered (in addition to gravity and electromagnetism). The Strong Nuclear Force acted like a glue, holding the protons and neutrons together inside the nucleus of each atom. The Weak Nuclear Force allowed neutrons to turn into protons, giving off radiation in the process. The Weak Nuclear Force is also involved in the mechanics of energy production in the stars. Four basic 'forces' of nature had been identified.

By the 1950s, with Einstein's death in 1955, almost no physicists were involved in the quest for unification. Physics was divided into two very different camps – one that used general relativity to study the big and heavy objects in the cosmos, and the other that used quantum mechanics to study the very finest level of nature like atoms and their constituent particles. While most scientists probably appreciated that gravity would have an influence at the subatomic level, its effect was far too weak compared to the other forces and simply did not fit into the conceptual models of the time. Remember that the apparent strength of gravity perceived by most of us is brought about because the huge mass of Earth is acting on relatively small masses on its surface. At much smaller size scales, the effect of gravity is billions and billions of times less than any of the other known forces. The discovery of black holes in the Universe would soon bring together the disparate disciplines of relativity theory (in its explanation of gravity) and quantum mechanics to form a new discipline called quantum field theory.

Scientists continue the process of unification
THERE ARE TWO MAJOR CATEGORIES OF QUANTUM FIELD: BOSE AND FERMI. Bose fields have traditionally been known as 'force fields' or 'gauge' fields – gauge meaning they act locally. Fermi fields are known as 'matter fields'. As I have discussed, however, any quantum field can play the role of a force or particle depending on the nature and degree of excitation of the field. Bosons (Bose virtual particles) like to exhibit collective coherent behaviour (such as a laser) whereas fermions are prevented from any collective behaviour by the Pauli Exclusion Principle. Hagelin says "bosons of a feather flock together".

It's just as well fermions like to exclude each other. Their exclusive behaviour accounts for the multiplicity and diversity we see around us. A look at the periodic table will reveal a vast range of different elements found on this Earth (and throughout this universe). The atoms differ from each other in their atomic number (the number of protons in the nucleus) and atomic weight (combined protons and neutrons). The number of circulating electrons exactly equals the number of protons. The electrons orbit the nucleus and occupy different 'shells'. The first shell will only permit two electrons, then the Pauli Exclusion Principle forces additional electrons to occupy the next shell. Only eight electrons are permitted in the second shell, after which extra electrons must occupy the next shell, and so forth. This reflects the inherent 'exclusion' behaviour of Fermi fields or particles of matter at this subatomic level. This behaviour accounts for the diversity of elements we see in nature, their different behaviour and hence the sheer diversity of material existence.

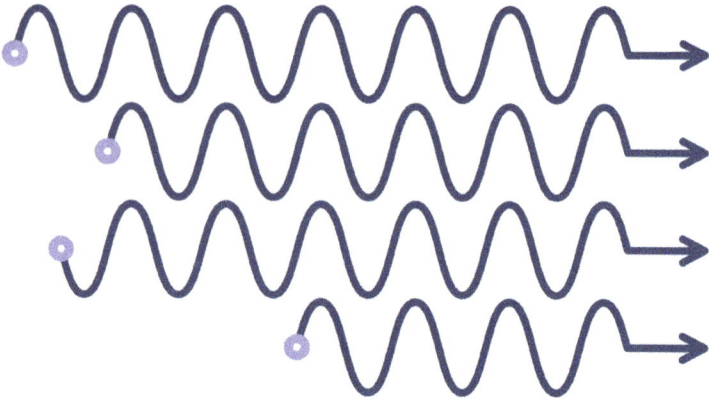

Coherent behaviour in lasers is illustrated by the tendency for light from different sources to align perfectly in their wavelengths.

Of the four fundamental force fields identified early in the 20th century (electromagnetism, the weak nuclear force, the strong nuclear force and gravitation), only electromagnetism (light, radio, X-rays etc) and gravity are familiar to us. Of the four main fermi fields, the up-type and down-type quarks (pronounced "kworks" as in "corks") were the essential constituents of the nucleons (protons and neutrons), neutrinos are almost zero-mass particles that travel at or almost the speed of light and interact with very little on their way from the Sun (which means they typically pass though us and the Earth easily), and the charged leptons are the electrons.

Note that there is a common ingredient to neutrons and protons within the nucleus – up quarks and down quarks. The difference between a proton and a neutron only relates to the particular composition of up quarks and down quarks. In their essence, protons and neutrons are one and the same thing.

AS WE CONTINUE OUR JOURNEY INTO THE PROGRESSIVE UNIFICATION OF all these laws of nature, it is probably helpful to discuss the concept of symmetry in nature. Most of us understand symmetry to represent a harmonising and usually aesthetically pleasing repetition of shape or parts of something facing each other or a centre. Take a snow-flake. Rotate it 60 degrees and it appears the same. Rotate a square 90 degrees and it will also appear unchanged.

Physicists have extended this usual meaning of symmetry to include not only an invariance of shape or appearance but also to an invariance (or sameness) of behaviour of the laws of nature when studied from different angles or in different circumstances. Scientists have discovered symmetry in the laws of nature that have persevered through time since the Big Bang. They have also observed symmetry in the laws of nature from one side of the universe to the other. We are referring to the inherent sameness and immunity to change with respect to space and time. These laws of physics remain the same, no matter from where or when we examine them.

We are told that attractive people usually exhibit symmetrical faces. Symmetry is aesthetically pleasing because it mirrors a quality of our essential Self – some universal, non-changing quality in the midst of superficial change. Symmetry with regard to the laws of nature also helps to explain the "unreasonable effectiveness of mathematics" (as Nobel laureate physicist Eugene Wagner called it in 1960) in making scientific predictions.

Unifying the electromagnetic and weak forces: electroweak theory
IN 1974, THE PREVIOUSLY VERY DIFFERENT ELECTROMAGNETIC FORCE AND weak force (among the bose fields) and the up quarks and down quarks and electrons and neutrinos (belonging to the fermi fields) were unified with the formation of the electro-weak theory[21]. W and Z bosons were the linking 'virtual' particles that unified the previously different forces and particles. These W and Z bosons were observed as particles in January of 1983, providing confirmation of this unified electro-weak theory.

By "unified" I mean that these once different force and matter fields are found to be indistinguishable at smaller distance scales. As we have already seen, at smaller and smaller subatomic distance scales, nature is found to be more energetic, and the increased energy (remember $E=MC^2$, which means that there is more energy needed for more mass) supports the expression of new heavier particles – the so-called W and Z bosons. They are not actually discrete particles but virtual. These extra particles (normally dormant in today's universe, but more active at smaller distance and time scales) are like the missing parts of a jigsaw puzzle. When present, the W and Z particles fill the gap in behaviour and appearance between the up quark and down quark particles and between the electrons and neutrinos, resulting in an indistinguishable entity – an identical wave of the same underlying quantum field. This one wave expression of the underlying quantum field has been called the "left-handed lepton doublet" (try remembering that!). Remove the W and Z bosons and the jigsaw puzzle appears broken or fragmented, giving the appearance of separate up quarks and down quarks, and electrons and neutrinos. With the absence of these heavier bosons, we say that the electro-weak symmetry has been broken. The bottom line here is that electrons and neutrinos are seen to be essentially the same at more fundamental distance scales and, because up quarks and down quarks are also identical at these scales, protons and neutrons are also unified. The "symmetry" here refers to the one underlying wave-functioning of an electro-weak quantum field. This electro-weak field is comprised of the massless photon (representing the EM force) and the heavy W and Z bosons.

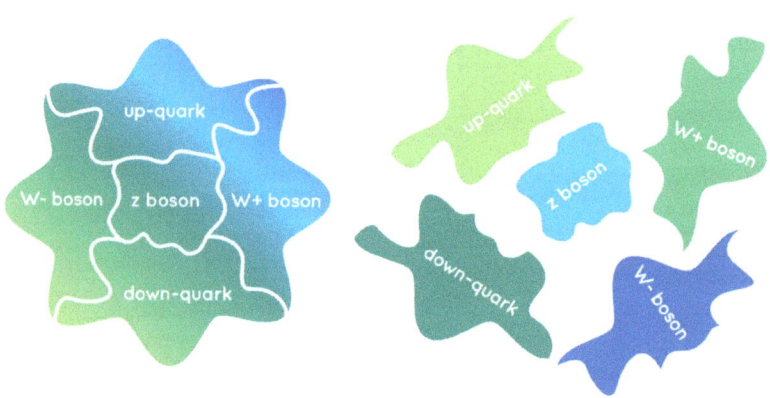

Without the presence of W and Z bosons, up quarks and down quarks appear as different particles and thus give rise to separate protons and neutrons. With the bosons actively present, the jigsaw puzzle is complete and symmetry is restored. The up quarks and down quarks are seen as one and the same entity – an indivisible whole.

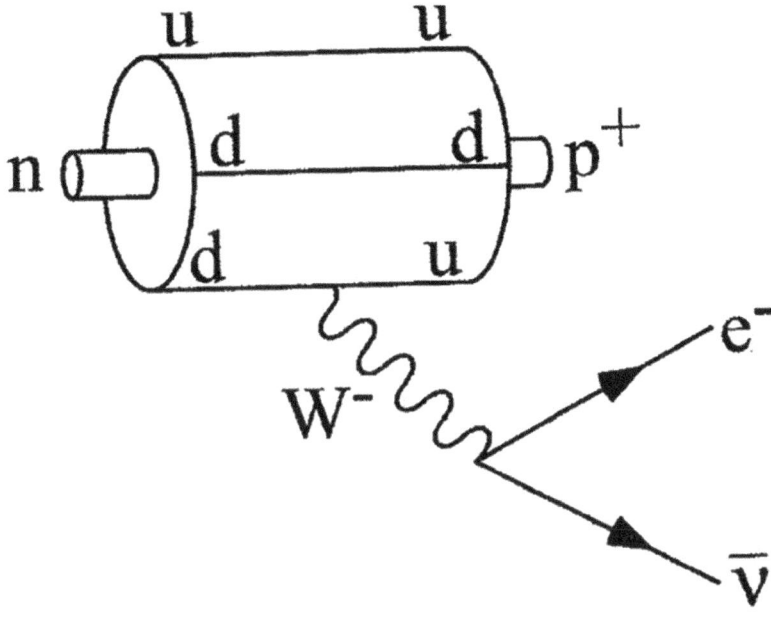

Shortly after the Big Bang, neutrons – comprising two down quarks and one up quark – quickly decayed into more stable protons – two up quarks and one down quark. It was the active presence of the W and Z bosons that upheld the symmetry (sameness) between the protons and neutrons, and between the electrons and neutrinos. In those first moments after the Big Bang, these bosons were very active, allowing the decay of the neutrons. The W boson here quickly decays into an electron and anti-neutrino. A positron also results from the decay of the neutron. This phenomenon is known as radioactive beta decay. (Illustration courtesy of Dr John Hagelin)

W and Z bosons are a hundred times heavier than a proton (the heaviest subatomic particle in our current universe). A much hotter, more energetic universe (such as existed for minutes after the Big Bang) would be needed to sustain these particles. They are now dormant. When they were around, they upheld the symmetry between up quarks and down quarks, and the electrons and neutrinos resulting in no discernible difference between protons and neutrons, and between electrons and neutrinos. W and Z bosons exist today at the finest subatomic scales and occasionally exert an influence. These particles have been re-activated in the super particle colliders at the European Organization for Nuclear Research (CERN).

Unifying the electroweak and strong forces: grand unified theory
ONE OF THE GREAT IRONIES IS THAT THE SMALLER THE TIME AND distance scale we explore, the more energy is needed to unravel that world. As we have mentioned there is also more energy inherent in that world. The smaller the 'thing', the bigger the energies involved. For example, a nuclear bomb has vastly more devastating power than a chemical bomb such as TNT.

The international scientific effort to unify the electroweak force and the strong force (leaving gravity on its own) and the quarks (found in the nucleons) with the much smaller leptons (electrons and neutrinos) has resulted in a number of Grand Unified Theories (GUTs), none which have been proven – yet. Proving any of these theories is going to be very difficult as the energies needed in collision experiments in even the world's largest collider – the Large Hadron Collider near Geneva, Switzerland – are far above what can be achieved now and in the foreseeable future.

The quest for a Grand Unified Theory connecting the electroweak and strong forces and quarks and leptons is motivated by two experimentally proven understandings:
1. Electrons and protons have precisely equal and opposite charges. Without grand unification, this must be viewed as nothing but a freak coincidence.
2. The strength of the strong, weak and electromagnetic forces all magically converge at a distance scale of about 10^{-29} cm.

ONE MAINSTREAM GUT FIRST PROPOSED IN THE EARLY 1980S AND LATER developed by Hagelin, Nanopoulos, Ellis and Antoniadis is the Flipped SU(5) model of grand unification. Hypothesised superheavy X and Y bosons, found at time-distance scales below 10^{-29} cm (that's one thousand million millionth of the proton radius) dynamically uphold the unity of quarks and leptons, and also unify the electro-weak and strong force fields. Because these new particles unify leptons and quarks, they are also called leptoquark bosons.

Using our jigsaw puzzle analogy, the superheavy X and Y bosons – some 15 powers of 10 heavier than the proton – fill the gaps between the leptons and quarks to form one single matter field (effectively unifying all the fermions) and also fill the gaps between the heavy and electro-weak gauge fields to form one grand unified force field. Symmetry (sameness) is thus restored to both the force and matter fields such that all matter particles found in nature derive from one quantum field and all the force fields in nature except gravity derive from the same unified quantum field. Because leptons (like electrons which are extremely light) are entirely different beasts from quarks (relatively much heavier) we can say that any symmetry which once existed between the two is badly broken.

Because the quarks found in the protons and neutrons, and the relatively light leptons comprising electrons and neutrinos become one and the same thing, proton decay becomes possible. The average proton lives for an extraordinarily long period – some 10^{33} years – before decaying. Considering the universe is only about 10^{10} years old, most protons have been around since (literally) the beginning of time. It has been considered – until recently – impossible for protons to decay. In the diagram below, it can be seen that an X boson mediates the decay of the proton (comprising two up quarks and one down quark) into a meson (a quark and an anti-quark forming what is known as a "pion" π) and a positron (positive electron).

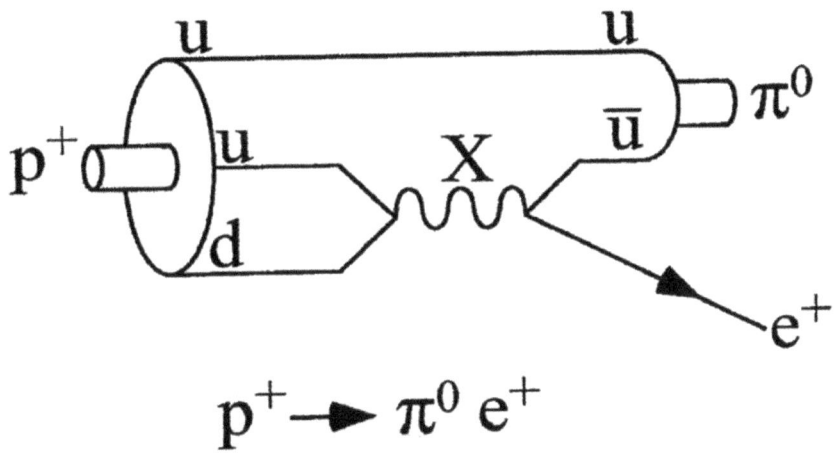

Even a proton, conventionally thought to be indestructible, can decay with the active presence of the hypothesised X and Y bosons. These bosons uphold the symmetry (sameness) between quarks and leptons (electrons and neutrinos) allowing such a transformation into a pion (quark-antiquark pair) and a positron. (Illustration courtesy of Dr John Hagelin)

When we say that an average proton lives for 10^{33} years, we can also interpret that as any proton has a 1 in 10^{33} chance of decaying at any time. Therefore, if you watch a tank containing 10^{33} protons for a few years, you should see some of the protons decay. 10^{33} protons are contained in just a thousand tonnes of water. Because protons could be disrupted by the cosmic rays that continually pour down upon us from space, an experimental lake has been constructed 1km under a mountain in Japan. That protons are given any life span at all depends on the rare appearance of super-heavy bosons that equate quarks with leptons and therefore allow the decay of quarks into leptons (and mesons). The hypothesised X and Y bosons would occasionally appear as faint twitches of the underlying quantum field, mediating such a rare and exotic transformation. Such an observation would prove the Grand Unified Theory and the existence of these super-heavy bose particles.

After a few years of no successful detection of proton decay, researchers have concluded that, if protons decay at all, the proton lifetime is greater than about 10^{34} years.[22]

NOTES

3   Capra, Fritzof, *The Turning Point*, p 59
4   Rodis-Lewis, Geneviève; 1978; *Limitations of the Mechanical Model in the Cartesian Conception of the Organism;* In Hooker, Michael, ed. Descartes. Baltimore: Johns Hopkins University Press.
5   Capra, Fritzof, *The Turning Point*, p 60
6   Garber, Daniel; 1978; *Science and Certainty in Descartes*, In Hooker, Michael, ed. Descartes. Baltimore: Johns Hopkins University Press.
7   Capra, Fritzof; *The Turning Point*; p 63
8   Hawking, Stephen; *The Sydney Morning Herald* – Health and Science – May 1, 2008 and TV documentary *Stephen Hawking – The Grand Design*.
9   Capra, Fritzof; *The Turning Point*; p 65
10   Visible to the naked eye, not needing any magnifying equipment
11   Recently, scientists have adjusted the time of the Big Bang from 13.7 to 13.8 billion years ago.
12   http://web.jjay.cuny.edu/~acarpi/NSC/3-atoms.htm
13   Haldane, J..B.S.; In *Possible Worlds* (1927), p 298.
14   Capra, Fritzof; *The Turning Point*, ps 91, 92
15   Jeans, James; *The Mysterious Universe,* 1930, Ch 5
16   Stapp, Henry Pierce, 1971, *S-Matrix Interpretation of Quantum Theory*, Physical Review D, March 15.
17   From a YouTube dissertation by Leonard Susskind
18   Mack, Katie, PhD; 'Catching Gravitational Waves'; *Cosmos – The Science of Everything,* Issue 68. April–May, 2016, p23.
19   Capra, Fritzof; *The Turning Point*, p76.
20   Greene, Brian; *Elegant Universe,* p 111
21   Physicists Glashow, Salam and Weinberg were awarded the Nobel Prize for their formation of Electro-Weak Theory.
22   Hawking, Stephen; *The Grand Design*, p 112.

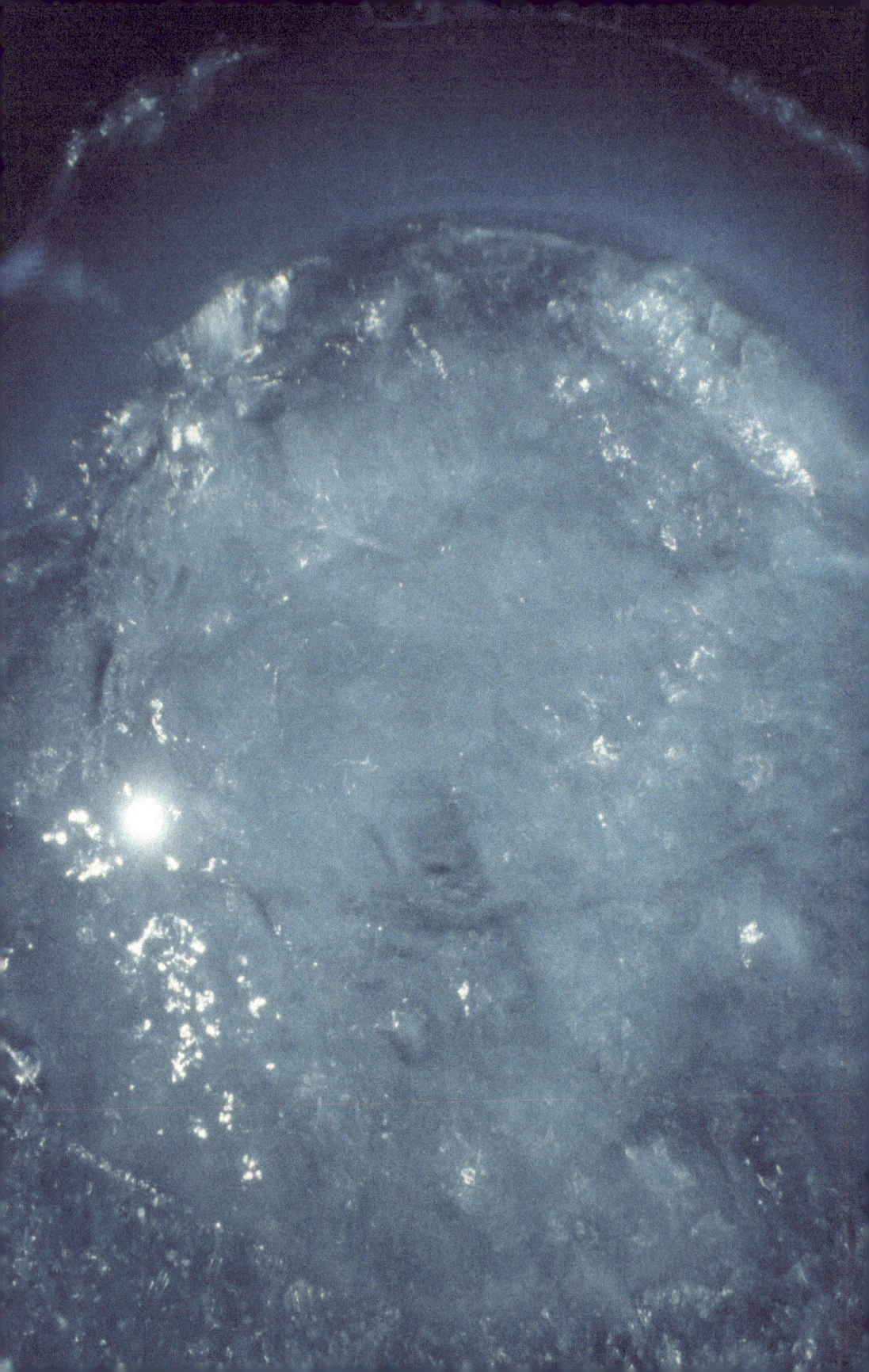

MODERN SCIENCE – PART TWO
SUPERSTRING THEORY AND COSMOLOGY: UNIFYING THE LARGE AND THE SMALL

"The universe begins to look more like a great thought than a great machine. Mind no longer appears to be an accidental intruder into the realm of matter. We are beginning to suspect that we ought rather to hail it as the creator and governor of this realm."

– Sir James Jeans (British physicist),
The mysterious universe (1930)

The development of superstring theory has equipped physicists with working equations to describe gravity as the very first manifestation of the unified field and therefore the most primordial entity of expressed material existence. It is from the field of gravity that all the other particles and force-fields arise. Quantum mechanics and cosmology have now been connected with the help of superstring theory.

Black holes
WAY BACK IN 1916, BLACK HOLES WERE FIRST PROPOSED BY THE GERMAN astronomer *Karl Schwarzschild*. He postulated that a massive star might shrink into a tiny space smaller than the eye could see. The centres of these black holes are therefore tiny, but massive. It was here that scientists realised that both general relativity (formerly used for studying massive objects in space) and quantum mechanics (formerly restricted to the study of the tiniest particles comprising atoms) would be needed to fully understand the behaviour of black holes. The existence of black holes is now accepted by scientists who have discovered evidence of them using satellite telescopes.

There is thought to be a black hole in the very centre of our own Milky Way galaxy. That centre, around which the whole galaxy rotates once every 200 million years, is some 27,000 light years from Earth. The radiation source that might be a black hole is called Sagittarius A* (pronounced "Sagittarius A star") and is millions of times heavier than our Sun, but is so small it would fit inside the orbit of the Sun's closest planet Mercury.

To appreciate the beauty and dynamism of our galaxy have a look at the Scientific American video link based on the magazine article: *The Dark Side of the Milky Way*, Oct, 2011 – http://bcove.me/00y909qp. The galaxy moves in a way that resembles some of the creatures I see while diving, although we must remind ourselves that the graceful movement shown graphically happens over many millions of years. Quite possibly, our attraction to the beauty of a jellyfish moving through the water reminds us – even unconsciously – of that similar beauty found at the greater cosmic scale of a whole galaxy. We are connected to that larger cosmos in more intimate ways than we have so far imagined. Again and again, I am drawn to the message from the *Upanishads* that "As is the microcosm, so is the macrocosm. As is the atom, so is the universe".

If we ignore the considerable effects of air resistance, a bullet needs to travel about 11km/sec (about 7 miles/sec) to escape the gravitational pull of Earth and continue into outer space. (A typical bullet in fact travels much slower than this – about 300m/sec, which is about the speed of sound.) Now imagine squeezing Earth into a smaller sphere. The more mass we squeeze into a tinier space, the more dense it becomes. The bullet would therefore need more velocity to escape the Earth because the total mass of the Earth is effectively closer to the bullet. Eventually, when the Earth is squeezed to, say, 1mm in size, even light could not escape, and if light cannot escape the Earth, nothing can, because nothing travels faster than the speed of light.

We can't be completely certain, but the general consensus is that at this level of density the Earth would catastrophically collapse into a mathematical point of zero radius – a 'singularity'. Such a point would represent a point of infinite gravitational forces, time would no longer exist and the classical laws of nature would no longer work. We know from the quantum principle that as we compact mass into an ever tinier space, we increase the amount of energy confined within that space. The singularity therefore would represent a state of tremendous dynamism. The tremendous energy at this scale would in fact re-enliven the hypothesised super-heavy X and Y bosons and the massive modes of the superstring. We are back to the Unified Field.

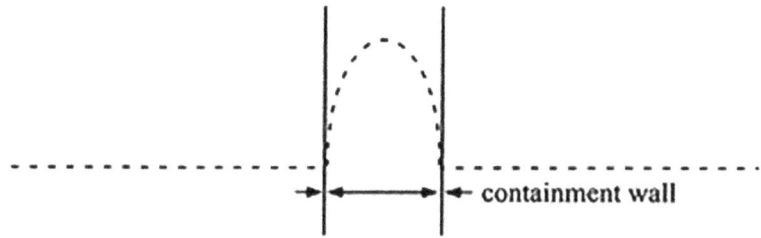

The quantum principle asserts that as a matter wave becomes more tightly confined, the more tightly peaked is the wave function with concomitant shorter wavelength. In this case, the shorter the resultant wavelength, the greater is the energy density.

The centre of a black hole probably contains a singularity of infinite density and is therefore unseeable. However, around the black hole is a so-called 'event horizon'. This is that point outside of which light can still escape.

When we talk about the size of the black hole believed to exist at Sagittarius A* being less than the orbit of Mercury, we are referring to the event horizon, since all its mass is presumed to have condensed to a singularity. If Sagittarius A* is a black hole, then – like most other black holes – it is actually not black to look at from a distance, but is radiating heat and brightness. Any gas nearby gets sucked into the black hole and the frantic energy resulting from the extreme speed of particles going into the event horizon emits much light and energy.

Black holes are therefore an oddity of nature. The extreme mass and size of a large star has collapsed into a point of zero dimension with presumably enough extreme energy to re-enliven all the heavy bosons and resume a state of super-symmetry – the return to the unified field. If you think this is a pretty amazing phenomenon in the study of cosmology, remember that if you take any point in space around you, that same unified field is also there at an almost infinitesimal scale.

Merging general relativity with quantum mechanics
The so-called "standard model" in physics described three of the forces that ruled the world (electromagnetism, and the strong and weak nuclear forces) and has come a long way in unifying these three forces. Gravity was the sole elusive force.

Gravity has stubbornly resisted any effort to define its exact nature or connect it with any of the other forces. Einstein proposed it worked by warping the space/time fabric around massive objects but its exact description still remained a mystery.

All forces and matter particles in nature are simply excitations of an underlying quantum field of some sort of energy. If excitation of this field gives rise to waves of energy or particles, what is the nature of this energy at rest? What happens when the wave flattens out to its unexcited state? Scientists call this state of least excitation the vacuum state. The classical view of this state is that it is lifeless, flat, inert and empty. After all, there is nothing being manifest when the quantum field is flat. It is not producing any forces or particles that comprise the manifest universe.

However, two principles change this view. The quantum principle notes that as we explore finer and finer time and distance scales, the underlying field appears more energetic and dynamic. The Heisenberg Uncertainty Principle states that we cannot know with precision both the position and momentum of any particle we are examining.

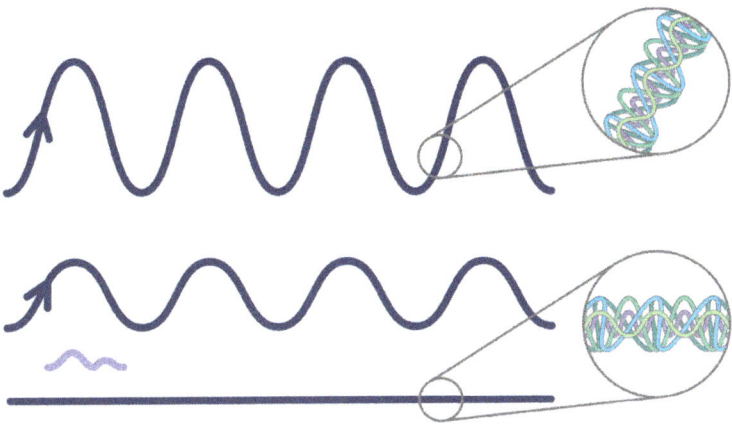

The vacuum state of quantum fields is the state of minimum excitation of the underlying field and therefore a state where no forces or particles are manifest. However, the vacuum state is in fact dynamic and brimming with liveliness and all-possible energy shapes. (Based on illustration courtesy of Dr John Hagelin)

So, even the flat line of a quantum field that we now call the vacuum state is full of brimming energy and liveliness. This liveliness is called "Zero Point Energy" or "Zitterbewegung" ("jitterbugging"). It is a state of no particles or forces, yet it is brimming with all possible shapes. Indeed, every possible shape cancels every other shape to form no specific shape. No other state has this quality of perfect balance. The vacuum state of a quantum field is a state of all possibilities and infinite dynamism, yet it remains unmanifest of any particle or force field and effectively silent.

IF I CAN REVERT JUST FOR A MOMENT'S REFLECTION ON THE SIMILAR experiences we have when entering the ocean of consciousness, you will hopefully remember that we mentioned experiences such as restful alertness (the dynamic quality of silence) and a sense of all possibilities. These experiences are also felt by explorers in the ocean environment and in other extreme environments.

We are now bravely exploring those very deep but fundamental levels of nature that give rise ultimately to the manifest world with which we are familiar. Gravity has remained stubbornly difficult to describe because it arises at this interface of the manifest/unmanifest level of existence. It arises somewhere among the first perturbations of this vacuum state that give rise to the elementary particles and forces. As you can now guess, gravity is closely linked with the emergence of space and time from this vacuum state.

This is a level of nature that is so small that we refer to its measurement as the Planck Scale (10^{-33} cm). Any distance smaller than this cannot be measured. Space – and therefore the concept of distance or measurement – does not exist at scales smaller than the Planck Scale. It is a scale that defines the very smallest of the smallest of manifest existence. It is at this scale where gravity is at its most dynamic. This is the level of the hypothesised unified field. Such a unified field is purely self-interacting. There is nothing else with which it can interact. At this scale, the self-interaction of the gravity field is so intense that space-time curves back on itself to form a bubbling cauldron of miniature black holes.

Space-time foam is an apt name for the frothing sea of micro black holes and every possible space-time shape seen at the Planck scale of nature's functioning. At this level, gravity (represented by different geometries of space-time) participates in a major way, producing the quantum geometry displayed at this level. (Based on illustration courtesy of Dr John Hagelin)

These micro black holes disappear as quickly as they form through the process of black hole evaporation. This activity resembles an incredible frothing sea of 10^{142} black holes per cubic centimetre per second, known as space-time foam.

This is the level of gravity that is known as quantum gravity, and – because it represents an expression of every possible shape and curvature of the space-time continuum – it is also called quantum geometry. This simultaneous co-existence of all possible field shapes of space and time makes space and time ill-defined. The Planck scale therefore marks the end of our classical notion of distance and time. With no definable concept of space and time at this level, the classical notion of causality also has no meaning, since an effect requires a cause to happen before it. Time, distance and causality are the three fundamental pillars of rational, deductive logic. Our so-called objective approach to gaining knowledge, which has successfully led us to ever more fundamental space-time scales, has transcended its own methodology. As physicist John Hagelin says, "Physics has '*walked the Planck!*'".

String theory

IN 1968, YOUNG ITALIAN PHYSICIST GABRIELE VENEZIANO WAS SEARCHING equations that would describe strong and weak nuclear forces. As the story goes, he happened on a dusty book on the history of mathematics and found a 200-year-old equation that seemed to describe the Strong Nuclear Force. Leonard Susskind (now at Stanford University) toyed with this equation and realised it described not a point source, but something that was elastic and vibrating. So began the evolution of string theory (or "superstring theory"). This is an example of where 'pure' mathematical formulations, while serving no practical application at the time, can later be used by scientists to better understand some aspect of nature. Another example of this was the application of knot theory[1] (developed since the 1860s) to the current concept of curled-up extra dimensions in string theory.

In 1973 only a few people were working with string theory. One of the puzzling outcomes of the theory was that it predicted a massless particle which was not allowed by the Standard Model. This massless particle turned out to be a graviton.

In the early 1980s string theory was riddled with mathematical anomalies. In 1984 Michael Green and John Schwarz removed the anomalies and were then able to describe all four basic forces in the one equation – including gravity. String theory became the "Theory of

Everything" and the hoped-for realisation of Einstein's dream of the unification of all the laws of nature.

While string theory represents an elegant model of the workings of nature and is – so far – mathematically consistent, it has not been proven by experiment or observation. The mathematical processes of deduction have been ahead of our ability to test this theory in the laboratory, although some of its predictions may realise themselves in the newly renovated and more powerful Large Hadron Conductor now operating in Geneva, Switzerland.

String theory sees the basic constituents of all material and phenomenal existence as tiny vibrating strings of energy rather than point particles. Exactly what this energy is has never been described, but I believe it is possible that consciousness itself is the underlying principle. The strings may be closed strings – forming loops – or open strings with free ends. The manner in which the strings vibrate – they can vibrate within their dimensional space or wrap around their dimensional space – and the frequency of vibration determine particular particles or forces. In string theory the universe can be seen as a grand cosmic symphony. After all, music is just vibrating air waves that our ears perceive as particular sounds.

In order to work, the mathematics of string theory demands another requirement that is truly incomprehensible. Apart from the four dimensions with which we are familiar, string theory requires another six dimensions. These have been proposed as tiny curled-up dimensions much smaller than normally perceptible. These extra dimensions might influence the nature of vibration of the tiny strings and be important to keep the cosmic symphony in tune. Strings need to move in more than three dimensions. Ten dimensions increases the degrees of freedom. The extra dimensions also allow the strings to stretch into a membrane (or 'brane' for short) which – with enough energy – can grow to enormous size, even as large as a universe. It has been further postulated that this brane may be only one inside many other universes – parallel universes. If it isn't mind-boggling enough to try to comprehend the size of this universe that we live in, now consider that there may be many more universes possibly operating with entirely different physical laws.

The five known quantum fields
IN STRING THEORY, THE SPIN TYPE OF A QUANTUM FIELD REFERS TO THE pattern of vibration that a string executes. A rotational movement is involved, but it would be misleading to suggest that an electron, for example, spins around a central axis like a frisbee spinning in space.

I've mentioned the concept of symmetry as it applies to physical laws of nature. Physicists have also introduced the concept of supersymmetry to make sense of some mathematical inconsistencies. It is now generally assumed that all elementary particles and forces have a supersymmetric partner, but these partners have not yet been seen. Calculations suggest they would be some 1000 times heavier than a proton, so we would never be able to reach those energies with our current particle accelerators.

The spin type of an elementary particle or virtual particle (force field) represents the very first expression of manifest existence from the unmanifest superstring field (or unified field). There are five spin types representing the five known quantum fields – Spin 0, ½, 1, 3/2 and 2. The five numerical values indicate – roughly – how fast the particles rotate[2]. Gravity – that bending of the space-time continuum around massive objects causing things to be drawn to the massive object – has its own 'particle' nature. That means, like other 'virtual' particles representing forces, gravity has its own vibratory expression of the underlying superstring field. The virtual particle representing gravity is called a graviton and is described as a Spin 2 particle, spinning twice as fast as Spin 1 particles. The graviton spins in a clockwise, vibrationary way.

Spin 1 expressions (integral spin) are the force fields (the gauge bosons). Spin 1 forces send the string in an anticlockwise vibration. Spin ½ expressions are the matter fields (ie the fermions). The matter fields arise from internal vibrations of the compact, six-dimensional space-time manifold (those folded-up extra dimensions that exist at the Planck scale).

The supersymmetric partners of the above spin-types have a value ½ lower than their principal. The Spin 2 graviton has a spin 3/2 gravitino partner. The Spin 1 gauge bosons have Spin ½ gauginos. The Spin ½ fermions have Spin 0 sleptons, squarks and sneutrinos. In addition, the Spin 0 Higgs boson is thought to give the property of mass to particles. The existence of the Higgs boson has recently been confirmed in the Large Hadron Collider.

Because we cannot have negative spin types, its supersymmetric partner is the Spin ½ Higgsino. String theory has now come up with a clearer concept of where gravity fits into the big picture. Many things, like light and matter (representing Spin 1 and Spin ½ particles and their super-partners), are made up of open-ended strings with the open ends tied down to our three-dimensional membrane. Closed strings (or loops) on the other hand have no free ends to be tied down and are free to move about on the brane. Gravitons are considered to be particular closed strings and are free to escape to other dimensions or even other worlds.[3] This would dilute the apparent strength of gravity and make it seem weaker than the other forces of nature. In its essential nature, gravity may be as strong as the other forces. It's just that it slips away from our own dimensional constraints and thus measures weaker than the other forces.

For so long now, the concept of one universe has been hard enough to comprehend. How can we possibly comprehend a universe that is infinite? Surely there must be an end somewhere? And if there is an end, what lies beyond?

The Big Bang itself has been seen as an incomprehensible event that happened some 13.8 billion years ago. We're inclined to think that there was probably only one Big Bang. But what existed before then? Now physicists are telling us that the Big Bang might be nothing more than colliding branes giving off vast amounts of energy with each collision. This has apparently happened a lot in the past and will happen again in the future. Again, it is important to emphasise that many physicists see this idea of multiple universes and colliding branes giving off multiple Big Bangs as a promising scenario, but not yet supported by mathematics.

It is hoped that the new Large Hadron Collider will record the brief existence of a graviton before it disappears into other dimensions. It is likely to be 'seen' by its absence. Likewise, it is hoped that small black holes might be created with high energy collisions. As gravity slips away into other dimensions, the mass of these black holes would diminish at a faster rate than otherwise expected. This observation would further support the existence of other dimensions. Astrophysicists are also looking at black holes in outer space for similar behaviour. The next few years will prove very interesting as scientists smash protons together at enormous speeds and with increasing energy to find further evidence of string theory. Even then, it's most likely that string theory will never be proven to the satisfaction of most scientists. If any of the predictions of string theory are proven in these colliders, then there will certainly be strong circumstantial evidence that scientists are on the right track with string theory. Physics has always had an impressive track record, with elegant mathematical predictions being eventually supported by observation or experiment.

Einstein's quest for the ultimate unification of all the laws of nature may have been achieved with string theory. Einstein talked of a "unified field". The term today has become somewhat antiquated, although scientists today appear to accept the distinct possibility or even probability that all the laws of nature are unified into one mathematical equation. It may be that the string field is a unified field in that it is a single field that determines the behaviour of all force and matter in the universe. But it may not be possible to prove string theory and the existence of a unified field through usual impartial observation and experiment.

The Big Bang
Black holes and similar phenomena compel us to accept that huge objects such as stars much bigger than our sun can collapse into themselves, and all that mass can somehow be confined to an immeasurable point in space. For this to happen, matter as we typically know it must convert to energy.

So far, I have shown the historical movement of scientific understanding from multiplicity and diversity towards unification. We can now reverse this process and imagine the material universe exploding from one unified source.

Scientists now know that the whole universe we occupy – not just this one galaxy – was born 13.8 billion years ago. What existed before then, if anything, is not yet known. It wasn't space, because our universe's space-time was born at the instant of this Big Bang. Because our time was born at the moment of the Big Bang, it's even hard to conceptualise what existed before the Big Bang, because there was no 'before' in our usual sense of understanding time. If there was no 'before', then it's hard to speak rationally of any cause of the Big Bang[4]. The current theory is just that the universe arose from a single point – a singularity. All of space-time and all the mass-energy of the present universe were squeezed into a cubic Planck length.

In 1931, the American astronomer Edwin Hubble established that the galaxies are receding from us at speeds proportional to their distances. Hubble's Law has been verified for galaxies up to 10^{10} light years away, which are travelling away from us at close to the speed of light. This gives rise to what is known as the 'cosmological red shift', where the familiar spectral line emissions from hydrogen and other elements have longer wavelengths, due to the Doppler Effect of them moving away from us. Hubble's Law supports the idea of an expanding universe and is therefore consistent with Big Bang theory.

The Big Bang scenario is also consistent with the observed cosmic microwave background radiation (CMBR). CMBR is a low-level radiation ever-present through the universe with a temperature of 2.7 degrees Kelvin (absolute zero).

With the help of the Unified Field Chart we can look at a theory of the extraordinary sequence of events following the Big Bang. The unified field represents a state of super-symmetry. Symmetry breaking started at a temperature of 10^{32} degrees Kelvin, with the emergence of gravity (space and time) first, then the Spin ½ and fermi fields and the Spin 0 and 1 bose fields. Within an inconceivably short fraction of a second, grand unified symmetry broke, resulting in the strong and electroweak forces, and lepto-quark symmetry broke into separate leptons and quarks. At this stage, the temperature had dropped to 10^{28} degrees Kelvin. By the time 10^{-12} sec had passed, electroweak symmetry had broken into electromagnetism and the weak force, leptons became separate neutrinos and electrons, and quarks became up quarks and down quarks. Gravity is still just gravity and provides the space-time arena upon which all these particles and forces play out their roles. The temperature has now dropped to 10^{15} degrees Kelvin, still enormously hot but now within the range of energies obtainable by humans with subatomic colliders. After about one second with temperatures still at 10^{10} degrees Kelvin (that's 100 billion degrees – twice as hot as the core of a massive star at the last moment of its life, when it's at its hottest), quarks combine to form more stable hadrons – notably protons and neutrons. Many of the neutrons in turn decay into protons, with a decay lifetime of about 15 minutes. Approximately 10 minutes after the Big Bang, the temperature is about one billion degrees Kelvin, at which point any neutrons that have not turned into protons participate in the process of helium formation, resulting in a universe with approximately 25% helium and 75% hydrogen. That's all the universe was for nearly 400,000 years – the so-called "dark ages" where only cold hydrogen and helium permeated the universe, appearing as a brightly shining fog of radiation (maybe not really so "dark").

Some 12.5 billion years ago, the first stars were born. Hydrogen and helium had coalesced into denser regions and then gravity further condensed the gases into hot, radiating stars. It was within the hot furnaces of these first-generation stars that heavier elements like carbon, silicon and iron were created. Their subsequent explosion and the resultant expulsion of these elements in the form of supernovas formed the ingredients for second-generation stars like our Sun and for inhabitable planetary systems and ultimately the emergence of biological life. We are all "the stuff of stars".

THERE HAVE BEEN SOME DEVELOPMENTS ON THE ORIGINAL BIG BANG theory. Generally accepted has been the variant of Big Bang theory known as 'inflationary cosmology'.

In this version of the Big Bang model, the initial expansion of the universe was considered to be enormous and practically instantaneous. The universe grew by an additional 100 orders of magnitude or so (10^{100})

in the first 10^{-35} seconds. Much faster than the blink of an eye, most of the magnitude of the current universe was established – albeit in that first dramatic instant just a huge expanse of hot, bright energy that within seconds was creating hydrogen gas – simple protons, each surrounded by an electron, and the most abundant element in the universe. Such an expansion from a single point is hard to conceive.

American-Australian scientist Brian Schmidt of The Australian National University in Canberra, as well as Americans Adam Riess of Johns Hopkins University and Saul Perlmutter of the University of California, have recently been awarded the Nobel Prize in Physics for their coincident discovery that the universe is not only still expanding, but is expanding at an accelerating rate. This is the other major twist that inflationary cosmology has added to the Big Bang theory. The implications of this latest finding are enormous. The known mass in the universe is considerably more than what we can see. Ordinary matter – the stars and their planets, helium and the free hydrogen still filling the universe – accounts for only 4% of the mass in the universe. The remaining matter is made up of what has been called "Dark Matter". Dark matter – believed to occupy 24% of the mass of the universe – may turn out to be the supersymmetric partners of photons (photinos) and perhaps the supersymmetric partners of other known primordial particles. Supersymmetric particles are quite heavy, but cannot be seen. These heavy, invisible particles may cluster and gather around galaxies, causing the warped but beautifully elegant rotation of galaxies.

Despite all this extra mass in the universe, it is expanding at an accelerating pace. The original Big Bang theory proposed that gravity would eventually take over from that initial explosive energy, and cause the universe to collapse inward, reversing the whole process and bringing about the 'Big Crunch'. Inflationary cosmology predicts we're all in for the 'Big Rip', where all our atoms will just rip apart. But don't worry – billions of years will pass before that happens.

What then, is overriding the gravitational pull of all that mass and causing this accelerating expansion? Dark Energy has been proposed as the anti-gravity influence and it is estimated to occupy 72% of the universe. While this repulsive force is currently considered mysterious by the scientific community, it is most likely the vacuum energy we examined earlier. Also called "quintessence", this vacuum energy fuelled the initial expansion of the universe and hasn't yet gone away. It represents the cosmological constant that Einstein introduced to his gravitational equation and later regretted. Einstein – like many others – thought that the universe was static in an overall dimensional sense, and yet his gravitational equation predicted an expansion. For this reason, he added a constant into his equation to offset that expansion. He would later call it the greatest mistake of his life.

$$G_{\mu\nu} = (8\pi G/c^4)\, T_{\mu\nu} + g_{\mu\nu} \Lambda$$

Einstein's gravitational equation with the gravitational constant (Λ) included to counter the attractive pull of gravity. Einstein believed that the universe was neither expanding nor contracting and so inserted this constant which he would later assert was the biggest mistake of his life. The gravitational constant is essentially the dark energy which is actually causing the universe to continue to expand rather than contract.

Vacuum energy is not the energy we are more familiar with. It isn't any of the spin coefficients we just described, and it's certainly not one of the by-products of those spin types. Vacuum energy transcends these levels and belongs to the proposed unified field. It does, however, have an important effect on those spin types and the quantum fields emitting from them. It has a big influence on how space curves and evolves. We learned that gravity is space curved in such a manner that massive objects are drawn to each other. It is possible, therefore, for space to curve in the opposite direction such that objects repel each other. This is anti-gravity, or more correctly, repulsive gravity. It isn't likely our technologies will be able to exploit it for hovering cars or space-craft any time soon. It's far too transcendental and we would never be likely to achieve the energies required.

The hypothesis that I have assumed is that vacuum energy represents the dynamic interplay of pure consciousness itself. If it is a field of consciousness, then that is great news for us, because our consciousness is connected to this field like a wave is to the ocean beneath it. We have the ability to dive into that realm of consciousness and work it any way we wish, to achieve anything – even to levitate!

In more recent times, some scientists are also entertaining a cyclic model of the Universe[5]. The Cyclic Model sees the universe expanding due to dark energy alone, but then contracting with a reversal of direction of dark energy. In this cyclic theory, the universe again collapses to a tiny size, but not as small as inflationary theory calls for. It then goes through a bounce and expands again into a new universe (a born-again universe). This re-cycling of the Universe may go on infinitely.

There are a couple of reasons for this departure from Inflationary Theory. One reason was the failure to detect any gravitational waves that would have been caused by the fantastic energy released as the Big Bang ripped space-time. However, in February 2016 gravitational waves were detected.[6] Although these gravitational waves are speculated to have arisen from colliding black holes, the newly emerging field that has been dubbed "gravitational astronomy" will surely throw more light on these variations of the Big Bang theory.

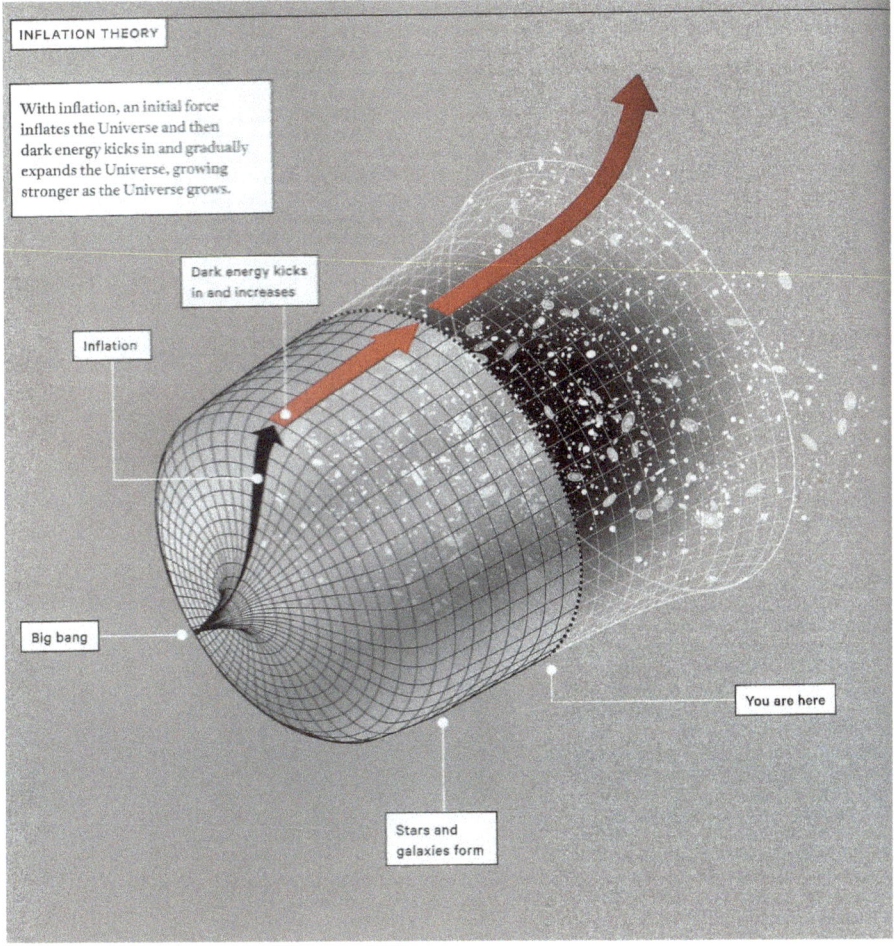

The Inflationary Cosmos model, (Illustration courtesy of *Cosmos* magazine / illustration: Anthony Calvert).

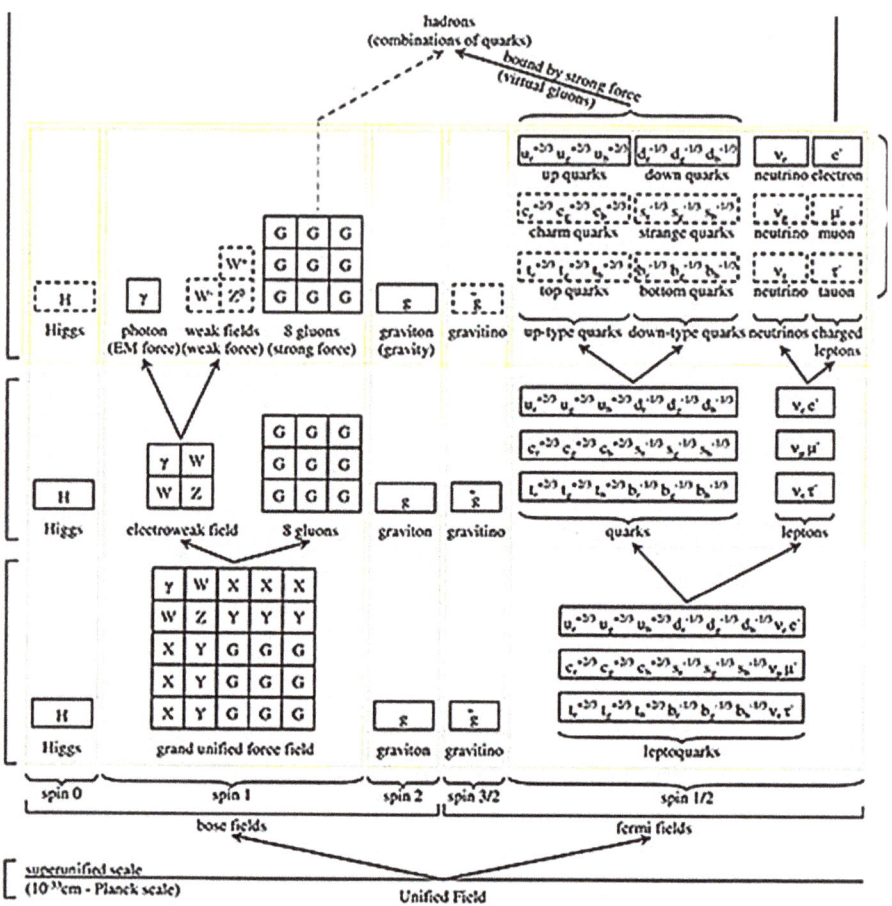

Unified Field Chart (courtesy of Dr John Hagelin, © J.Hagelin)

NOTES

1. Livio, Mario, 'Why Math Works', *Scientific American,* Aug 2011
2. Greene, Brian; *The Elegant Universe*, Vintage UK, Random House, p 172.
3. Greene, Brian, *The Elegant Universe*, TV documentary, SBS, 2004.
4. A comment made by Stephen Hawking in the TV documentary *Into the Universe* (2010)
5. Lemonick, Michael D., 'The Universe that Begins Again', *Cosmos*, Issue 64, Aug–Sept 2015, p 62–71
6. http://news.discovery.com/space/weve-detected-gravitational-waves-so-what-160213.htm

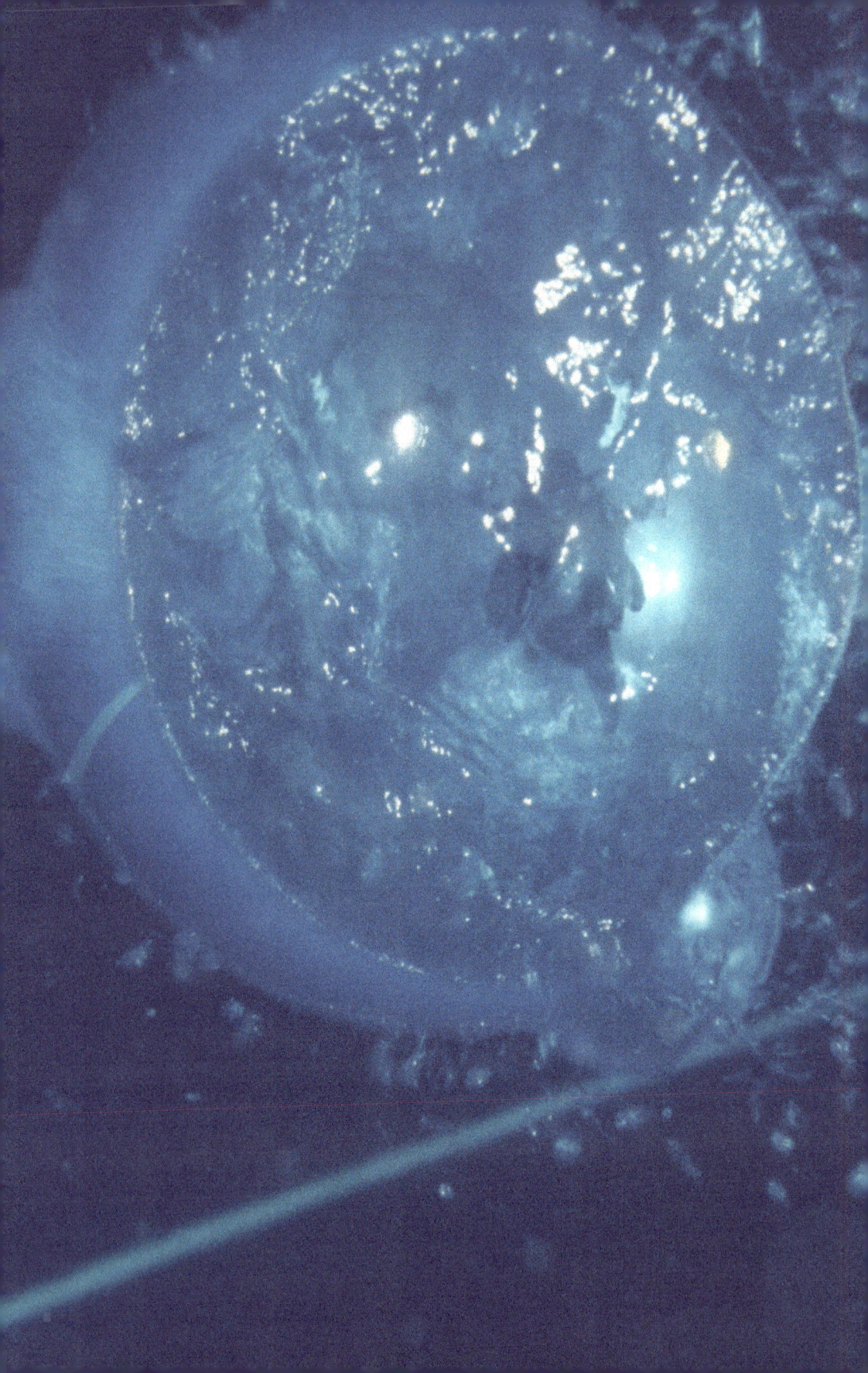

Chapter Eleven

VEDIC SCIENCE – PART ONE
CONSCIOUSNESS AS THE UNIVERSE'S BASIC INGREDIENT

"I glide downward a few feet and leave what looks like a trail of stardust behind me. By moving my hand in spirals, I conjure up a Milky Way. Smiling now, I swing my arms about in wide strokes, and the sea around me brightens with thousands of sparkling lights. I am the creator of a cosmos."

– Jacques Yves Cousteau (Undersea Explorer and Documentary Producer)

A remarkable correlation has been established between the latest findings in quantum field theory and the recordings of the first manifestations of the physical universe described in the ancient Vedic texts. The hypothesised unified field of all the laws of nature is proposed as none other than a field of self-interacting pure consciousness.

IS CONSCIOUSNESS A PHENOMENON THAT ARISES FROM WITHIN THE BRAIN, as a function of brain cells? Or is consciousness fundamental to all aspects of nature and therefore found everywhere and in everything, but requiring a brain for its expression through the physical senses and a nervous system?

Great advances have been made in the field of neuroscience. Most, if not all, neuroscientists would hold the firm view that the genesis of consciousness is "all between the ears".[1] In other words, neuroscientists see the brain as the source of consciousness and therefore the location of our essential identity of self.

The following summary in the open online encyclopaedia *Scholarpedia* reflects the conventional understanding of this perplexing aspect of our existence: "At present, however, no single model of consciousness appears sufficient to account fully for the multidimensional properties of conscious experience. Moreover, although some of these models have gained prominence, none has yet been accepted as definitive, or even as a foundation upon which to build a definitive model".[2]

I am going to outline a set of arguments that I believe strongly support the notion that the hypothesised unified field is a field of consciousness and that our essential identity of 'self' – our consciousness – is the one unified field at the base of everyone else's identity of 'self'. We can call it the big Self or simply "Self" with a capital S.

This concept has profound ramifications. It gives us, ultimately, the power to control nature at its most fundamental level of creation. In short, it explains how and why 'miracles' are possible. It also means that *we are all one.* We are separated from each other only in the sense that we have different nervous systems and tend to identify ourselves with our bodies, but in reality our essential "Self" is the one entity. We are individual "selves" on the one ocean of "Self". We can substitute "Self" for "pure consciousness", "Ātmā", "ocean of being" or "ocean of spirit". I will also add "ocean of life" to this list.

I will develop the arguments in favour of a unified field as a field of consciousness along four themes, as proposed by renowned physicist Dr John Hagelin[3]:

1. Common sense.
2. Correlation of descriptions (both qualitative and quantitative) of the unified field in modern science and Vedic science.
3. The Maharishi Effect – a super-radiance social phenomenon verified by many carefully controlled statistical studies that suggest a bosonic field of consciousness is created when transcendental consciousness is attained by large groups gathered in one place.
4. Yogic levitation and flying.

Common sense
JOHN HAGELIN POINTS OUT THAT IT WOULD BE INCONSISTENT AND unlikely that the basis of all the material and phenomenal world – the unified field (or superstring field) – would not also be the basis of our very notion of self, our being. Our most irreducible sense of self is our consciousness (remember Descarte's "Cogito ergo sum"). We also happen to be part of nature. Doesn't it appeal to common sense that the most basic perceived aspect of our own existence should also be the most basic aspect of all the rest of nature?

Continuing this same theme, modern physics has demonstrated a definite trend towards unification of all the separate laws of physics and diversity of particles and forces. Indeed, as we have already said, this progressive unification of all the separate particles and force fields may have culminated in the discovery of one field of complete unification – a unified field – a field that contemporary scientists might refer to as a field of superstrings. We are going to add further weight to the argument that the unified field (the ultimate source of atoms, molecules and cells) is a field of consciousness. If we accept the convincing arguments in favour of this unified field as a field of consciousness, it would seem strange, especially given our understanding of the concept of symmetry in nature[4], to pursue the genesis of consciousness at the relatively gross level of multi-cellular interaction. Nature works more efficiently than this. Why would it reinvent something that already defines it? Rather, it would appear more reasonable to see its one essential nature expressed in diverse ways. The diversity by which consciousness expresses itself as our unique individualities is where the brain makes it appearance. In this unified field model of consciousness, the brain can be seen more as a reflector or mediator of consciousness. One universal consciousness makes multiple individuals of itself, diversifies itself and expresses the multiple versions of itself by enabling individual consciousness to operate through a complex nervous system. Our brains and attached nervous systems in turn enable experience and enrich experience with a full palette of emotions, feelings, memories, desires and creativity.

My second point in this common sense argument is best promoted by what we might call a "thought experiment". Let's imagine that the unified field is all there is. There is nothing manifest from this field, not even the first excitations of the field that bring about time and space or gravity. To manifest from this state, there must be some interaction with something, and that something has to be something else or itself. There can't be anything else, because this field is the source of everything else and has not yet manifest anything. It can only interact with itself. How does it interact or refer to itself unless it is conscious? Think about this, especially in light of what we have said about the interaction of elementary particles in the last chapter. The interaction of two particles – even identical particles – involves the participation of a third virtual particle (the quantum field acting as a force between the two particles). Consciousness is surely the only thing that can interact with itself without the participation of anything else.

If the unified field is conscious, then it can refer to itself. That is, consciousness can be aware of its own nature. The one consciousness becomes the 'knower', the 'process of knowing' and the 'known'. This is what we mean when we refer to pure consciousness. Pure consciousness is a state in which consciousness knows itself in a completely self-sufficient manner. Consciousness is its own subject (the knower), its own object (that which is known) and its own subject-object relationship (the process of knowing). This might sound like wordplay, but purely self-referral consciousness can be experienced by all of us when we allow our awareness to settle to the least-excited state in meditation.

In Vedic science, the 'knower' is the *Rishi* value of consciousness. The process of knowing is the *Devata* value and the 'known' is the *Chhandas* value. The wholeness that is the reality of all three together as the one consciousness is the *Samhita* value. This self-referral dynamic interplay becomes exponential in its rate of interaction and is highly energetic. The quality of consciousness that is known (*Chhandas*) takes on the role of *rishi* and refers back to the knower and the process of knowing, bringing about another value of awareness and a second *Devata* value. The *Devata* value from the first referral can become aware of this second *Devata* value and so it goes on and on with an exponential explosion of self-referral interaction.

This energetic self-interacting process is the explosion of life itself. This is how multiplicity and diversity arise from unity – the one essence. The dynamical interplay of pure consciousness knowing itself may be the vibrational essence of what physicists are calling the superstrings. This may be the unknown energy that physicists refer to when discussing the vibrating strings of energy. The manner in which the superstrings then vibrate or spin eventually manifests first as space-time, and then the earliest particles and force fields. Everything, therefore, is made up of consciousness.

Quantum field theory and Vedic science

'*VEDA*' IS SANSKRIT FOR 'KNOWLEDGE' OR 'WISDOM', RECORDED AS THE oldest Sanskrit texts from ancient India and also the oldest scriptures in Hinduism. The fact that the Vedic literature is associated with a religion should not be cause to instantly dismiss it. A close examination of the texts and an attempt to understand the knowledge does not require anyone to change their religious or irreligious views. Vedic knowledge can, and should be, adopted by all inquiring minds, whether such inquiry is directed to the material world or the spiritual. It describes – from an experiential subjective perspective – the underlying reality that is the foundation and ultimate goal for all material or spiritual pursuits. Just as an agnostic would not dismiss Isaac Newton's laws of motion because Newton was Christian, so it would be illogical and self-defeating to dismiss the insights of the Vedic texts because of any association with a religion. Any Hindu would admit that they have no propriety on the knowledge of consciousness or its subjective exploration, just as a biotech company does not have ownership over the nucleotide sequence of any section of the human genome. (Not that that has stopped the biotech companies trying!)

Veda can also be interpreted as 'life'. I refer to Vedic texts to correlate the subjective discoveries of seers living long ago with the discoveries and hypotheses of modern science. These ancient texts were written by those with amazing ability and insight, but such insight is not beyond what is possible today by enlightened[5] individuals. Indeed, we will shortly look at the comments of some more recent individuals who have achieved great insights into the nature of reality. All these past and present seers have explored deep within the ocean of consciousness and have glimpsed the very workings of the unified field at the level of first manifestation of the physical world. Their inner journey in consciousness has represented the subjective path to knowledge, and that subjective path might well be the ultimate way ahead to explore firsthand the full gamut of the superstring world.

One might ask why these illuminated seers lived so long ago. Why don't they show up these days? Well, there are some remarkable current day seers whose insights also correlate with modern understandings in science. But it might well be that the world 3000 or more years ago was simpler and less stressful, with fewer distractions. It might be that more societal emphasis was placed on deep meditation as a path of self-discovery back then. Perhaps, too, the natural environment surrounding them was more conducive to deep meditative experience. And human beings have experienced cycles in terms of what they consider important. Currently, we place considerable emphasis on technological improvement for our material wellbeing. In the past, more emphasis was probably placed on reflective, spiritual and subjective means of gaining knowledge. The path was more of an inward exploratory journey as opposed to today's predominantly outward, objective path in seeking knowledge.

> *"What is the difference if I wear a visible or invisible wave on the ocean of my spirit?"*[6]
>
> – Mahavatar Babaji

The Lagrangian formulas
THE LAGRANGIAN[7] IS A MATHEMATICAL FORMULA USED TO DESCRIBE THE structure and dynamics of any cause/effect system in the physical universe. The Lagrangian is used to predict the likely action out of all possible actions. Take a guitar string, for example. The Lagrangian will allow the possibility that one end of the string will vibrate twice as fast as the middle of the string, but that is very unlikely. The Lagrangian formulas will predict the most likely modes of movement or action out of any object or entity.

The very fact that scientists have been able to use mathematics to describe this as-yet unproven (unseen and untested) unified field theory for the first expressions of natural law from an un-manifest state is testimony itself to the theory that our 'mind' as we know it is intimately connected to this most fundamental level of nature's functioning.

Physicists use the Lagrangian equations to predict the likely modes of vibration of the superstrings. Already, physicists have had great success using these formulas to predict vibrationary modes that describe already known and measured quantum values, for example the electron. Essentially, each of the vibrational modes of the string is one of the elementary particles of physics. Dr Hagelin has identified certain qualities of the unified field in its Lagrangian[8], and these derived qualities of the unified field match those qualities describing the subjective experience of Pure Consciousness in meditation.

Again, 'pure consciousness' refers to purely self-referral consciousness, that is, consciousness that is not directed to anything but its own nature.

Through meditation, everyone can experience this state of purely self-referral consciousness.

One aspect of the vacuum state in physics is the quality of all possibilities. Anything seems possible at the level of pure conscious awareness. Anything is also possible at the most fundamental level of nature's functioning. In the grossly perceived world with which we are familiar, reality is based on a statistical probability that certain events will occur or that nature will function in a certain way. We should no longer say that "something is impossible", only that "something is improbable" – even if those things are highly improbable.

Freedom is another quality described in the Lagrangian of the superstring and also experienced in transcendental consciousness. There are simply no barriers. Since everything is made of consciousness, once one gains mastery of this state of pure, transcendental consciousness, one can fulfil all desires. It certainly feels that way when one reaches this "ground" state of consciousness.

'Fully Awake Within Itself' is a quality described by the Lagrangian and also experienced by anyone transcending consciousness. The experience is often described as a state of "restful alertness". There is silence and a great sense of peace and calm. The mind (and body) is fully relaxed, yet it is not asleep but very much alert. This reflects the ultimate level of dynamics at the Planck scale we referred to in our description of the vacuum state in quantum mechanics. We also saw it in our description of quantum gravity and the concept of space-time foam, which represented all possible space-time shapes or geometry. The very notion of space-time foam suggests a highly dynamic process. This dynamism – the expression of all possible space geometry – is experienced as a state of amazing alertness and that subjective sense of "all possibilities".

Another quality that is experienced in meditation (and very much when I dive in the ocean) is a sense of timelessness. This quality is described in the Lagrangian as the ancient and eternal quality of intelligence, which in turn reflects the "time-translational invariance" of the Lagrangian. The sense of timelessness is also a quality of the unmanifest nature of the superstrings (since time and space are manifest qualities of the laws of nature; they are not absolute qualities). Immortality and invincibility are also qualities described in the Lagrangian that explain that sense of timelessness.

Deepak Chopra has used the term "endless wonder"[9] to describe the experience of this state of pure consciousness. I like this description, because I too feel this sense of wonder enlivened in my meditations and also in my underwater diving experiences. In reference to the qualities of the superstring as described in the Lagrangian, this quality of "endless wonder" could be matched in those listed qualities, such as all possibilities, omniscience, analysing, bountiful, fully awake within itself, infinite creativity, unboundedness and bliss.

Is everything conscious?
THERE HAS ALWAYS BEEN A NAGGING QUESTION IN MY MIND THAT IF everything is made of consciousness, wouldn't everything *be* conscious? Surely it is preposterous to think that a rock might be 'conscious'? Without a nervous system, a rock will not feel pain or psychological hurt if you crush it with a hammer. It's not going to 'feel' anything. Clearly, we need to delineate different levels of consciousness.

At least two contemporary and independent sources support the notion that everything is indeed conscious. In Neale Donald Walsch's *Conversations with God* series, God[10] confirms that "everything is conscious". I found further reinforcement of this notion in Deepa Kodikal's book *A Journey within the Self*. Deepa is a science graduate, a mother of four children and the wife of a successful Indian industrialist. She is hardly an ascetic or recluse, as she enjoys Indian dance and music, play-writing and directing, glider flying, ceramic art and gourmet cooking. Although throwing herself actively into many aspects of 'life', Deepa Kodikal has undergone some dramatic advances in her spiritual development throughout her life. It would appear that she might have attained or is close to attaining the level of Unity Consciousness.[11]

On the subject of all-present, all-pervasive consciousness, Deepa Kodikal writes from the conviction of her own deep level of awareness:

> *"If the particle is not aware of the glowing Self within itself, it is because the awareness, hardly developed in minerals, is sleeping as it were. But the Self and the awareness are alive alright.*
> *In the plants, it is stirring. Plants being more evolved than minerals, there are the beginnings of perceptions, feelings and visible life.*
> *In animals it is awake. More prominent. Their perceptions, emotions, their instincts, behaviours, intellect, awareness are quite active.*
> *In man it is divine. He excels other species in his perceptions, intuition, awareness. He can feel the presence of a superior force within him. He is aware of the divinity within him."* [12]

So, it remains safe to throw a rock, crush a rock or even abuse a rock! The awareness within minerals is self-contained and probably mostly – if not all – self-referral consciousness. I wonder, however, if the foreboding 'mood' or 'feeling' that some people claim to encounter when they enter a room or building that has been the scene of a horrific crime, has been caused by a certain absorbance by the bricks and mortar, influenced by the malevolent waves of consciousness generated by stressed humans.

Modern-day seers
Deepa Kodikal is an excellent example of an extant, current-day seer. Her experiences reinforce or even add to those of the ancient Vedic seers. She writes of her insights into the very genesis of the cosmos.

> *"At night, I experienced within me the existence and non-existence and the emergence and convergence of the universe. I felt that I was non-existent, but not dead in the usual sense of the word and then that I came into existence as I was breathed out by some entity. As I was flung out, I formed into a luminous point having all the potential of the universe, as a seed has the potential of a mighty tree. This luminous point quickly expanded and fragmented into a myriad luminous points, which in turn expanded and spread with lightning speed, widening and spreading into stars and planets speeding away from each other and from that entity. But the more I sped and the more I spread out, I still remained close to that entity. In fact, there was no distinction between Him and me. We were one principle occupying one space and form. There was no duality. Both were one."*[13]

Here, Deepa experiences through her own awareness the genesis of a universe, which is nothing ultimately but the expression of consciousness – *her* consciousness, but at that deep level, *our* consciousness too. Current thinking among those who accept the unified field model of consciousness is that the birth of our universe some 13.8 billion years ago resulted from the creative self-interacting dynamics of the unified field – a field of pure consciousness – our consciousness.

Deepa then continued to describe the dissolution of the universe. "The infinite vastness that was me was now converging towards the original point at which I had been flung out of the entity, being drawn back by its inhaling breath." She added: "Slowly I became aware that this inhaling and exhaling action was not of some other entity but my own. The universes came from and went back into my own self".

CURRENT COSMOLOGICAL THEORY HAS OUR UNIVERSE FOREVER expanding and eventually pulling itself apart (inflationary cosmology) or going through a cyclic expansion/contraction pattern (cyclic model). Can either of these current theories be accommodated by Deepa Kodikal's extraordinary insights?

Deepa's insights come as direct first-person experiences (for example the experience of the genesis of a universe) and related, or second-person, communications. Deepa refers to a "voice", but I don't think she meant that she heard a voice with her ears. She would have been communicating with a deeper more fundamental level of her own self – the Ocean of Self.

She relates some further knowledge of the genesis of the universe when she says, "a voice spoke, 'The Big Bang theory cannot be! In the Big Bang theory, the universe burst forth from a point so tiny that it was non-existent. The matter was compressed so densely that it all fitted into that point of nothingness. The force of the burst flung the matter apart, forming planets and stars and galaxies, evolving in a pattern to form the ever-widening universe. And when destruction finally comes, the universe falling back upon itself, the matter will again converge and disappear into this mighty density of nothingness. The resultant force of this high density reduced to the compressed ultimate nothingness is the potential of the birth of the next universe.

'But to what centre will the universe converge when each point is itself the centre of the universe? And from which special point has it been flung apart when the all-pervading Infinite is spread across all infinities in equal force and evenness? Just as a grain of rice taken from a sackful will contain all the attributes of all the grains of rice in the sack, each point in the universe is an entire whole of this mighty Infinite, and is capable of being that special point from where can be born universes and into which can disappear universes. The Big Bang is only a local action going on all the time in different places. In miniscule ways and in stupendous magnitudes.

'When destruction finally comes, each atom will disappear where it is, transforming itself into energy which, in turn, will become so subtle that it becomes nothingness, for, after all, that is how it was born. And when the birth of the next universe takes place, each atom, that is already there within that nothingness[14], at that point, in the form of unmanifest energy and eventually matter, like the cream is already present in the milk, will precipitate forth in the form of matter and universe, as expansive, dynamic and ever-evolving as before. It would be something like the light suddenly being put off and the world shut off from our eyes, and then switched on again only to lay before our eyes the magical extravaganza of creation, no doubt, each process involving enormous time, and being accompanied by traumatic upheavals and cataclysmic changes. Till then, the perpetual pattern of birth and death goes on every moment, everywhere, in smaller and bigger magnitudes.

'This is the divine breathing…'

'This process goes on. So does the evolution, once the universe takes its birth, much like man continually evolves from birth, till death finally merges him into the divine matrix, and he once more comes back with a new body to further the process of evolution."

MY READING OF PHYSICIST BRIAN GREENE'S LATEST BOOK *THE HIDDEN Reality*, revealed some semblance to the above experience of Deepa Kodikal in regard to the birth of the Universe. Greene discusses the current theories of physicists and cosmologists on the possibility of many universes, not just the one we live in.

Einstein's General Relativity theory tells us that an enormous expenditure of negative pressure at the beginning of the Big Bang brought about a repulsive gravity (rather than the attractive gravity we are familiar with), causing the Universe to expand. The energy released by the action of this negative pressure in bringing about the rapid inflation "condenses into a uniform bath of particles that fill space". Greene compares this phenomenon to "a cooling vat of steam condensing into water droplets". It is therefore a two-step process: enormous and rapid expansion of space-time followed by energy conversion to particles.

Could this contemporary understanding of the Big Bang accommodate Deepa Kodikal's description? Note the similarity of words used by the two different experts in their respective fields – "condenses" like "a cooling vat of steam condensing into water droplets" by Greene and "precipitate…like the cream is already present in the milk" by Kodikal.

The cyclic model has dark energy reversing its direction after a long period of expansion, causing the collapse of the Universe and the disappearance of physical particles. It postulates a rebound of the Universe with another expansion/contraction period that goes on in a cyclic fashion, possibly for eternity. This model certainly fits nicely with the concept of "divine breathing" and also the mirroring of the human body (breathing) and the cosmic body as mentioned in the *Upanishads*. It is also possible though to fit inflationary cosmology into this "breathing" analogy, with space-time alone contracting back to its source.

As a mere mortal, I find it difficult to get my mind around some of these cosmological concepts. This is because space-time itself begins and ends in the various scenarios proposed, and how do we visualise that? Kodikal's direct experience and divine explanation for the behaviour of the Universe might accommodate both the current inflationary and cyclic models.

In the past decade, physicists have predicted (based on mathematical calculations) that the expanse of the Universe as we know it would be subject to minor fluctuations in energy or temperature because of the frenetic and unpredictable behaviour of the quantum field (aka: space-time foam). If we assume the Universe was born from the unified field, it would carry with it the fluctuations and variability present at the level of the space-time foam, that jittery expression of space-time also known as quantum geometry or quantum gravity. The "quantum uncertainty" prevalent at the microscopic level of nature would have been stretched to the macroscopic level of the universe.[15]

Indeed, their predictions were found to be extremely accurate as measurements taken of what is known as the "cosmic micro-wave background radiation" – that measurable energy remnant today that is left over from the very first rapid inflation of the universe – confirmed the predictions. The temperature variations predicted and ultimately verified vary by no more than one thousandth of a degree. If the temperature is 2.725 Kelvin in one region, a nearby region might be a touch colder at 2.7245 Kelvin or 2.7255 Kelvin in another. These slight variations in energy across the universe result in different mass concentrations of hydrogen and helium in different areas of the universe ($E=MC^2$), which in turn would have caused these gases to condense into denser regions and the resultant attractive gravity causing the extreme compaction of these gases into stars and galaxies. The spread of the galaxies in the universe today is an expression of the quantum uncertainty present at the level of the unified field at the time the universe was born 13.8 billion years ago.

This adds literal meaning and verification to the following verse from the *Upanishads*[16]:

> *As is the human body, so is the cosmic body*
> *As is the human mind, so is the cosmic mind.*
> *As is the microcosm, so is the macrocosm.*
> *As is the atom, so is the universe.*
>
> – Upanishads

Physicist and popular author Fritzof Capra relates a transcendent moment in his life in the preface of his first book *The Tao of Physics*. As a disciplined researcher in arguably the most exacting of all the sciences, Capra acknowledged that his understanding of the subatomic world was based largely on "graphs, diagrams and mathematical theories". Yet, on one special day in 1969, sitting on a beach watching the ebb and flow of the waves, and at the same time aware of the inhaling and exhaling of his own breathing, he "'saw' cascades of energy coming down from outer space, in which particles were created and destroyed in rhythmic pulses; I 'saw' the atoms of the elements and those of my body participating in this cosmic dance of energy; I felt its rhythm and I 'heard' its sound, and at that moment I *knew* that this was the Dance of Shiva, the Lord of Dancers worshipped by the Hindus."

Dr Capra wrote that this particular experience and further experiences like it led him to a study of the comparisons of Eastern mysticism with modern science. His is yet another example of the profound insights demonstrated by intelligent, accomplished people. It is not an easy task to communicate transcendent experience. Our language is very often found to be limited in its ability to cope with anything outside normal 'waking state' experience. Some of the mystical poets however do a pretty good job at it.

Was it an expanded state of consciousness, an over-worked imagination or some pathological state of mind that prompted 18th-century English poet William Blake to craft the following verse? It is certainly a verse that stuck with me ever since learning it as a young teenager at school back in the 1960s.

> *To see a World in a grain of sand,*
> *And a Heaven in a wild flower,*
> *Hold Infinity in the palm of your hand,*
> *And Eternity in an hour.*[17]
>
> – William Blake

Blake could have been describing the all-pervasive nature of Ā*tm*ā (the unified field), with the potential of a world or universe at any point in space, beyond time ("eternity") and without boundary ("Infinity"). His was clearly a transcendent or mystical insight.

I believe that many, if not most, people have experiences throughout their lifetime that appear to clash with their normal perception of 'reality'. They either dismiss the experiences or hold them tightly as secrets, too afraid to talk about them for fear of ridicule. Indeed, many psychiatrists would categorise such experiences as pathological for the simple reason that these unexplained experiences are abnormal and lie outside our mutually agreed paradigm of what is considered real.

NOTES

1. I read this very statement in the newspapers made by a prominent international neuroscientist visiting Australia a couple of years ago.
2. Scholarpedia review of models of consciousness http://www.scholarpedia.org/article/Models_of_consciousness
3. Hagelin, John S., 'Is Consciousness the Unified Field? A Field Theorist's Perspective', *Modern Science and Vedic Science*, Vol, 1, No. 1, January, 1987, Maharishi International University, Fairfield, Iowa. Hagelin, John Ph.D., *Foundations of Physics and Consciousness*; MUM Online course, Physics 110.
4. See p 17, Chapter 10.
5. By 'enlightened', I mean those with an experiential understanding of the concept of unity we have been discussing, not just an intellectual understanding based on reading or what we hear from others.
6. From *Autobiography of a Yogi*, Paramahansa Yogananda, Ch 33, "Babaji, the Yogi Christ of Modern India." Mahavatar Babaji is a recently living, centuries-old saint identifying himself as the ocean of being rather than a separate wave of being. He was asking his sister if he should relinquish his corporeal form and "plunge into the Infinite Current". With the encouragement of his also spiritually advanced sister, he maintained his youthful body.
7. The term honours the Italian mathematician Joseph-Louis Lagrange (1736 –1813)
8. Forty qualities of Intelligence in the Self-Interacting dynamics of the Unified Field are listed, along with the Lagrangian equations in *Celebrating Perfection in Education*, Maharishi Vedic University Press, 1997, ps 26-27
9. In an early audio-tape series narrated by Dr Chopra, MD.
10. For the reader who finds any reference to communication with God as incredulous, I will have more to say about this subject in the last chapter.
11. Unity Consciousness is defined as that state where we experience the infinite, absolute level of life, pure consciousness itself, in everything and everywhere. It is in this state that one has mastery over natural law. See Appendix for a further description of the different states of consciousness.
12. Kodikal, Deepa, *A Journey within the Self – A Saga of Spiritual Experiences* (Revised Edition), 2006, p 265.
13. Kodikal, Deepa, *A Journey within the Self – A Saga of Spiritual Experiences* (Revised Edition), 2006, p 87
14. Recall the principles of supersymmetry from the chapters on modern science.
15. Brian Greene, *The Hidden Reality – Parallel Universes and the Deep Laws of the Cosmos*, Ch 3, p 59
16. The *Upanishads* (more than 200 Upanishads are known) are a collection of philosophical texts which form the theoretical basis for the Hindu religion. They are also known as Vedanta ("the end of the Veda"). The *Upanishads* are considered by Hindus to contain revealed truths ("Sruti") concerning the nature of ultimate reality ("Brahman").
17. William Blake (1757–1827); *Auguries of Innocence*

Chapter Twelve

VEDIC SCIENCE – PART TWO
CONSCIOUSNESS AS THE UNIVERSE'S BASIC INGREDIENT

"In the beginning there was desire, which was the first seed of mind; sages having meditated in their hearts have discovered by their wisdom the connection of the existent with the non-existent."

– (*Rig-Veda* Translation, X. 11. 1. 4)

A detailed analysis of the ancient Vedic texts reveals a strong correlation with the findings of quantum field theory and superstring theory. This supports the contention that individual consciousness is firmly established at nature's most fundamental level of functioning – the unified field itself.

Correlation of quantum field theory with Vedic science

THE INCREDIBLE JOURNEY OUR SCIENTISTS HAVE MADE IN THE PHYSICAL sciences has depended greatly on mathematics. Mathematics works precisely because there is structure, rhythm and 'law' in the way our Universe works. It is with precise mathematical correlation that we can further correlate the qualities of the proposed unified field with those of pure consciousness.

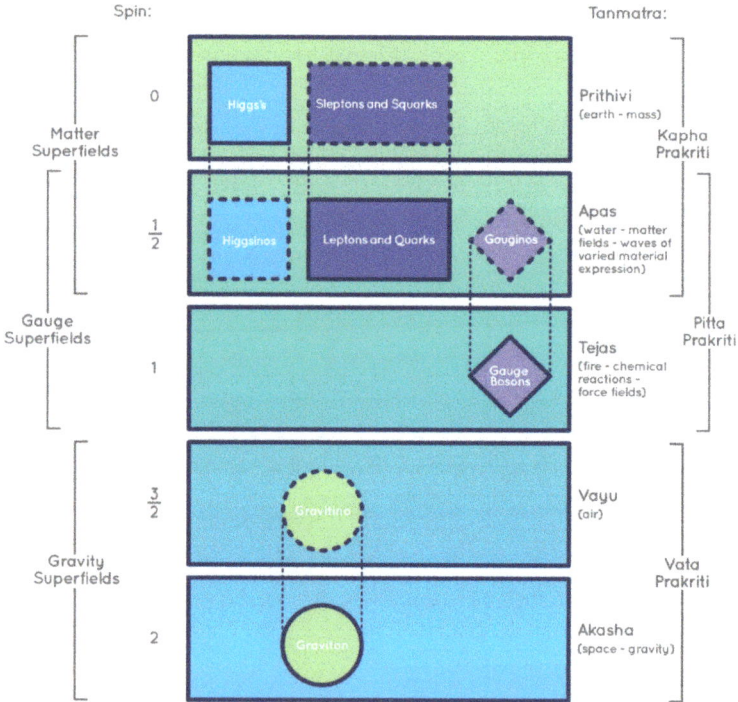

Diagram: Comparing the five quantum-mechanical 'spin types' and the three theorised 'superfields' with the five 'subtle elements' or tanmatras and the three 'prakritis' in Vedic science. Diagram based on an illustration[1] courtesy of Dr John Hagelin; © J. Hagelin.

There is a precise quantitative correspondence between the fundamental vibrational modes of the unified field *within* the domain of classical space-time geometry[2] (the five quantum-mechanical spin types) and the fundamental modes of consciousness responsible for material creation (the five subtle elements or *Tanmatras*).[3] The correspondence is even more profound in supersymmetric theory, in which there is a natural and unique pairing of these five spins into three, more holistic *superfields*, which correspond precisely to the three *Prakritis* in Vedic science. The probability that this structural correspondence could be due to coincidence is less than 1:1000 [4]

THE SEQUENCING INVOLVED IN THE EXPRESSION OF THESE *TANMATRAS* ALSO matches the sequencing of the five spin types of the underlying unified field. The *Tanmatras* are effectively the 'bricks' of the tangible, physical universe. The great philosopher of non-dualism Sankaracarya[5] explains that *Akasha* (space) is the first element to be expressed from *Atma* (the field of pure self-interacting consciousness), and then it evolves to *Vayu* (air). Space (and time) provides the stage upon which the unfoldment of life as we know it can take place, so it isn't surprising that space or *Akasha* is the first brick in the manifestation of material reality. From *Vayu* evolves *Tejas* or *Agni* (fire). From *Tejas*, *Apas* (water), and from *Apas*, *Prithivi* (earth). It might seem that breaking down material existence into such simple descriptions as space, air and water is rather primitive and over-simplistic. The Sanskrit terms attempt to describe the qualities of the vibrational modes of the unified field that bring about the first elements of material creation. They are not necessarily meant to be interpreted as literally "water", "air" and so forth.

Note in the diagram that this sequence exactly matches the numbering of the spin types. Spin 2 graviton matches the 'space' Tanmatra (gravity is bent space) and its supersymmetric Spin 3/2 partner the gravitino matches the 'air' *Tanmatra*, then Spin 1 bosons (the force fields like electromagnetism and hence chemical reaction, which is what 'fire' is) match the 'fire' *Tanmatra*, and Spin ½ fermions (the matter fields) match the 'water' *Tanmatra*. The recently confirmed Higgs particle has been described as giving mass to the matter fields, and so is not surprisingly related to the 'earth' *Tanmatra*.

The matching of the three superfields (gravity, gauge and matter) with the three *Prakritis: Vata* (space and air), *Pitta* (fire and water) and *Kapha* (water and earth), is also of more than academic interest. Practitioners of the ancient Indian health-care discipline of Ayurveda[6] are able to use pulse-diagnosis to determine the balance of the three *Prakritis* in individuals and in different organs or parts of those individuals. A person with a prominent *Kapha* Prakriti[7] is likely to be big and heavy with smooth, oily skin and hair – consistent with the more expressed water and earth elements. A person with a prominent *Vata* Prakriti is more likely to be wiry, with faster movement and mental processes, but also with a tendency to be more forgetful or confused – all consistent with the space and air elements. In all of us, *Kapha* tends to predominate earlier in life (remember those pictures of you as a chubby baby?) and *Vata* as we get older (skin and bones).

The *Vedas*

THE MATHEMATICAL CORRELATION BETWEEN QUANTUM FIELD THEORY and Vedic science does not stop at the five fundamental spin types described in physics and the matching of these spin types with the *Tanmatras* described in Vedic science. With the developments in superstring theory over the past few decades, scientists have been able to mathematically describe the different vibrational degrees of freedom of the superstring. We referred to this earlier as the *Lagrangian of the Superstring*. Again, we can demonstrate a quantitative match between the calculated vibrational modes of the superstring and the first sounds emanating from the field of pure consciousness described in the Vedic texts.

I am now referring to the 'unmanifest' realm before space-time up to the point of creation of space-time and the manifesting realm past that. Space-time becomes the 'canvas' upon which the material and phenomenal world crystalises. These different vibrational modes of the superstring represent the varied fluctuations of self-interacting pure consciousness we have described. If we attempt to break down superstrings any further, we're basically left with self-interacting consciousness as the essential 'stuff' of the universe. The dynamic interplay of *Rishi*, *Devata* and *Chhandas* – consciousness being aware of its own nature – causes a vibrational 'hum'. This humming – heard by many in transcendental consciousness – may well be the highly energetic variations of space-time geometry we described as "space-time foam", "zero-point energy" or "zitterbewegung" of the vacuum state in our chapter on modern science. This is the field of "all possibilities".

The sages of long ago developed such fine perception of this hum that they were able to identify structure in the hum, representing a code or language that formed the primordial packets (or quanta) of energy that became the first particles or force fields. These unmanifest fluctuations of consciousness, as well as the first manifestations of consciousness, were cognised by sages long ago (perceiving the "connection of the existent with the non-existent") and recorded in the *Rig Veda*.

Maharishi Mahesh Yogi – one of the world's foremost scholars of the Vedic texts and Vedic science –described the *Rig Veda* or *R̞k Veda* (as he has referred to it for phonetic reasons) as the fountainhead of all the other Vedic texts and the "Constitution of the Universe". *Veda* means 'life' but generally is understood to mean the very foundations of life or the genesis of life – the whole field of existence around us and including us, as well as that from which all that exists was born.

The code defining the structure of our Universe
"Veda" or "Ved"[8] was perceived by the highly attuned rishis as sounds – the sounds representing a particular structure in the humming. These 'sounds' were not sounds produced by vibrations of air as sensed by the ears, but rather vibrations that represented the dynamic and rhythmic self-interaction of consciousness itself, interpreted by the brain as sounds. These sounds were perceived with such clarity that the Vedic rishis were able to reproduce the sounds as syllables in speech, which were then recorded in the Vedic texts. As Maharishi emphasised, the Vedic texts need to be appreciated for these original Sanskrit sounds, not for any translated meaning in the texts. Many of the Vedic texts don't make a lot of sense when read as a translated document. Attempts by different scholars to translate and interpret the texts have generally resulted in the Vedic texts being seen as nothing more than quaint poems by simple, relatively uneducated people. This is not so, as we will shortly see.

It is difficult, however, to comprehend how the unfolding of special packets of energy that become space/time and primordial particles could be perceived and translated into spoken language and texts. For example, the passage quoted at the beginning of this chapter, from the *Rig Veda* translation, 10th Mandala, has a conversational and informational emphasis about it, and thus seems unlikely to be part of basic code structuring the most subtle levels of material existence. The answer to this lies in the understanding that mathematical language can ultimately be structured into spoken language. The spoken language in the *R̞k Veda* translations might represent stories or comments inspired by essential sounds and rhythms perceived by the ancient rishis. Again, attempting to interpret particular messages or knowledge from the translated texts misses what the Vedic texts actually represent. This is the perspective of contemporary Maharishi Vedic Science, which is the discipline that has resulted from the scholarly guidance of Maharishi Mahesh Yogi.

The syllables (*Akshara*) we speak of are the packets (or quanta) of information that constitute the code that ultimately dictates the laws of nature relevant to our particular universe and the expression of material particles. The syllables are perceived as sounds, the sounds are vibrations, and the vibrations represent the rhythmic self-interacting dynamics of consciousness itself. When you think carefully about this, 'life' began with consciousness knowing itself in the manner we have described, and here we are at a faraway, evolved stage contemplating it all! In Carl Sagan's words, "We are a way for the cosmos to know itself"[9]. Strictly speaking, the cosmos has been "knowing" itself all along. Even now, as we wonder about the 'mechanics' of life, isn't that again, in essence, consciousness reflecting upon itself?

The important gaps
MAHARISHI EMPHASISED THAT IT IS NOT ONLY THE SOUNDS THAT ARE important, but the gaps between the sounds. The purely self-referral quality of consciousness is just as energetic in those gaps as it is in the expressed syllables or words forming the code that become the Laws of Nature. Compare this with our understanding of the vacuum state of quantum fields (Chapter 11).

The energetic interplay of consciousness being aware of itself is forever and always dynamic. Within that silence between the sounds is a state of dynamism that is simply unmanifest. It remains intelligent, fully self-contained, brimming with all possible expressions (potential energy). The gaps represent the fully awake nature of Ā*tm*ā[10] within each of us and within everything. The gaps represent the totality and unity (*Samhita*) of *Rishi*, *Devata* and *Chhandas* (the knower, known and process of knowing aspect of pure consciousness). Ā*tm*ā, although highly dynamic and energetic, contains all possibilities of eventual expression and therefore – being totality and wholeness – remains unchanging. Into each of these gaps (called *Sandi* in Sanskrit) a syllable dissolves and from each gap the next syllable emerges. Consciousness needs to be lively and intelligent for the creation and dissolution of these syllables. Within these gaps therefore lies Creative Intelligence – the abstract nature of Veda.

The 'gap', in the context of Vedic science, is far from 'nothing', just as a straight line representing the vacuum state in quantum physics is far from 'lifeless'. It represents the source and wholeness of all intelligence and creativity.

The syllables, words and verses formed by these sounds represent the first expressions of individuality and separateness that arise from the wholeness that is the unmanifest, silent field of consciousness (Ā*tm*ā). These sounds are expressed sequentially and simultaneously. That something can be sequential and also simultaneous seems contradictory, but remember that this level of existence is beyond space and time.

One sound (*Akshara* or 'syllable') goes through a process of disintegration or decay after it has been expressed. This process is referred to as *Pradhwaṁsa-Abhāva*. A particular sound or *Akshara* offers itself (so to speak) in a process of dissolution or dissolving that is *Pradhwaṁsa-Abhāva*. It then is completely destroyed so that there is only the unmanifest state of pure consciousness remaining. This state of complete annihilation of the previous sound is known as *Atyanta-Abhāva*. The previous sound – while no longer existent – is remembered in this field of pure intelligence. This memory is known as *Smriti* (memory of everything).

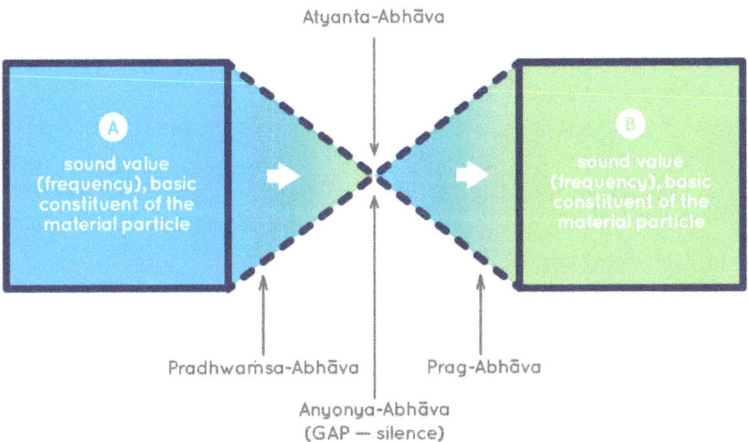

(Caption: The transformation of one sound value to another taking place in the silent dynamism of the GAPS between sounds in the nature of consciousness. Based on diagram in "Celebrating Perfection in Education", MUM Press.)

Absolute destruction (*Atyanta-Abhāva*), in the spirit of destruction, destroys the absolute state of nothingness (*Atyanta-Abhāva*) and in this unmanifest liveliness of all possibilities, the memory of what was before inspires the self-referral state of consciousness.[11] This is *Anyonya-Abhāva* – the state of unmanifest intelligence lively with the memory of what was before, the memory of all possibilities and what should be the next sequential step in evolution. So, *Anyonya-Abhāva* contains the memory of the sound before it and the inspiration for the sound that follows. At this point, creation of the new sound starts and is fully expressed from *Prag-Abhāva* as the more evolved value of the previous sound.

This concept of destruction of one entity, followed by the birth of a new entity with the memory of the previous entity influencing the qualities of the new entity, can be seen in contemporary cosmology. The black holes I described in chapter 11 represent the death of enormous stars (more massive than our Sun) collapsing under the effect of their own gravity to a point known as a singularity. The in-falling matter is totally destroyed (*Pradhwaṁsa-Abhāva*), leading to total annihilation *(Atyanta-Abhāva)* at the point singularity. As we learned in our discussions of quantum fields, at their most fundamental Planck level, these fields are highly energetic and lively, brimming with all possibilities of space-time geometry (*Anyonya-Abhāva)*. The unmanifest quantum dynamism causes the black hole to radiate, leading to the emergence of fresh new matter (*Prag-Abhāva*).

What then of 'memory'? According to conventional black hole physics, only the total mass-energy, total spin (angular momentum) and total electric charge of the in-falling matter is 'remembered' or conserved[12]. The initial state would determine the final or renewed state to some limited extent. However, more recent advances in black hole physics based on superstring theory augment this quality of memory (*Smriti*). As superstring theory provides the first true quantum theory of gravity, it gives us a more comprehensive picture of what happens at the level of the singularity. Superstring calculations reveal that, in the singularity, no information is destroyed – just reprocessed and regurgitated. What comes out truly depends on what went in![13]

This is yet another example (along with our earlier reference to the cosmic microwave background radiation) of the mirror behaviour of nature at its smallest and largest.

The reverberating Self

THE LAWS OF NATURE EVOLVE AS A SEQUENTIAL EMERGENCE OF SOUNDS, submerging in gaps, emerging as sounds, submerging in gaps and then emerging again as new sounds. In this fashion, the whole creative process can be seen as pulsating and vibrational. With every expressed sound, there is constant referral back to its source – the unexpressed, purely self-referral state of whole creative intelligence. This reverberation of sounds represents the primordial impulses of natural law that form the first expression of material existence. It is the reverberating quality in the expression of this code, resulting from the alternation of gap and sound, that gives rise to the special vibrational modes modern science has been uncovering at the most fundamental level of nature.

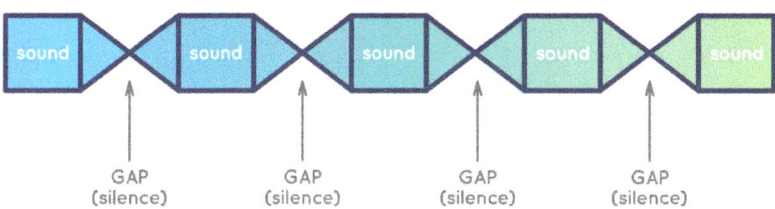

(Caption: The sequentially evolving (reverberating, wave-like) structure of the laws of nature emerging as sounds, submerging in GAPS. Based on diagram in "Celebrating Perfection in Education", MUM Press.)

We should now be able to appreciate the profound depth of meaning in the following verses:

> Dūrē dṛishaṁ gṛihapatim atharyum (Ṛk Veda, 7.1.1)
>
> "Far, far away the in-dweller of the house, the Self, is seen reverberating."

The constant referral back to the source of pure intelligence is also described:

> Prakṛitiṁ swām avashtabhya visṛijāmi punaḥ punaḥ (Bhagavad-Gita, 9.8)
>
> "Curving back upon My own Nature, I create again and again."

Like a wave curling back on itself and merging back into the formless ocean, so too does a wave of individuality or a wave of creation curl back on itself and again unite with its source. That wave can be viewed as one of the primordial sounds arising from Ātmā, or it can represent your or my individual consciousness (the small self) on the ocean of consciousness, or it can be anything materially manifest – a particle, a star, a whole universe or your body. After all, consciousness is the essence of everything material too. But 'life' is both the gap and the creations, not just the creations.

British explorer Sir Laurens Van der Post urged fellow explorer Sir Wally Herbert to "look between the lines" for the transcendent messages in the experiences of fellow explorers, and poets such as William Blake and T.S. Eliot valiantly attempted communication of the sublime and lofty in their skilful use of the language. To me, "the voice of the hidden waterfall and the children of the apple-tree" represent quintessential life, perhaps also those dreamlike memories of life, and perhaps too the possibilities of life dormant in the stillness between two waves of the Ocean of Self.

> *The voice of the hidden waterfall*
> *And the children of the apple-tree*
> *Not known, because not looked for*
> *But heard, half-heard, in the stillness*
> *Between two waves of the sea.*[14]
>
> – T.S.Eliot, Little Gidding, Vs 5

The flicker book model
MANY OF YOU WILL RECALL THE 'FLICKER' OR 'FLIP' PICTURE BOOKS WE used in our younger years to see a moving picture out of a series of still figures drawn on consecutive blank pages of paper. By flicking rapidly through the pages, the figures would appear to move relatively seamlessly.

If, in our flip picture book, (example: https://youtu.be/U7F298wy291), a "gap" appears after every expressed sound (to reflect the changeless, unmoving gap appearing between every differently expressed sound), and we then flip quickly through the pictures, we will notice the unmoving gap (in our picture book represented symbolically as the sun) as the unchanging, immovable background to the ever-changing, impermanent expressions of sounds (represented by their syllables or *Akshara*). This is the nature of 'life'. Life is filled with actions, but we tend to see only the actions. Behind all the activity and separate from activity is the self-referral field of consciousness known as Ātmā. It is the source of all that is, including action, but it remains uninvolved and removed from it. Lord Krishna – representing the wholeness of Ātmā – speaks about this very subject to the archer Arjuna on the battlefield of life in the *Bhagavad Gita*[15]:

*"The fourfold order[16] was created by Me
According to the division of gunas and
Actions. Though I am its author, know Me
To be the non-doer, immutable."*

Lord Krishna's use of the word 'author' seems particularly relevant to the writing of a script or code that is the collection of syllables, words and verses forming the *Ṛk Veda* – the Constitution of the Universe. Again, this code represents what physicists would describe as the varied vibrational modes of the superstring.

Life not an illusion
THIS FLICKER BOOK VISUALISATION OF THE MECHANICS OF CREATION WITH Ātmā remaining uninvolved in the background conjures another perspective – that of life as a motion picture projected onto a stationary screen. This analogy is useful to appreciate the non-moving and unchangeable ultimate reality behind the activity of manifest life, but it may also allow one to see manifest life just a projected image on an immovable background screen that is the only 'reality'. But maintaining a healthy perspective in one's adoption of this profound knowledge (or any recorded knowledge for that matter) is vital for a happy and balanced life. To view our current lives and the world around us as unreal or an illusion (like a movie on a screen) drastically diminishes the dignity and purpose of life. Such a philosophy could set the ground for a mood of non-involvement, listlessness and isolation.

Life as we know it – physical, changing, happy, sad, varied and complex – is all 'real'. However, the material and phenomenal world around us, including our bodies, is ever-changing, transient, impermanent, and therefore should be seen in context as not total reality. Total reality is Ātmā plus creation, the unmanifest along with the manifest, the wholeness of the ocean of Self along with the expressed waves of individual self. Total reality is the Unity that combines the source of all diversity and the diversity itself. We do not speak of the ocean as a collection of changing and transient waves, we speak of the ocean in its wholeness along with its expressed waves – one total entity. Transient though the waves are, they – along with the ocean beneath them – are all a real part of the ocean.

The first sounds of the *Ṛk Veda*
I AM NOT A PHYSICIST, NOR AN ADVANCED MATHEMATICIAN. FOR THIS reason, I will outline the corresponding findings in both Vedic science and

modern sciences as simply as I am able. I will admit what follows here in this section is intellectually demanding, but the ramifications are highly significant towards our acceptance of consciousness as a unified field underlying all of material existence. The mathematically gifted reader can refer to a chart published in one of the Maharishi Vedic University (Iowa, USA) publications for a more detailed elaboration of the correlations.[17]

I'll mainly stick to the familiar English words and only occasionally use Sanskrit words such as *Sūkta* (means "hymn"), *Richā* (means "verse"), *Pada* (means "phrase"), *Shabda* (means "word"), *Akshara* (means "syllable").

The very first words and sentences of the *Ṛk Veda* will be correlated with the very first vibrational expressions of the superstring proposed by string theorists. The first phrase (or *Pāda*) is also known as the *Rishi Prakriti* and it contains three words – AGNIM ĪLE PUROHITAṀ. These three words can be broken down to eight syllables (*Akshara*), expressed thus – AK NI MĪ LE PU RO HI TAṀ.[18] These *Akshara* are the very first sounds of creation.

The single and initial *Akshara* "Ak" is highly significant. The "A" vowel (pronounced *Ah*) denotes infinity and the "K" consonant ends that expression and denotes a point. The *Akshara* therefore denotes infinity collapsing to a point or infinity arising from a point. Musical expressions of "Ah" by voice or instrument can be highly emotive and tend to resonate favourably at a deep level of our awareness. Maharishi describes this first *Akshara* "Ak" as being a "highly compactified, one-syllable version of total Veda" within Ātmā – the self-referral consciousness of everyone. The whole structuring dynamics of the *Ṛk Veda* emerge from this one syllable.

IN THE CHAPTER ON MODERN SCIENCE I MENTIONED THAT MODERN quantum field and superstring theory postulates 10 dimensions rather than the four space and time dimensions with which we are familiar. The Lagrangian must allow 10 dimensions in order to produce the known fundamental fields in nature (or if you like, the known particles and forces in nature). The other six dimensions are considered by scientists to be tightly bound up inside the familiar three space dimensions and therefore not perceptible by our senses.

Dr Hagelin has described the possible vibrationary modes available to the superstring.[19] Of the 10 dimensions fundamental to our universe, if we exclude the time dimension, we are left with nine dimensions. When considering the degrees of freedom of a vibrating string, let's compare a superstring to a guitar string. One dimension is taken up by the length of the guitar string (essentially a one-dimensional straight line). That now leaves us eight degrees of vibrational freedom of the superstring – eight ways in which it can express itself. These eight essential modes of vibrational freedom of the superstring represent the first eight *Akshara* – or syllables – forming the code of vibrations that will eventually manifest as discrete particles of forces. These particles or forces are – you will recall – particular expressions of vibrating energy or quantum fields.

The likelihood that this is just coincidence becomes less as we move through the verses of the *Ṛk Veda* and compare the development of these verses with the progressive unfoldment of vibrational modes of the superstring.

This first unfoldment of eight syllables is called the *Rishi Prakriti* because, here, consciousness from the perspective of the knower, interacts with itself and unfolds in eight steps (Maharishi often referred to it as "eight summersaults"). These eight steps appear different when consciousness is considering itself as the process of knowing; and they appear different again from the perspective of consciousness as the known. Hence, there is a further unfoldment of eight syllables in the *Devata Prakriti* (representing consciousness in the process of knowing), and yet a further eight syllables in the *Chhandas Prakriti* (representing consciousness as the known). These (8 x 3) equals 24 *Akshara* are represented in their phrases (PĀDA) as follows:

PĀDA 1: AGNIM ĪLE PUROHITAṀ (the Rishi Prakriti)

PĀDA 2: YAGYASYA DEVAM RITWIJAM (the Devata Prakriti)

PĀDA 3: HOTĀRAṀ RATNA DHĀTAMAM (the Chhandas Prakriti)

These nine words (representing 24 syllables) are the first verse (ṚICHĀ) of the Rk Veda.

In the field of physics over the past few decades, string theorists have calculated the different vibrational modes of the superstring using the Lagrangian formulas. They too have introduced three different perspectives in which the superstring can vibrate, given the eight essential modes of vibrational freedom. Physicists call these three perspectives Hilbert Space, Operators and States. They match exactly the concepts of Rishi, Devata and Chhandas, but just in a different language.[20] Contemporary physics does not acknowledge the unified field as a state of consciousness, although there are many physicists who entertain the concept or are open-minded about it.

Modern physics assumes (8 x 3) equals 24 values of vibrational freedom of the superstring in its ten-dimensional existence.[21] This matches the total number of syllables (or sounds) in the first verse of the *Ṛk Veda*. What we're seeing is a direct correlation between the unfoldment of vibrational modes of operation of the superstring with the sequence of sounds perceived by the early Rishis. It's all the same code, perceived directly by the Rishis or derived through mathematics by modern scientists.

Between each of the 24 syllables, representing the nine words that form the first verse of the *Ṛk Veda*, is the gap (*Sandi*), and each gap contains a further eight syllables of expression. There are 23 spaces or gaps between the 24 syllables, but we include the first syllable "Ak" as well because it contains within it the whole *Veda*. This is 24 x 8 syllables (Akshara) – 192 further syllables – representing the "first level of elaboration" of the *Ṛk Veda*. These 192 syllables form 24 phrases (PĀDA) and represent verses 2–9, which is the first *Sūkta* (Hymn) of *Ṛk Veda*.

IN THE CORRESPONDING EVOLUTION OF SUPERSTRING THEORY, WE HAVE now reached that stage where space-time has been created, and in the process, the 10 dimensions are reduced to four dimensions with the remaining six dimensions curled up inside. According to the most recent advances in superstring mathematics, there are 64 fermionic degrees of freedom of the string corresponding to this compactification of 10 dimensions to four. By "fermionic", physicists mean the vibrational mode of the superstring that is responsible for producing fermions (discrete primordial particles). If we now assume the three perspectives (Hilbert Space, Operators and States) in which these 64 degrees of freedom operate, then we have (64 x 3) equals 192 values of vibration of the superstring. This expression of the most basic Laws of Nature derived by modern science exactly matches the progressive unfoldment of the *Ṛk Veda* – 192 syllables forming the first *Sukta* (Hymn) of the *Ṛk Veda*. This sequential expression of sounds was of course perceived by the early rishis and is capable of being perceived in our own still awareness.

There are three further levels of elaboration of the *Ṛk Veda* which give rise accordingly to the 192 *Sūkta* (or Hymns) of the First *Mandala* of the *Ṛk Veda*, the 192 *Sūkta* of the Tenth *Mandala*, and then all the remaining *Mandalas* from 2–9. Correspondingly, string theorists have calculated further elaborations of the vibrational modes of the superstring which exactly match this sequential unfoldment of the 10 *Mandalas* in the *Ṛk Veda*.

Some physicists throw their hands up and say: "just about anything can be proven with string theory". Could my attempt to correlate superstring theory with the Vedas be an attempt to custom fit mathematics to an ancient Hindu text? I would say definitely not. The descriptions of the unified field with regard to the vibrational characteristics of the superstring have been derived by string theorists over the decades and are widely known by physicists throughout the world. There is a remarkable quantitative correlation between these findings in physics with the sequential elaboration of sounds recorded in the Vedic texts so long ago. Such a matching could not be contrived, nor could it be seen as sheer coincidence.

People who are of a devout religious faith tend to be very cautious of entertaining any philosophy attached to another religion. The Vedic literature might be sacred to Hinduism and Buddhism, but that does not mean that it 'belongs' to those faiths. The *Vedas* were not invented or created by anyone. The literature represents nature's sounds, interpreted and recorded by those with finely tuned perception. Vedic science should be the foundation for modern science. It could also ideally be seen as a foundation for all our religions. Vedic science is really ultra-modern science and should not be seen as something that undermines the essential premises of established religions.

In summary, "the languages of Vedic Science and of modern Unified Field Theories may be different, but the striking parallels lead us to the conclusion that the self-referral dynamics of the field of consciousness described in Vedic Science, and the self-interacting dynamics of the Unified Field explored by modern science, are one and the same thing."[22]

NOTES

1. Hagelin, J., Is Consciousness the Unified Field? A Field Theorist's Perspective; Modern Science and Vedic Science, Vol 1, No. 1, January, 1987
2. "Within the domain of classical space-time geometry" meaning familiar four-dimensional space-time along with the curled-up extra space dimensions as described in Superstring theory.
3. Hagelin, John. *Foundations of Physics and Consciousness* (MUM Iowa course), Lesson 12, 'Is Consciousness the Unified Field?'
4. Hagelin, John. *Foundations of Physics and Consciousness* (MUM Iowa course)
5. *Self-Knowledge* of Sri Sankaracarya.
6. Maharishi Mahesh Yogi has revitalised and reintegrated this noble and effective health care system, which is now practised as Maharishi Ayurveda by many medical practitioners around the world. For more information on Maharishi Ayurveda, see www.imavf.org (or in Australia www.ayurveda.org.au)
7. *Prakriti* in Ayurveda is also referred to as *dosha* when referring to the particular balance of all three prakritis (vata, pitta and kapha) in the body that someone carries through life.
8. The "a" is typically dropped and thus pronounced "Vād" (as in "Vaid")
9. Carl Sagan, *The Cosmos* (TV documentary series), Episode 1: The Shores of the Cosmic Ocean.
10. Ātmā: The innermost reality of life; the essence not only of human consciousness but of all reality; the unified field (or superstring field) identified by modern physics; pure self-referral consciousness.
11. *Celebrating Perfection in Education*, Maharishi Vedic University Press, 1997, p14.
12. John Hagelin, *Foundation of Physics and Consciousness Course*, MUM, Iowa
13. John Hagelin, *Foundations of Physics and Consciousness Course*, MUM, Iowa
14. T.S. Eliot, "*Little Gidding*" from *FOUR QUARTETS*, Vs 5, *The Complete Poems and Plays by T.S. Eliot*; Excerpt reprinted by permission (world rights) of publishers Faber and Faber Ltd. Copyright 1936 by Houghton Mifflin Harcourt Publishing Company; Copyright © renewed 1964 by T.S. Eliot. Copyright 1940, 1942 by T.S. Eliot; Copyright © renewed 1968, 1970 by Esme Valerie Eliot. Reprinted by permission (USA rights) of Houghton Mifflin Harcourt Publishing Company. All rights reserved.
15. *Bhagavad Gita*, Ch 4, Vs 13.
16. *Maharishi Mahesh Yogi on the Bhagavad-Gita*; Penguin Books, 1969. The "fourfold order" Maharishi explains and expands on in his commentary on this verse, represents the four degrees of interaction of the three *gunas*. The "*gunas*" – *sattva, rajas* and *tamas* – are vital for the evolution of life and all activity. They represent the creation of a new state (*sattva*), the destruction of the created state (*tamas*) and the neutral balancing role of *rajas* maintaining balance between the two opposing forces.
17. *Celebrating Perfection in Education*; MUM Press, Iowa, USA; p152-153
18. The apparent discrepancy here – "Ak" instead of "Ag" ("Agnim") – is permitted in Sanskrit, by what is known as "regressive assimilation". The voiced sound "n" (in "Agnim") includes the previous sound, which is more "g" than "k". The "k" turns into a "g" because the "n" requires a voiced sound in front of it.
19. John Hagelin, *Foundation of Physics and Consciousness Course*, MUM, Iowa
20. 'Hilbert Space' can be considered ordinary space. 'Operators' are rules that govern the transformations of states – the creation or destruction of specific states in Hilbert Space or change of position within the space. Operators are therefore "process" orientated. 'States' refer to the particular quality of a quantum system within the Hilbert Space.
21. Three perspectives of the eight fermionic fields propagating on the string of the D=10 Heterotic Superstring Theory (8 x 3 = 24 values).
22. *Celebrating Perfection in Education*; MUM Press, Iowa, USA, p153

Chapter Thirteen

THE MAHARISHI EFFECT

"Tat sannidhau vaira tyagah"
In the vicinity of coherence (Yoga), hostile tendencies are eliminated.[1]

— Patanjali, Yog-Sutra

The so-called Maharishi Effect is probably the most tested and verified phenomenon in contemporary sociology, yet remains under the radar of most society leaders and policy makers worldwide. The Maharishi Effect demonstrates the field nature of consciousness and provides evidence that individual consciousness is intimately linked to a unified field underlying all the laws of nature.

> *"I think the claim can be plausibly made that the potential impact of this research exceeds that of any other ongoing social or psychological research program. It has survived a broader array of statistical tests than most research in the field of conflict resolution. This work and the theory that informs it deserve the most serious consideration by academics and policy makers alike."*
>
> –David Edwards Ph.D., Professor of Government, University of Texas at Austin

I'VE INCLUDED THIS COMMENT BY PROFESSOR DAVID EDWARDS EARLY IN this chapter because, on first reading about the Maharishi Effect, there is a natural tendency to consider the claims far-fetched.

The Maharishi Effect refers to the scientifically measurable benefits to society produced when a small percentage of the population practise Transcendental Meditation and the TM-Sidhi Program. How could a group of people ostensibly sitting down, seemingly doing nothing, create a profound positive influence on society on a broad scale?

Maharishi Mahesh Yogi was always interested in the connection between Vedic science and modern science, seeing both as an exploration of the fundamental mechanisms of nature's functioning. While Maharishi was primarily a scholar of the Vedic sciences, he also studied physics at India's esteemed Allahabad University and obtained a degree in that subject in 1942. Maharishi surrounded himself with contemporary scientists of sharp intellect and was constantly exploring correlations and similarities between the two disciplines.

In 1960, Maharishi predicted that only 1% of a population practising the Transcendental Meditation (TM) technique would produce measurable improvements in the quality of life for the whole population. The phenomenon was first noticed in 1974 and published in a paper in 1976[2]. It was found that when 1% of the community practised TM, crime rate was reduced by an average of 16%. The phenomenon was called the Maharishi

Effect in honour of Maharishi, who predicted the effect and promoted its implementation.

It was not until 1976 that Maharishi introduced the advanced TM-Sidhi[3] program, which also included the yogic flying sutra[4] of Patanjali. The radiance effect of the TM-Sidhi and yogic flying program appeared to be very strong, and – comparing the effect to some field phenomena in nature – scientists estimated that merely the square root of 1% of a population practising the TM-Sidhi program would have a significant beneficial effect on the whole population[5]. The square root of 1% relates to a phase-transition effect commonly observed in nature, such as water boiling and turning to steam at 100°C or turning to ice at 0°C. A particular temperature must be reached before any change in the state of the water is observed. So too, with the Maharishi Effect, a certain critical number of practitioners of the TM-Sidhi program is needed before significant measurable changes can be observed in the surrounding community.

The square root of 1% of a population means that, for example, 200 people practising the TM-Sidhi program together in a city of four million (100 x 200 x 200) would be sufficient to produce a measurable influence on the whole city; a group of 1,769 in the U.S. would influence 313 million (100 x 1769 x 1769) people – the whole population of the U.S.[6]; and a group of 8,367 would influence 7 billion (100 x 8,367 x 8,367) people – the population of the world.

How does it work?

WHILE THE PRECISE PHYSICAL MECHANISM FOR THE MAHARISHI EFFECT is not yet known, we will look at a broad conceptual framework for understanding how it could possibly work. This framework is consistent with the principles of Vedic science as expounded by Maharishi Mahesh Yogi[7] and does not disagree with any physical measurement so far.

We have been developing the principle that consciousness is a field phenomenon and that each and everyone's consciousness is like a wave on the ocean of that one field. We have also explored the hypothesis that this one ocean-like field of consciousness is also a unified field described by the mathematics of string theory and proposed as the one universal field giving rise to all the laws of nature throughout our universe, and possibly other universes.

A notable feeling of harmony is experienced in transcendental consciousness, and this harmony is also seen and measured in electro-encephalogram (EEG) studies of the human brain in this state of consciousness. It just so happens that during the yogic flying stage of the TM Sidhi program, the brain-wave coherence (harmony) between different parts of the brain is particularly profound and very pronounced on EEG recordings. While the brain registers this harmony as coherence in the firing of neurons in various regions, things are happening at a deeper, more fundamental level too, because participants in the TM-Sidhi program notice the coherent effect rather dramatically. Meditators participating in large groups practising the TM-Sidhi program will typically find their transcendence deeper and more restful – more powerful – because each of the meditators has a reinforcing effect on the other.[8] Some meditators prefer solitude for their journeys into the Self, but for many, the more the merrier.

A field coherence effect happens among the TM-Sidhi practitioners. It is argued that this same field coherence effect shared by the meditators radiates further afield into the surrounding community well beyond the meditating group. It is highly unlikely that the electromagnetic (EM) spectrum is responsible for this 'action-at-a-distance' phenomenon. The power of the EM field emitted by neuronal activity, giving rise to the typical electro-encephalogram (EEG) recordings, is orders of magnitude too small to affect other brains at a distance. Likewise, the other three force-fields (the strong and weak nuclear fields and gravity) are all too weak at the scales of distance we are referring to with the Maharishi Effect.[9,10]

A plausible explanation for such a radiating influence of consciousness can be found at that level where consciousness is assumed to operate at a much more fundamental scale of nature's functioning – the Planck Scale of 10^{-33} cm and 10^{-44} sec, where the different quantum fields become unified and space-time assumes a 'non-local' quality.

If we assume that space is truly 'non-local' at this unified field level of existence, we might expect the radiating coherence effect of consciousness to reach across the universe. During the emerging period of quantum mechanics in the first half of the last century, English physicist Sir James Jeans (1877–1946) once commented that, "When an electron vibrates, the universe shakes". The effect of group practice of a technology of consciousness like the TM-Sidhi program would likewise have an influence across the universe, but it has been found that any measurable effects of this influence diminish with distance, even on an Earthly scale.

Is this mind control?
THERE IS NO REASON TO BELIEVE THAT BEING POSITIVELY INFLUENCED BY a harmonising 'atmosphere' would result in loss of one's free will. Similarly, an influence of harmony on the level of consciousness would not take away from one's free will. Accordingly, the Maharishi Effect could not sensibly

be seen as a form of mind control. Anyone being positively influenced by this coherent wave of harmony is perfectly able to make their own decisions and freely execute their own wills. For a comparison, imagine being situated in a beautiful rainforest with clear running water and the musical sounds of birds. Compare that to being situated in a war zone or even a noisy, aggressive, angry and crowded environment. In both situations, you are still free to make your own decisions and think how you wish. It's just that one environment is more likely to influence you positively and the other is more likely to induce stress. The radiant effect of harmony and coherence in the underlying field of consciousness just provides that harmonising foundation or background that will naturally influence everything that arises from it – which is everything. From a social point of view, its main positive effect is a reduction in stress.

Maharishi put this another way: "we are not speaking of interference in the natural tendencies of people here and there. We leave it to nature. After all, it's natural law that guides and governs all the different tendencies of life".[11]

What about prayer?
I AM PERSONALLY A BIG BELIEVER IN PRAYER, BUT I DO NOT SPEAK FOR fellow practitioners of TM or the TM-Sidhi program, who may or may not have religious beliefs. As I have stressed before, meditation is a mental technique and not the propriety of any religion. I also strongly feel that prayers are not always answered the way we would like them to be. I believe there are reasons for this, and it might have something to do with an apparent conflict between our soul's agenda – not known at our superficial levels of awareness – and the way life appears. I do believe in giving thanks or expressing through prayer our love for God and those persons we know and even those we don't.

The *Bhagavad-Gita* has a statement relevant to the question of God apparently allowing suffering in our lives and not always intervening. "He who has conquered his self by his Self alone is himself his own friend; but the Self of him who has not conquered his self will behave with enmity like a foe."[12]

The Self – that core, universal aspect of our very identity, that ocean of consciousness underlying and giving rise to our individual consciousness – "unfolds Itself by Itself to Itself".[13] The ultimate answer and solution to our problems lie within each and every one of us. As long as we identify only with the small self, which acts "through the senses, encouraging them and enjoying the variety of objective experience", then we remain susceptible to the buffeting of the sometimes tempestuous waves on the surface of the ocean.

After looking through some of the available information on this subject, I am aware that the few studies that have been done on the effectiveness of prayer relate mainly to "intercessory" prayer, that is – praying to God or a divine entity to intercede on behalf of another person for their improved wellbeing or health. There appear to be very few carefully monitored studies on the effectiveness of intercessory prayer and certainly not enough studies to draw confident conclusions with a meta-analysis (conducting a review of existing research) of the literature.

Meditation – at least the way I practise it and the way TM is taught – does not involve prayer, canting or conjuring, nor for that matter, any form of contemplation or concentration. Prayer on the other hand is a mental or spoken request or attempt at communication with a divine entity. Meditation and prayer are therefore very different concepts.

If group or "common" prayer works – and I suspect it might – then it may be possible to explain it scientifically in terms of the unified field model of consciousness. It could be that, in prayer there is also a transcending of consciousness, and with sufficient numbers also transcending during their praying, a radiating coherent field effect is occurring. It might also reflect what I have mentioned before – that the power of consciousness, especially in a 'collective' sense, is such that it can create reality. If the identity of pure consciousness and the unified field proposed in the chapters on modern science[14] is true, it would strongly suggest that even thought can work powerfully from the most fundamental levels of nature.

Continuing on this assumption of a unified field model of consciousness, if we 'believe' something strongly enough, then often we make it so. We would also assume consciousness to be more powerful in its ability to create when we work from a more transcendent, universal level of consciousness.

Evidence for the Maharishi Effect
I MENTIONED THAT THERE IS AMPLE EVIDENCE TO SUPPORT THIS phenomenon and we will examine a couple of the 23 published articles supporting different exercises of the Maharishi Effect. We will also examine critically how the statistics in these studies stands up to scrutiny despite the well acknowledged assumption that "statistics can be used to lie".[15]

When I first read about the profound social effect of groups gathering together to practise what I was practising daily, I was both fascinated and suspicious. I had to address two issues to satisfy myself that this was a phenomenon worth serious attention:

1. The legitimacy of the statistical studies supporting the Maharishi Effect.
2. The underlying premise that consciousness is a field phenomenon and indeed that our consciousness operates at the level of the proposed unified field.

Reviewing the references to the 23 published articles on various demonstrations of this social phenomenon, I was particularly interested in two of them – one article published in the *Journal of Conflict Resolution* on the results of group practice of the TM-Sidhi program in Jerusalem in 1983 and its effects on social conflict in Israel and neighbouring Lebanon; the other article published in *Social Indicators Research* on the results of a huge group of 4,000 practitioners of the TM-Sidhi program gathering together in Washington DC in 1993.

I chose these articles because both journals were internationally respected peer-reviewed publications with stringent criteria regarding acceptance of submitted material. I had also heard that the editor of the *Journal of Conflict Resolution* had written a special comment preceding the article and that one of the journal's (formerly) anonymous reviewers had also written a comment at the conclusion of the article. I was deeply curious to read every word to see what ideas they held about this "technology of consciousness".

The other journal (*Social Indicators Research*) appeared to address a complaint of the reviewers in the former journal (that the authors of this Middle East study were all from the one organisation) and so included independent authors from other respected universities and the Metropolitan Police Department in Washington D.C. It also discussed the results of one of the largest congregations of TM-Sidhi practitioners of all time.

If you are interested in this potentially powerful social 'technology' – and I hope you are, particularly if you are a politician or another person of influence in society – then I would encourage you to also have a look at these articles in full, and if necessary, have them reviewed by scientists or statisticians you respect.

Basically, the editor and reviewers of the *JOCR* were content that the methodology applied to the study was "competent". Furthermore, the data was in the public domain, so the data was unlikely to have been 'cooked'. For this reason, they felt they had no choice but to publish the article because it had passed the "standards to which manuscripts submitted for publication in this journal are normally subjected". If a hypothesis is wrong or errant, then it is up to future researchers to nullify that hypothesis with properly executed replicated tests or new tests. That is how science works. So far, it appears no-one has published anything to adequately refute the statistical methodology or premise associated with this published study.

THE PREMISE UNDERLYING THE PROPOSED MECHANISM FOR THE Maharishi Effect appears to have presented the main stumbling block. In editor Bruce Russett's words[16]: "This hypothesis has no place within the normal paradigm of conflict and peace research. Yet the hypothesis seems logically derived from the initial premises, and its empirical testing seems competently executed." In the words of reviewer Robert Duval[17], who wrote a short comment at the end of the article: "The fundamental assumptions of a 'unified field' and a 'collective consciousness' are not within the paradigm under which most of us operate. Yet if one will, for the sake of argument, accept these premises as plausible, then the research conforms well to scientific standards."

The premise – that consciousness is a field phenomenon with its genesis in a unified field – lies outside the prevalent paradigm assumed by most modern-day scientists working in the fields of engineering, medicine, psychology, politics and Earth sciences. The predominant Cartesian-Newtonian paradigm for understanding the world is insufficient when it comes to understanding the workings of nature at its most miniscule level or its most cosmic level. We have had to assume a broader paradigm – that of relativity, quantum field theory and more recently superstring theory – to make any sense of the subatomic world or the universe as a whole.

My question to these noble and accomplished social scientists is this: can we afford to totally disregard 20th century science as it applies to the very fundamental levels of nature, when studying a subject like consciousness, which all of us would surely agree is fundamental to our very notion of self? Surely, it's time to come out of the 19th century, with its reliance on Newtonian science, and integrate our modern theories and scientific pursuits with the amazing discoveries of the past century? It might be harder to test behavioural hypotheses, but these social experiments on the Maharishi Effect have proven it is not impossible. We just have to get our heads around a new premise – the possibility that consciousness is not solely a product of the brain, but has its genesis at the hypothesised level at which superstrings work – the level Einstein referred to as a "unified field". Neuroscientists and behavioural scientists in particular would ideally expand their scientific paradigm or at least accept that the explanation given for the effectiveness of the Maharishi Effect is not necessarily from a "quasi-scientific" or "quasi–religious sect".[18]

Here's a comment from another academic removed from the TM organisation, Dr Ken Pease, Professor of Criminology, University of Huddersfield, U.K: "My first reaction to work in this tradition was one of total disbelief. However, its proponents have shown themselves prepared to subject programs to empirical test, and the technique already has a sounder basis than many less exotic approaches. At the minimum, courtesy and humility demand interest and attention to its progress and testing. If favourable results keep coming, we should not shrink from using them, or from seeking to understand them."[19]

In the face of substantial empirical evidence that something works, surely we can all employ that "courtesy and humility" in regard to our understandings of nature, and allow ourselves to enjoy the considerable benefits on a global scale?

In the first part of the 19th century, electricity was little understood, and was thought to behave as a fluid. Despite this paucity of knowledge, the electrical telegraph – transmitting Morse code – transformed communication over distances and sparked the information technology revolution. Even if we have trouble getting our heads around the proposed mechanism for the Maharishi Effect, then why not apply the technology – simply because it is shown to work – and then continue the research and efforts to understand it?

The International Peace Project

THERE IS AN ACUTE NEED FOR ALTERNATIVE APPROACHES TO THE reduction of violence at domestic, national and international levels. We can do better. All existing methods have been only partially effective at best. Blight speaks of the "policy irrelevance of available approaches to resolving enduring civil and international conflicts".[20]

By the early 1980s a number of published studies had confirmed the effectiveness of the Maharishi Effect in positively affecting society in a number of ways, e.g., reduced incidence of car accidents, violent crime, fires, absence from work (all reflecting a reduction in societal stress). All those studies had been retrospective studies. In other words, researchers had decided, after the fact, to study the effects of large groups of yogic flyers.

While these studies presented strong evidence of the effectiveness of the programs, scientists also like to see prospective experiments, where the experiment has been deliberately created and predictions made in advance. The first such experiment was reported in the *Journal of Conflict Resolution* in 1988.

By the beginning of August, 1983, about 40,000 people – mostly in Israel, but also in neighbouring Lebanon – were practising the Transcendental Meditation (TM) technique. Of those, more than 200 had gone on to learn the TM-Sidhi program. At the time of the study, Jerusalem had a population of 429,000 (including the Arab population), Israel had a population of 5,304,000, consisting of 4,024,000 plus 1,280,000 for the West Bank and Gaza Strip. Israel and Lebanon combined had a population of 7,905,000. For Jerusalem, Israel, and Israel and Lebanon combined, the square root of 1% is 65, 230 and 281 respectively. The researchers took into account the 1% contribution of TM (alone) practitioners with their calculations, and concluded that a mere 197 yogic flyers were needed to positively and measurably affect changes throughout Israel and Lebanon combined. A group of 122 was needed to see measurable changes throughout Israel alone.[21]

The social variables being studied were crime, automobile accidents, fires, stock prices, national mood, war intensity and war deaths. All this data was available from independent sources within the public domain. In Jerusalem, crime statistics were obtained from the Social Research Division of the Israel Police Department; auto accidents from the Municipal Government of Jerusalem; fires from the Jerusalem District Fire Extinguishing Service. Being accessed from public sources, all the data was available to be checked by future reviewers or scientists wishing to replicate the study.

The original experiment was designed to have 200 yogic flyers maintained as a group for two months in August and September, 1983. All the yogic flyers were accommodated in a hotel in the Arab quarter of Jerusalem, the Arab hotel owner being quite supportive of the exercise. Contrary to the experimental design however, the group numbers fluctuated throughout the two months. Despite sponsorship from a corporate entity back in the USA, participants – for work or study reasons – participated only as long as they were able. Over the two-month period, the numbers varied from 65 to 241. This initially concerned the scientists, as they were uncertain of their ability to measure the effects with such a fluctuating group size. As it turned out, the variation in numbers of yogic flyers closely matched the fluctuations in the dependant variables studied.

Independent research scientists in both Israel and the USA were prepared months in advance of the project and given the research hypotheses, dates of the assembly, statistics gathered and results predicted. The organisers would also forward to these scientists the yogic flying attendance numbers mid-way through the experiment and also at the end.

THE RESULTS – AS SEEN IN THE GRAPH – WERE VERY COMPELLING. THE researchers combined the statistics for all the variables into a single Quality of Life index. As the numbers of flyers went up, so too did the Quality of Life index. When the numbers of flyers went down, so too did the Quality of Life index, pretty much in lock-step. The statistics also demonstrated an inverse correlation between numbers of flyers and both war intensity and war death figures. In all examined variables, the numbers of flyers preceded the social effects examined. It wasn't the other way around.

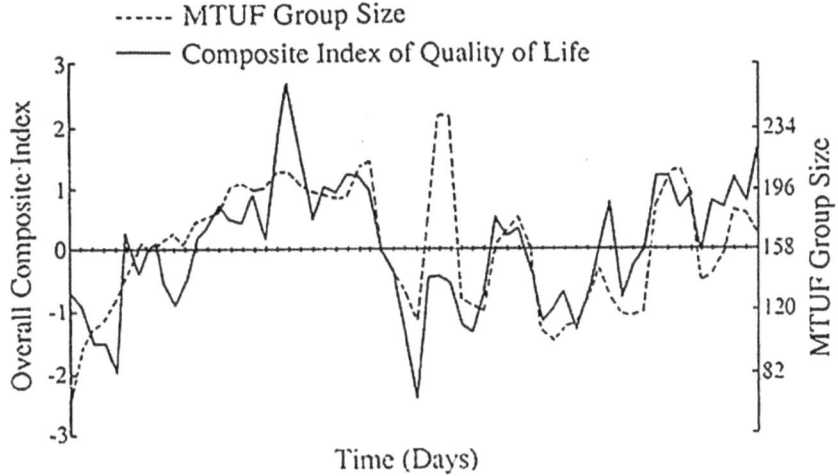

Figure 3: Standardized Daily Time Series of the Overall Composite Index Plotted Against the MTUF. An Overall Composite Index composed of six variables was constructed so that a positive deflection on the graph represents global improvement in quality of life. It can be seen that the index showed a positive correlation with the MTUF (r = .57).

From Orme-Johnson et al, 'International Peace Project in the Middle East', *J. of Conflict Resolution*, Vol. 32 No. 4, December 1988, p795.

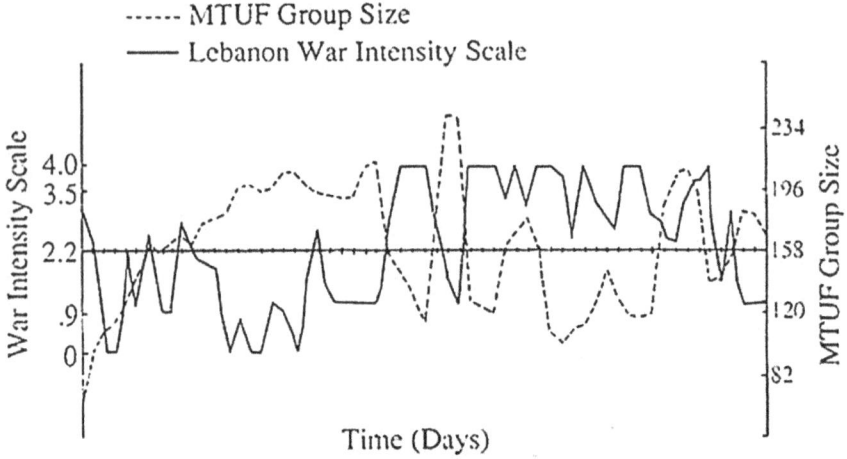

Figure 2: Standardized Daily Time Series of the MTUF and the Lebanon War Intensity Scale. These graphs show a tendency toward an inverse correlation between the MTUF group size and the war intensity in Lebanon (r = −.48).

From Orme-Johnson et al, 'International Peace Project in the Middle East', *J. of Conflict Resolution*, Vol. 32 No. 4, December 1988, p794.

As one would expect with any physical field phenomenon, the greater the strength of the field, the greater is the range of effect. When attendance of yogic flyers was low, the positive effects were felt only in Jerusalem. As attendance rose, the effects were felt throughout Israel as a whole. When attendance reached its peak, the effect reached into Lebanon with decreased war deaths and intensity of fighting.

During the high-attendance periods, crime rate in Jerusalem dropped 8.8% (with a p<.023). In statistics, the *p* value indicates the probability that an effect occurs purely by chance, meaning in this case that the chance that pure coincidence was involved was less than 2.3%), the crime rate in the whole of Israel dropped 12.1% (with a p<.0016 or chance of coincidence less than 16 in 10,000), automobile accidents in Jerusalem dropped 34.4% (p<.024), and fires in Jerusalem dropped 30.4% (p<.045). More dramatic was the effect on war deaths and war intensity across the border in Lebanon. During overall high-attendance days, war deaths dropped 76% (p<.02, reflecting the smaller sample of 40 deaths per day reduced to 9.7 deaths per day). War intensity dropped 45% (p<.0045).

Let's look at possible criticisms of this study:

1. The data fed into the statistics might have been 'cooked'.
Because all data was collected from public institutions within Israel or Lebanon, such data is freely available at all times for future reviewers to examine. The independent variables in this study are the numbers of yogic flyers attending at different times, and this was also reported to scientists in both Israel and the USA midway through the experiment and at the end.

One of the journal referees, political scientist Associate Professor Robert Duval from West Virginia University, was originally concerned that the numbers of yogic flyers might have increased as a result of an increase in the war intensity rather than the other way around. Duval suggested that, when the flare-up passed, it would seem that the yogic flyers had caused the decline. At the request of Dr Duval, the authors provided a revised "transfer function analysis" of the project, which indicated that the time lags between flyer numbers and social effects supported the direction of causation from flyer numbers to social effects recorded in the study.

2. The correlation between improvement in Quality of Life parameters and yogic flyer numbers could have been coincidence.
There was such a strong correlation demonstrated between flyer numbers and positive social changes that calculations show that the chance that this could happen by coincidence was only one in 10,000. In the social sciences, a $p<.001$ (that is, a probability of coincidence is less than one in one thousand) is considered very highly significant. For a correlation to occur by chance only one in 10,000 times is very strong evidence for a cause-effect relationship. Additional support for the findings in this study come from the results of almost 50 other exercises of this social technology replicated in many parts of the world by different researchers using different research designs. Some 23 of these exercises were published in respected science journals.

3. Were other influencing factors like weather, change of season, holidays and predominance of younger people at certain times of the year taken into account?
Yes. The researchers measured the normal variations in social parameters over similar lengths of time to determine patterns that might normally occur during that period. For example, crime might increase during the hotter periods of the year, or during school or university holiday periods. These normal changes are incorporated into the mathematical analysis called a time series analysis. Such an analysis allowed the researchers in this study to filter out cyclical patterns in social effects even if the causes are unknown.

Fales and Markovsky[22] claimed that the authors of the Middle East study omitted other possible influences, specifying certain social, political and military events at the time. The original authors responded in detail and stressed that Fales and Markovsky's conjecture "does not hold up with simple inspection of the published data nor with decisive statistical tests".[23]

4. Did the yogic flyers advertise their activity to the broader public, somehow influencing society's behaviour?
All participants in the study were asked not to discuss the precise nature of the study with non-participants. Remember too, that this was a time when cell phones had only been around a few years and were owned by very few people. Social media such as Twitter and Facebook had not even been thought of. It is unlikely that any real impact would have been made by even a few participants sharing the details of their project with outsiders. Certainly, there does not appear to have been any newspaper or television media reports of the project during the study period.

5. Might there be mysticism or divine intervention involved here?
I very much doubt this was entertained at all by any of the yogic flyers involved in this study, so natural and innocent is the technique of transcending. It seems far more likely that a natural scientific explanation would account for the results of this experiment. While an explanation for the Maharishi Effect is still wanting within the materialistic Newtonian paradigm, the broader understanding of nature's functioning apparent in quantum field theory and cosmology does accommodate the proposed explanation for the Maharishi Effect.

We have already discussed the differences between prayer and meditation. In Transcendental Meditation the mind is simply allowed to disengage itself from outside sensory input and thereby gain a simpler, quieter state of self-referral stillness. The researchers of this phenomenon have good reason to believe that a coherent field-effect is occurring not too dissimilar to other known field effects in nature. The only distinction is that the researchers have concluded that the yogic flyers must be enlivening a very fundamental level of the quantum fields – a level that is also shared with everyone else's consciousness.

> *"If it only happened once or twice, you could argue coincidence. In these studies it's the continual correlation, replicated many times over a long period, that gets your attention."*
>
> – Dr Mark Novak, Sociologist, *University of Winnipeg, Canada.*

What is empirical evidence?
EMPIRICAL EVIDENCE IS A SOURCE OF KNOWLEDGE ACQUIRED BY MEANS OF observation or experiment. An *empiricist* would contend that one can only have a belief if that belief is based on empirical evidence. The *empiricist's* view stands in contrast to the *rationalist's* view, under which reason or reflection alone is considered to be evidence for the truth or falsity of some propositions. While we might expect that empirical evidence alone should convince or highly persuade people to see the validity of a hypothesis, prior beliefs and experiences of the investigators also determine the conclusions drawn from empirical studies. In other words, we see a mixture of rationalist and empiricist philosophies in the acquirement of knowledge. The role of observation alone as a "theory-neutral arbiter" may not be possible.[24] This assertion is strongly supported by the reaction of sociologists and politicians to the conclusions of these studies on the Maharishi Effect.

> *"One possibility is that there has been a gigantic fraud. Personally, I cannot believe that because I know these people, and I know them to be careful and dedicated researchers. The second possibility is that we have made one of the most important discoveries of our time. If these findings are accurate, we can change the mood of the whole world."*[25]

– Juan Pascual-Leone, MD, PhD, Professor Emeritus in psychology, *York University, Canada,* and one of the independent scientists who reviewed the research design and monitored the course of the study.

The national demonstration: Washington, D.C., 1993
This study, reported in the *Social Indicators Research* journal[26], is worth noting for three reasons:

1. This was a prospective study with predictions made in advance to a panel of scientists uninvolved with the TM and TM-Sidhi programs. The previous time this was done was with the International Peace Project in Israel, 10 years earlier.
2. The sheer scale of the project made it a landmark experiment with 4,000 yogic flyers from 80 countries gathering in one place.
3. The authors of the study included scientists from outside the TM organisation, including from the University of the District of Columbia, Washington, D.C., University of Maryland and from the Crime Research and Statistics Section of the District of Columbia Metropolitan Police Department, Washington, D.C.

Washington D.C. is, of course, the location of the US Government, where important decisions affecting the whole world are made. This city also happens to have one of the highest rates of violent crime in the world. Each year, the city was spending more than $1 billion to combat crime. In Dr John Hagelin's opinion, "Our leaders cannot make balanced and farsighted decisions in Washington's stressed and criminal atmosphere".[27]

The organisers of this project put together an independent 24-member Project Review Board to objectively evaluate the research. This board consisted of some of the nation's leading sociologists and criminologists from the University of Maryland, Howard University, the University of the District of Columbia, American University, Temple University, the University of Texas, the University of Denver College of Law and the D.C. Metropolitan Police Department, and local government and civic leaders. The organisers lodged their predictions with this Project Review Board and faxed their predictions to 1,900 points in Washington, including all U.S. Senators and Congressmen, members of the diplomatic corps, many senior government officials and 375 media offices throughout the U.S. and the world.[28]

The participants bore most of the $5.98 million costs, including the international or domestic travel, accommodation and meals. They were housed in eight facilities around the city. Again, the participants had virtually no behavioural interaction with the wider population being studied. An additional $2.5 million was donated by individuals for wide publicity of the results of the experiment to governments around the world.

There was of course wide scepticism of the predictions by members of the Review Board. The Police Chief of Washington, D.C. remarked: "It will take more than mental harmony to reduce crime by one-fifth. We'll probably have to have 20 inches of snow to keep people off the streets".[29]

Again in this study, all data assessed for indications of improved "quality of life" in Washington D.C. was obtained from public sources and so could always be checked by future scientists or reviewers of this project. The gathering of data and the statistical method employed was supervised by an independent Project Review Board. This board comprised 27 members, including sociologists and criminologists from leading universities, representatives from the District of Columbia Metropolitan Police Department and District government and civic leaders.

President Clinton had not long been elected president and, in the time immediately preceding the project dates of June/July, 1993, was not expected to last more than one term as president, with significant disapproval ratings. He was continually making apologies for mistakes. Almost from day one of the Yogic Flying demonstration, the president's approval ratings began a turn for the better. His performance locally and internationally even became impressive. Americans began to rally behind their president.

On July 18, *Washington Post* columnist Sally Quin wrote: "The Clinton administration appears to have revived…Washington has relaxed. But such a swift reversal of political fortune is not easy to account for. [We] may logically wonder whether Clinton really turned things around or if something else is going on…Almost mysteriously and almost overnight, in the face of government distress, the press seemed to be transformed". Based on the evidence, we could suggest that, that "something else" going on was the powerful radiating effect of coherent waves of consciousness positively influencing the population. With the reduction in societal stress, fewer mistakes were made, there was more orderliness and calm in decision making and the general feelings of animosity towards the president were also declining. It made no difference, by the way, if the incumbent government was Democrat or the Republican. Other studies during leadership by a Republican president proved that the same improved level of public support resulted from the nearby gathering of a critical number of practitioners of this technology of consciousness.

Crime throughout the city was predicted to drop by 20% as a result of the project. It actually dropped 23% when the numbers of flyers peaked to 4,000. Time series analysis showed that no other factors, including increased police efforts, changes in temperature and annual cycles such as summer vacations, could explain this change. The odds that such a decline in violent crime could have occurred by chance were less than two in a billion ($p<2 \times 10^{-9}$). It was calculated that, if the yogic flyers had stayed beyond the end of July, the incidence of violent homicides, rapes and assaults (HRA) would have dropped 48% and remained at that level.

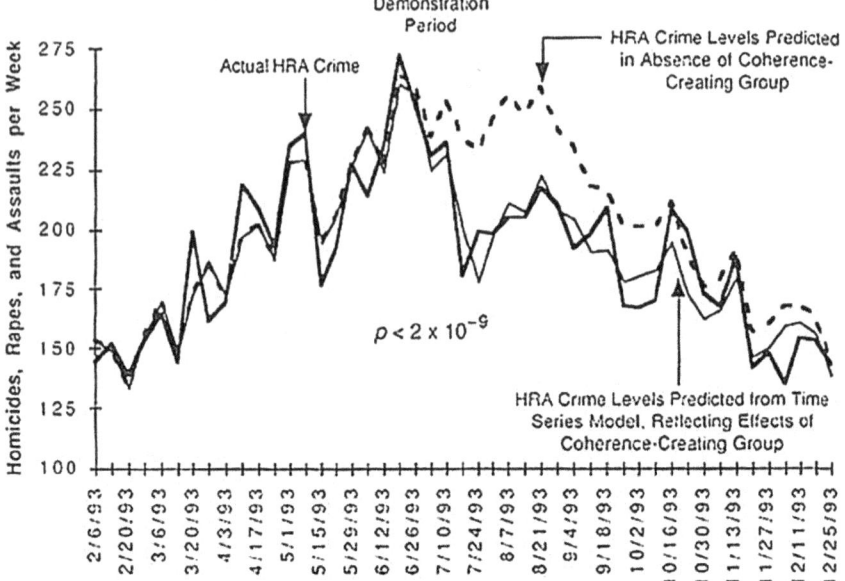

Figure 1. Effects of the National Demonstration Project on 1993 HRA crime levels in Washington, D.C. *Dark solid line* – actual HRA crime levels. *Light solid line* – predictions (or "fitted values") for HRA crime based on the time series model, reflecting effects of the coherence-creating group. *Dotted line* – HRA crime levels predicted to occur in the absence of the coherence-creating group. *Shaded area* – the period of the Demonstration Project.

From J.S. Hagelin et al, 'The Effects of Group Practice of the Transcendental Meditation Program on Preventing Violent Crime in Washington, D.C.: Results of the National Demonstration Project, June–July, 1993,' Social Indicators Research 47(2) (1999), p 172

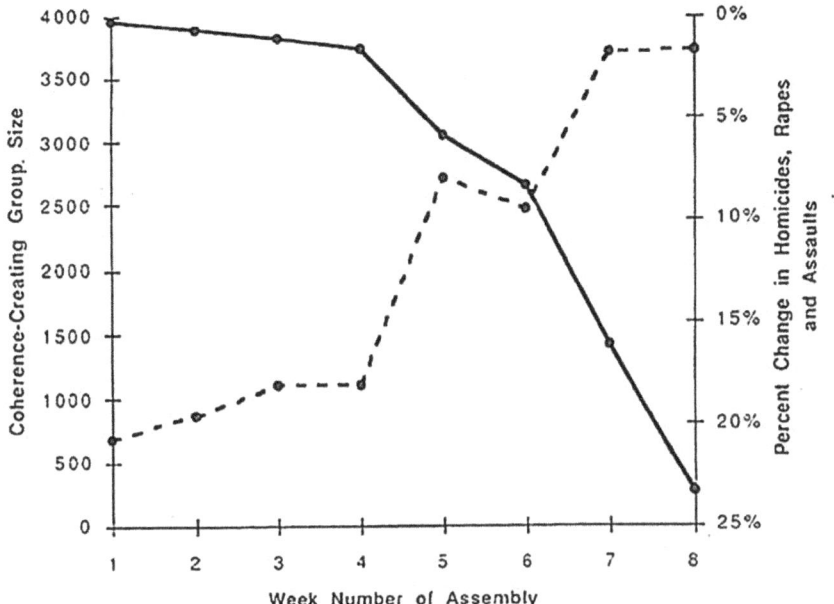

Figure 2. Percentage change in HRA crimes (*solid line*) in relation to the size of the coherence-creating group (*dotted line*) over the 8 weeks of the Demonstration Project.

From J.S.Hagelin et al, 'The Effects of Group Practice of the Transcendental Meditation Program on Preventing Violent Crime in Washington, D.C.: Results of the National Demonstration Project, June–July, 1993,' Social Indicators Research 47(2) (1999), P 173

Consider the financial aspects here – the city spends $1 billion a year fighting crime. This represents more than $83 million a month. The cost of running this National Demonstration Project over the two months was $8 million and it reduced crime by 23% – nearly one quarter. Had the project been maintained, that level of crime reduction was expected to reduce to 48% and remain at that level. That's nearly a half! That's a saving of some $80 million every two months for the outlaying of $8 million. That's a pretty good public investment.

Robberies throughout the city did not change with the concurrence of the two-month yogic flying project. This unchanging parameter was explained by the fact that "robberies are less strongly related to societal stress than are HRA crimes…Also, robberies are often related to long-established drug abuse habits and involve a degree of prior planning. Therefore, we hypothesize that a longer intervention period may be required to reduce them."³⁰

Apart from crime, which was considered independently, a "quality of life" index was also measured based on publically available data on four variables: emergency psychiatric calls, complaints against the police, trauma cases (assaults and vehicle accidents) at the District of Columbia General Hospital and accidental deaths (including suicide). All four variables were shown to decline in correlation with increased flyer numbers.

> *"I want to express my support for this research. What we are really looking at here is a new paradigm of viewing crime and violence…I would like to recommend that this new model being offered here, which is supported by a number of exhaustive and very carefully controlled studies, be considered and that we think of ways that it might be implemented in the inner city…*
>
> *"The Demonstration Project in D.C. as well as the demonstrations elsewhere hold promise for assisting with society's problems. To a skeptic I would say, 'What is your solution?' I haven't seen one yet. We need to consider other possibilities than the conventional wisdom."*

– Ann Hughes, PhD, Professor of Sociology and Government, *University of the District of Columbia;* one of the authors of the paper who does not practise TM.

What was the experience like?
Yogic flyers came from all over the world and included school teachers, medical doctors, scientists, business people, tradesmen and students. Even the close proximity of one other yogic flyer during my own TM-Sidhi program increases the quality of experience and depth of meditation. It also seems to make my flying program more active and vibrant. When I write 'flying', I do not mean that I am maintaining a hovering position or truly 'flying', but managing a series of hops which are spontaneous and effortless, and accompanied by remarkable changes in brain functioning.

I have meditated with large groups of 200 or more, and I recall the experience as being truly vibrant and blissful. Flying appears effortless. I can't imagine what it must be like to participate with 4,000 fellow flyers, but here are some comments from some of the participants in Washington in

1993: "I've had very good flying. My body's been hopping up and down for the whole flying session. I've found that the more I fly, the more I go into this deep inner ocean of bliss inside. The more I fly, the more refreshed and energetic I feel…I'm finding huge amounts of energy".

Another participant in the Demonstration Project made a reference to the ocean and even fish, which of course appealed to me! "There was no breath, just Being, moving within itself. My heart was totally open, infinite love, at one with everything – no boundaries, restrictions, individuality, just universal cosmic Being…It feels more natural, more comfortable in the air. Cosmic intelligence is filling my body. I am the ocean and all the fish in the ocean are transparent fluctuations of my transparent Self."

It's interesting this person expressed that they were "more comfortable in the air" because Maharishi has described hovering or floating as "a more natural phenomenon, and coming down is unnecessary". Maharishi explained that the body comes down only when there is some stress in the body. "This [flying] is the most natural state of human physiology," he said. "Anything unnatural will cause the body to come down."

Did civic leaders take notice?

OF COURSE NOT! WE HAVE ALREADY EXPLAINED THE POTENTIAL CLASH OF empirical evidence with innate bias related to our world view or preconceptions on how nature works. Many believe that the workings of society are not able to be effectively studied with science[31], let alone able to be influenced by 'technology' that has its explanation in something as far removed as physics.

Although several U.S. mayors and several non-government groups expressed interest in the technology of Yogic Flying for reducing crime, in the end, no one adopted the program. Dr John Hagelin and politician Dr Mike Tompkins met with city officials and chiefs of police in a number of cities. Dr Tompkins said, "Government leaders are bound by the quality of society's collective consciousness – and the collective consciousness still was not sufficiently coherent to permit them to act responsibly".

And this about sums it up! If you still have problems getting your mind around the concept of a "collective consciousness" in society, then consider it a kind of societal mindset. Politicians will act according to what they think is the prevailing set of values or expectations of the community that elected them. Until we change the mindset or values of society as a whole, I don't think we will ever get a politician acting responsibly outside of those rather strict constraints. If most people in society won't think outside the box, don't expect politicians to.

Maharishi and the TM organisation had performed enough demonstrations of the Maharishi Effect. It took time, money and considerable effort to implement these studies. Governments just dismissed the whole phenomenon as the misguided antics of some religious or pseudo-religious organisation.

My own project
IN 1999, I DECIDED TO MAKE A PERSONAL EFFORT TO INITIATE YET another test of the Maharishi Effect. I would gather the necessary funding and, if the test proved once again that the phenomenon works, would approach leading public figures and politicians to commit to continuing public support of this social technology. In my letters and meetings, I asked the government to nominate the most sceptical and respectable university departments or scientific organisations to specify the parameters of the test and to be responsible for the statistical analysis of the findings. I firmly endeavoured to eliminate any possible bias at any level of the study.

I knew that elected governments are naturally conservative in spending the public's money. They have to be, as they are continually audited and checked by opposition parties. I was proposing that this test would cost the government nothing. If the test proved a success, and actuaries determined that so many hundreds of millions of dollars would be saved by the community over a year, then the investors of my project would be paid back with appropriate interest. It would clearly be a win-win for everyone.

I'm clearly the fool for thinking it was all so simple. I approached a leading state politician. I approached the then commissioner of police. I approached a leading political journalist, whom I knew and respected. I approached another respected state public servant who had been a leading figure in the armed forces. I knew and respected him also. I approached the Rotary organisation, to which I still belong as a member. I approached a major insurance council in Australia. I approached my local Catholic priest in the hope that a referral to some higher representatives might happen.

In all the above cases, I got a confused and basically impotent response from those I directly approached, and a polite shrug-off from Government representatives, with their usual referral of the matter to other government departments they considered more appropriate.

I soon discovered that such attempts to inspire public figures had been done before. The Washington study was met with the response from politicians that government support of such a social technology would be "politically unacceptable". After the September 11, 2001, terrorist attack of the USA, John Hagelin, accompanied by biomedical researcher Peter

Salk, and David Edwards, a highly respected professor of political science at the University of Texas, all met with congressional leaders, senior military officials from the Pentagon, and members of the White House staff. The Government representatives' inability to think outside the box quenched any support of the technology proposed by the scientists.

My personal efforts back in Sydney were a total failure in one sense, but gave me a very clear picture of how ingrained the prevailing Cartesian paradigm was. It also demonstrated to me that how we see the world through our fundamental assumptions about how it works will override all scientific evidence that questions those assumptions – no matter how rigorously derived and logically presented that evidence is.

If we can't convince people with scientific observation or test, how can we convince them? It can take more than a century for society to adopt a new paradigm of seeing the world that is based on new developments in science. Noted physicists like Werner Heisenberg,[32] Thomas Kuhn,[33] and Fritjof Capra[34] have all commented on the connection between societal attitudes and scientific discoveries.

We can improve our knowledge of how the world works by reading and going to lectures and undertaking courses, but I firmly believe that we also need to experience new realities so that we don't just know about new paradigms, but 'become' that new paradigm. In other words, that new understood reality must be fully consistent with our sense of being. Maharishi has long emphasised the importance of complementing knowledge with experience to truly reinforce our understanding. "Knowledge", he said, "in its entirety comprises both understanding and experience"[35]. It is only after understanding *and* experiencing that we can 'be'. Our whole sense of self relates to that broader reality. Meditators experience firsthand the powerful effect of group practice of TM and the TM-Sidhi program. Even just meditating with one other person adds considerably to the experience of transcendence. We know at a very practical experiential level that some coherent field effect is working among fellow meditators. It is therefore not a huge leap for us to comprehend that a meditating group might also be radiating a coherent influence beyond the group.

> *"Success awaits man not on the basis of what he does, but on the basis of what he is."*
>
> – Maharishi Mahesh Yogi

In light of this new unified field as consciousness paradigm, a basic understanding of modern physics and cosmology should be a prerequisite for anyone professing expertise in the social sciences. That intellectual understanding alone will be insufficient however. Experience should also complement this understanding. The best way to experience and really know this expanded reality is to better familiarise ourselves with the depths of our own nature. That will most practically be done with regular meditation.

A new approach
Maharishi developed a different tactic. He decided to create $\sqrt{1\%}$ of the world's population in India and through them to gradually bring about positive changes in the world's collective consciousness. The $\sqrt{1\%}$ of the world's current population of 7 billion is 8,367. Maharishi was aware that this population number is growing exponentially and so an initial target of 9,000 yogic flying Vedic pandits has been chosen as a permanent coherence-creating group for the whole world. This number is planned to increase considerably in the future.

India was chosen because several hundred thousand Vedic pandits have already been trained there. Also, India can provide a lower cost of living for a permanent group of this size.

A look at the website www.vedicpandits.org reveals that this amazing project is well underway, with an impressive number of buildings constructed to house 2,000 Vedic pandits, of which 1,500 pandits are already housed. Construction has begun on two more campuses to house an additional 6,000 pandits. The website lists the details of an endowment fund that anyone can support. To create permanent support for a group of 9,000 Vedic pandits, nearly $1 billion is necessary. The interest from such an endowment will be sufficient to maintain this group for all time.

The overall plan includes 100–200 yogic flyers in each of the world's major cities. Like watering the roots of a tree to obtain the benefits for all the branches and leaves, a 9,000 coherence-generating group in India should generate a global upwelling of interest and receptivity for the added satellite groups of flyers throughout the world. Despite the sometimes depressing news of global social and environmental events, this technology of consciousness can be seen as a viable measure to implement and so lift the quality of life for everyone.

At the time of this writing, and in response to the recent terrorist attacks in Paris, Dr John Hagelin submitted a letter addressed to "President Hollande, President Obama, President Putin, the leaders of all nations and the philanthropic peace-loving citizens of the world". It was published in the *International New York Times*.³⁶ Dr Hagelin again directed attention to the endowment fund as a means to support a permanent force of peace-creating professionals for the whole world. In this letter however, Dr Hagelin proposed that 16,000 permanent peace-creating professionals be established and supported by this endowment fund.

NOTES

1. Patanjali, *Yog-Sutra*, 2.35
2. M.C.Dillbeck, G.Landrith III, and D.W. Orme-Johnson, 'The Transcendental Meditation Program and Crime Rate Change in a Sample of Forty-Eight Cities,' *Journal of Crime and Justice* 4, 24-45.
3. "Sidhi" is more often seen transliterated from the Sanskrit as "siddhi".
4. Sutra means an aphorism introduced during transcendental consciousness.
5. In physics the "N-squared" (N^2) effect is the phenomenon of the increased intensity of coherent emitters. A hundred photons are 100 times brighter than a single photon unless they are behaving in complete coherence. In that case, they are 10,000 times as bright (100 squared) – hence the effectiveness of lasers. This coherent wave phenomenon and N^2 effect can also be found in sound waves, water waves, etc. It was believed that by practising the advanced (TM) meditation technique together in one place in synchrony, the meditators would effectively be behaving in coherence with one another and would therefore follow the N-squared law. Experiment later supported this hypothesis. This is like a phase transition of consciousness.
6. The population in the USA in 2013
7. Usually referred to as "Maharishi Vedic science" to distinguish Maharishi's clarifications of Vedic science in light of his knowledge of modern physical science.
8. This reinforcing effect between any meditators in a group is noticed by all those who effectively transcend, but appears to be very pronounced with the TM-Sidhis program.
9. Orme-Johnson et al, International Peace Project in the Middle East, *J. of Conflict Resolution*, Vol. 32 No. 4, December 1988, p 784.
10. J.S. Hagelin, *Modern Science and Vedic Science*, Vol 1, No 1, January, 1987, p 67-68.
11. Maharishi Mahesh Yogi, *Life Supported by Natural Law*, page 161.
12. *Maharishi Mahesh Yogi on the Bhagavad-Gita; A New Translation and Commentary, Chapters 1-6*; Penguin Books, 1969: Ch 6, Vs 6.
13. Maharishi Mahesh Yogi; commentary on the *Bhagavad-Gita*, Ch. 5, p396.
14. Chapters 10 and 11.
15. Benjamin Disraeli (1804–1881) said, "There are three kinds of lies: lies, damned lies, and statistics." Charles H. Grosvenor said, "Figures won't lie, but liars will figure."
16. Bruce Russett, *Journal of Conflict Resolution*, Vol 32 No. 4, December 1988, page773.
17. Robert Duval, *Journal of Conflict Resolution*, Vol 32 No. 4, December 1988, page 813
18. Robert Duval, TM or Not TM? A Comment on "International Peace Project in the Middle East.", *Journal of Conflict Resolution*, Vol 32 No. 4, December 1988, page 814
19. Ken Pease PhD, Professor of Criminology, School of Health and Human Sciences, University of Huddersfield, U.K., Board Member, Home Office National Crime Prevention Board.
20. Blight, J.G. (1986) 'How might psychology contribute to reducing the risk of nuclear war?' *Pol. Psychology* 7 (4): 617-660. Blight, J.G. (1987) 'Toward a policy-relevant psychology of avoiding nuclear war: lessons for psychologists for the Cuban missile crises.' *Amer. Psychologist* 42 (1):12–29.
21. Orme-Johnson et al, 'International Peace Project in the Middle East', *J. of Conflict Resolution*, Vol. 32 No. 4, December 1988, p787.
22. Fales,E., & Markovsky,B., Evaluating heterodox theories. *Social Forces*, 1997, 76, 511-525
23. Ormes-Johnson, D.W., & Oates, R.M., A field-theoretic view of consciousness: Reply to critics. *Journal of Scientific Exploration*, 2009, Vol 23, No.2, 139-166
24. http://en.wikipedia.org/wiki/Empirical_evidence
25. Craig Pearson PhD, *The Complete Book of Yogic Flying*, page 303, Maharishi University of Management Press, Fairfield, Iowa, USA.
26. J.S.Hagelin, M.V.Rainforth, D.W.Orme-Johnson, K.L.Cavanaugh, and C.N. Alexander, S.F. Shatkin, J.L.Davies, A.O.Hughes, and E.Ross, 'The Effects of Group Practice of the Transcendental Meditation Program on Preventing Violent Crime in Washington, D.C.: Results of the National Demonstration Project, June-July, 1993,' *Social Indicators Research* 47(2) (1999), 153-201.

27	Craig Pearson PhD, *The Complete Book of Yogic Flying*, page 374, Maharishi University of Management Press, Fairfield, Iowa, USA.
28	Craig Pearson PhD, *The Complete Book of Yogic Flying*, page 376, Maharishi University of Management Press, Fairfield, Iowa, USA.
29	Craig Pearson PhD, *The Complete Book of Yogic Flying*, page 375, Maharishi University of Management Press, Fairfield, Iowa, USA.
30	J.S.Hagelin et al, 'The Effects of Group Practice of the Transcendental Meditation Program on Preventing Violent Crime in Washington, D.C.: Results of the National Demonstration Project, June–July, 1993,' *Social Indicators Research* 47(2) (1999), 184 (with references).
31	Brown, C.L. 'Overcoming Barriers to Use of Promising Research among Elite Middle East Policy Groups,' *Journal of Social Behaviour and Personality* 17(1) (2003), 489–546.
32	Heisenberg, Werner; *Physics and Philosophy*
33	Kuhn, Thomas; *The Structure of Scientific Revolutions*
34	Capra, Fritjof; *The Turning Point – Science, Society and the Rising Culture*; *Uncommon Wisdom – Conversations with remarkable people.*
35	*Maharishi Mahesh Yogi on the Bhagavad-Gita, A New Translation and Commentary*, Chapters 1-6, Penguin Books, Page 249.
36	Hagelin, John, PhD; *A scientific Solution to Terrorism and Conflict*; International New York Times, December 3, 2015

Chapter Fourteen

LEVITATION AND FLYING

"Life is a miracle...Life is a miracle"

– Maharishi Mahesh Yogi

It is quite possible for human beings to lift from the ground and maintain a state of unassisted levitation – even to the extent of flying – with mere intention. The physics of today says it is possible and the assumption that consciousness has its genesis in a unified field underlying all the laws of nature makes it plausible.

THE PREVIOUS CHAPTER ON THE MAHARISHI EFFECT PRESENTED SOLID empirical evidence that the attainment of transcendental consciousness by a sufficiently sized group has a harmonising influence on a broad population around that group. It was further reasoned that this super-radiance phenomenon demonstrates the field-like nature of consciousness operating at the level of the hypothesised unified field – a field that is currently described by the mathematics of superstring theory. The Maharishi Effect strongly supports the proposal that pure consciousness is this conjectured unified field giving rise to all the laws of nature and the material world we experience.

Human levitation or flying represents a further argument that consciousness is intimately linked with a unified field underlying all the laws of nature. Admittedly, it's an 'argument' rather than evidence, because sustained levitation would have to be demonstrated before a scientific audience before it could be accepted as evidence. For this reason, I could be accused of placing the cart before the horse. While the science of yogic flying might be acceptable and allow us to entertain the possibility that humans can levitate, are there any actual examples of such ability to truly add to our arguments that consciousness is based in a unified field? If so, why haven't we seen it demonstrated in today's world? Or have we?

There have actually been hundreds of historical and contemporary reports of yogic levitation and flying throughout the world.[1] If even one of the hundreds of reported incidences of human levitation is legitimate, then we can accept that human beings are, in principle, capable of levitating. The only way gravity (or the space-time fabric) can be consciously influenced[2] is at the level of the unified field. Space-time is the very first of the classical quantum fields or spin-types that emanate from an underlying superstring field. For this reason, if we can control gravity with sheer intention, then we should be able to control all the other forces of nature. Remember that the closer we approach the unified scale of nature's functioning, the higher are the energies involved. More 'power' is needed to work at more fundamental scales. Because all the other 'gauge' forces like electromagnetism, and the strong and weak nuclear forces arise out of space-time and are – in a relative sense – more "gross" fields, they should in theory be more easily accessed and manipulated.

Miracles

Maharishi's comment that "life is a miracle" – which I heard in a video recording of a lecture he delivered over 20 years ago at the Maharishi International University[3], Iowa, USA – is one of the most profound statements I have come across. Most of us would see human levitation or flying as either a miracle or clever trickery if we ever did witness it. This is because most people see the concept of levitation as defying gravity or defying the laws of nature. Certainly Isaac Newton would have seen it that way, but Albert Einstein may not have. Einstein's General Theory of Relativity, describing gravity as a warping of space-time, also allows for space-time to be bent in the other direction around massive objects, repelling rather than attracting objects[4].

Modern science allows for the concept of 'repulsive gravity'. Indeed, repulsive gravity in the form of 'dark energy' may well be the predominant force in the universe, causing its continuing expansion. It should be stressed here that dark energy is not being presented as a possible explanation for human levitation. Dark energy operates at a cosmological scale and there is much yet to be understood about its nature. Human levitation more likely has its explanation at the level of quantum gravity, where the statistical outcome of all possible geometries of space-time can be influenced.

If consciousness does arise from a unified field, and we can actualise our intentions at this level, then not only is flying possible, but any other so-called 'miracle' is possible too. In fact, when viewed in the light of the unified field model of consciousness, they are no longer 'miracles', but just the operation of natural law by individuals or groups of individuals. It's just the fulfilling of human potential, as Jesus Christ demonstrated and asserted: "I assure you, most solemnly I tell you, if anyone steadfastly believes in Me, he will himself be able to do the things that I do; and he will do even greater things than these, because I go to the Father".[5]

So, yes! It is possible to walk on water or fly through the air. We only refer to them as 'miracles' because we do not understand the science behind what really are natural abilities. Miracles can be performed by each and every one of us when we achieve that state of consciousness that enables us to operate at the level of the proposed unified field.

Maharishi's words imply not only that miracles are possible, but that this Life we all take for granted is truly a miracle. Inspired by his words, I say: "We're all miracles, living within a miracle, wondering if miracles exist".

Life – with all its wondrous diversity, complexity and splendour – is a miracle because it arises from unity and remains interconnected and essentially one. Unity seems such a simple concept – and it should be – but the dependency most of us have on our senses has equipped us so well with the ability to discriminate among this amazing diversity, that unity with all its implications is actually a difficult concept for us to grasp.

"We're all miracles, living within a miracle, wondering if miracles exist".

– Mark N. Spencer, 2015

The physics of yogic flying
IN THE CHAPTERS ON MODERN SCIENCE, I NOTED THAT THE UNIFIED OR superstring field was said to give rise to a complex bubbling cauldron of miniature black holes that disappear as soon as they form. The comparison was to a "frothing sea of 10^{142} black holes per cubic centimetre per second, known as 'space-time foam'".[6]

This is gravity as it behaves at the quantum level of nature and hence is known as 'quantum gravity' or 'quantum geometry'. This level of nature is so miniscule that it is said to belong to the Planck Scale (10^{-33} cm). At this scale, distance starts to lose any relevance because it represents a field of all possible geometries of space. The distance measured between A and B depends on which geometry we lay our ruler on. Since all geometries are simultaneously present and equally valid, it is impossible to assign any distance between two points.

The world we are familiar with has a smooth space-time curve that bends around massive objects in such a way that other objects are attracted to them. This is classical gravity, which causes an apple to fall to the ground. It is also the gravity that is responsible for the seasons and the ocean tides and our very existence on this planet.

Without the benefit of modern scientific knowledge, the 'law of gravity' – that is, attractive gravity – would be seen as an inviolable law of nature. This, however, is not correct, for exactly the same reason that space and time are not absolute qualities.

What we have typically described as classical laws of nature, like attractive gravity, represent nothing more than a statistical likelihood that a particular event will happen. Classical laws are macroscopic laws that are really only approximate laws, or 'rule of thumb' laws. They represent the likely behavioural outcome of many possible microscopic variations of behaviour. At the microscopic level space-time presents as all possible shapes and geometries – including space bent in such a way that objects are repelled from each other rather than attracted.

Dr Hagelin describes dropping about an ounce (28 grams) of water at random into two jars. An ounce of water contains about 10^{24} molecules. We would expect, if the water molecules were dropped truly at random into the two jars, both jars would end up with an equal share of water.[7] As Dr Hagelin says, if we didn't know better, we would assume that the world is governed by the law of "Equal Water in Every Jar".

Now imagine we had a microscopic friend who gave a tiny well-timed nudge to each water molecule, causing every molecule to fall into the one jar. Physicists call such an assistant operating at these microscopic levels as 'Maxwell's Demon'.[8] If such a nudge by Maxwell's Demon was utilised, then all water in one jar would be seen as a miracle, because the law of "Equal Water in Every Jar" was violated.

Hagelin's metaphor was designed to emphasise that the macroscopic expressions of the laws of nature that we have come to see as inviolable are really only statistical probabilities. With nothing different to influence the fundamental level from which these laws arise, these laws will almost never be seen to change.

At the quantum level of gravity, all possible shapes of space-time exist, and therefore all possible behaviours of gravity exist. In the creation of our Universe some 13.8 billion years ago, repulsive gravity became the primary and predominant force causing the ongoing expansion of the universe. Dark energy occupies some 72% of the matter and energy in the known universe, so it is certainly a predominant phenomenon, even if not commonly witnessed at the human sensory level.

Our own subtle influence at the level of the unified field could be Maxwell's Demon. If our consciousness – our awareness – does operate at nature's most fundamental level, we can in principle insert a slight microscopic nudge of intention to affect the outcome of space-time curvature at the level of our gross world. We could cause an outcome where space-time is curved in such a way that we are repelled from the Earth rather than attracted to it. In fact we could cause space-time to curve in a way that we simply elevate or move forward in motion.

Maharishi mentioned that flying was "the most natural state of human physiology". Initially I found this statement a bit hard to swallow, but now I believe he was speaking quite literally. If the predominant expression of space-time curvature is such that gravity is primarily repulsive at the level of the whole universe, then this expansionary quality of the universe (its 'natural' state) should reflect at some level in our own nature – even if the exact mechanisms operating to bring about repulsive gravity differ.

Perhaps repulsive gravity, with the outcome of 'flying' is our natural state too, and of course I refer to intentional and controlled flying where we can enjoy the freedoms attached to both attractive and repulsive gravity. This proposed correlation between the nature of the cosmic body and the human body is yet another example of the universal presence of symmetry – that invariance or commonality of behaviour of natural law at all levels of its expression.[9]

Flying should be possible. But we have to know it is possible. Then we need to have constant and repetitive experience of transcendental being in order to be able to operate at that level. 'Knowing' is not enough by itself.

Rabi'a al-Adawiyya al-Qaysiyya

A REVERED SAINT IN ISLAM, RABI'A (C. 717–801) WAS BORN TO VERY POOR parents within the first hundred years after the Prophet Muhammad's life on Earth. She was the fourth born and her father – himself a holy man – died when she was quite young. Rabi'a's mother was later killed during a raid, at which time Rabi'a and her sisters were taken as slaves. Her life was then one of hardship and servitude until she reached her mid-30s, when she was released as a free person.

Rabi'a dedicated herself entirely to Allah, responding thus to a marriage proposal by friend Hasan al-Basri, "The tie of marriage is for those who have being. But here being has disappeared for I have become as nothing to my self, and I exist only through Allah for I belong wholly to Him, and I live in the shadow of His control. You must ask for my hand from Him, and not from me".[10]

She also said, in reference to Allah, "You are my Joy and my Life to Eternity. You were the Source of my life; from You came my ecstasy. I have separated myself from all created beings, for my hope is for Union with You; for that is the Goal of my searching".

Such was the love and devotion of Rabi'a to Allah that she knew all things were possible through that complete devotion and confidence in Allah. Such devotion and love for God can itself bring about transcendental consciousness, because the knowledge and experience and consequently the person's individual wave of being becomes entirely identified with that Oneness and Wholeness that is the Ocean of Being or Self.

One day Hasan al-Basri saw Rabi'a near a lake, and throwing his prayer rug on top of the water said, "Rabi'a come! Let us pray two ruk'u[11] here". She replied, "Hasan, when you are showing off your spiritual goods in the worldly market, it should be things which your fellow men cannot display". Then she threw her prayer rug into the air and flew up onto it. "Come up here, Hasan, where people can see us," she cried. Acknowledging Hasan's despondency, she said, "Hasan, what you did fishes can do, and what I did flies can do. But the real business is outside these tricks. One must apply oneself to the real business".

This remark by Rabi'a implies that the ability to levitate or even fly – as she demonstrated – should not be seen as a final goal in itself, with the risk of elevating the ego. Rather, emphasis must be directed towards "the real business". The "real business" might very well have been the helping of others gain the same spiritual development in their lives, to strive towards an awareness of their oneness with God.

St Rabi'a radiating coherent waves of consciousness

It is interesting that the goal of yogic flying, as incorporated into the TM-Sidhi program by Maharishi Mahesh Yogi, was not to create a circus act. Its prime inclusion was to accelerate the development of consciousness in the meditators and also to make the radiance effect of group practice of the program much more powerful, so benefiting the whole of society. Perhaps Rabi'a was thinking of this positive radiating influence too.

Earlier, I referred to Deepa Kodikal who currently lives a busy and active life in India, and has been experiencing a rapid evolution of consciousness with concomitant growth in spiritual experiences. The prime goal of spiritual growth is the knowledge and experience of our Union with the All – with God – and any acquisition of extraordinary powers (*Siddhis*) along the way can hinder such growth if the ego becomes enthralled with its newfound "tricks". Deepa had at one stage lamented that she had not even acquired the elementary power of telepathy or intuition as part of her growth in consciousness. She was reminded by God (her own Self) in a thought message that she had been given everything that was worthwhile. "The greatest boon in life is True Knowledge, peace, tranquillity of mind and contentment. You have been bestowed with these. '*Siddhis*' are a hindrance and a harbinger of unhappiness, ego, and temptation…Yogis who acquire powers have to negate them before being shown the higher realities."[12]

Maharishi Mahesh Yogi has also commented on the nature of the *Siddhis* – those abilities that would have traditionally been referred to as superhuman or supernatural. "To handle the whole of cosmic life is within the range of everyone's nature, because it is the same nature." The performance of the *Sidhis (sic)* has given us such a practical philosophy. It is not the power element, but the wisdom element that has greater power. It is the field of pure knowledge, not the ability of action that is more powerful. This is the philosophy that we are giving to the world now. Success awaits man not on the basis of what he does, but on the basis of what he is."[13]

The yogic powers called the *Siddhis*, including levitation and flying, are therefore not something we have to necessarily avoid in our spiritual evolution. Rather, their development should be carefully balanced with our prime goals in life and managed with wisdom and responsibility for our own continued development. That said, the continuing development of flying ability by the practitioners of Maharishi's TM-Sidhi program is vital for the effective radiation of harmony and coherence to broader society. It is therefore an important task for our present world.

The flying friar
THE 17TH CENTURY WAS A RISKY TIME FOR ANYONE DEMONSTRATING supernatural abilities. The Church's attitude was such that anything that might threaten its status quo or appear to entertain demonic forces was dealt with firmly. The Church was not certain whether St Joseph of Cupertino's flying ability was gained from demonic forces or from God. Fortunately, he was trusted to the guardianship of other professional religious in the Catholic Church and escaped harsh judgement.

Joseph was born in 1603 in a small village in the then Kingdom of Naples. As early as the age of eight, he experienced ecstatic visions at school.[14] This abnormal behaviour earned him the derision of fellow students and even his mother and relatives were concerned for his future. He apparently also had a reputation for a hot and irascible temper, which his mother made great efforts to control.

After a difficult and tenuous effort to be accepted as a professional in the Church, Joseph was eventually ordained as a priest in the Franciscan Convent of La Grotella near Cupertino. His continued ecstasies however proved problematic, especially when he would lift into the air saying Mass or when simply hearing church bells, hear any mention of the name of God or of the Blessed Virgin or any event in the life of Christ.

Joseph's levitations were not brief occurrences, as he would often fly to the ceilings of cathedrals or to the tops of trees. "Witnesses to his levitations include three cardinals, his personal physician, the Spanish ambassador to the Papal court and his wife and retinue, and many others. There can be no question about what he did."[15]

"He could not be allowed to say Mass, to take part in processions, or even to share in the meals of the community, for at any moment he was apt to rise into the air and remain suspended for a long time…Nothing would bring him back to them except sometimes a sharp order from his Superior. The accounts of his flights are numerous and amazing…He frequently flew up to holy statues in order to embrace them, and, carrying them off their stands, floated about with them; he sometimes picked up a fellow-friar and carried him around the room."[16]

I do not believe that anyone demonstrating such ability publicly these days would be treated much differently. Flying would still be regarded as against nature and therefore likely seen as an embarrassment to family or any organisation to which the flyer belonged. In the absence of proper understanding of the science behind it, fear could arise.

How extraordinary then is it that Maharishi has described hovering or floating as "the most natural state of human physiology"?

Milarepa

As a young man, Tibetan Saint Milarepa (1052 – c.1135 CE) engaged in some vengeful practices that caused harm to others. As he grew older and wiser, he clearly regretted his earlier behaviour, and pursued a spiritual path. After a 12-year period of meditation under the guidance of a teacher, he achieved an advanced state of consciousness known in Buddhism as *Vajradhara* (complete enlightenment). At the age of 45, he began living in a cave that would forever become known as Milarepa's Cave. He subsisted on nettle tea, which gave his skin a green colour later depicted in many paintings and sculptures of him. Milarepa said he "zealously persevered in my meditations…until, finally, I could fly".[17] He was seen flying high in the air by several people, but decided to avoid fame and soon retired to a Himalayan mountain. He wrote, "If I stayed where I was when it was known that I could fly, people would come flocking to me to see me work miracles, and fame and prosperity would impede any further progress".[18]

Belgium explorer Alexandra David-Néel (1868-1969) mentioned[19] that Milarepa had "crossed in a few days, a distance which, before his training in black magic[20], had taken him more than a month. He ascribes his gift to the clever control of 'internal air'". David-Néel apparently witnessed a monk doing just that while she was in the area Milarepa lived. "He seemed to lift himself from the ground. His steps had the regularity of a pendulum… the traveller seemed to be in a trance." This particular skill, known as Lung-gom-pa ("wind meditation") in Tibet – and also known as running levitation – is said to allow a practitioner to run at an extraordinary speed for days without stopping.

Jesus walks on water

The *Bible* relates the episode when Jesus walked on water towards his disciples, while they were in a boat many hundreds of metres from shore, crossing to the other side of the Sea of Galilee. Peter, seeing this remarkable feat, said to Jesus, "Lord, if it is You, command me to come to You on the water". And when Jesus told Peter to come, Peter too successfully walked on the top of the water towards Jesus. But when Peter let his awareness become distracted with the strong wind and his precarious situation, he began to sink. Jesus reached out to hold him, saying, "O you of little faith – why did you doubt?"[21]

This well-known demonstration by Jesus of a super-human feat can be explained through His conscious control of the gravitational force and also most likely, the electromagnetic force.

Dennett reports a number of other historical instances of people walking on water[22]. In one account shared by Baird Spaulding, an expedition of 11 men were undertaking "metaphysical research" in India in December of 1894. After some prior investigation, they had come across a group of yogis who appeared to exhibit numerous "supernatural" powers, including communication with animals and seemingly appearing out of nowhere. Spaulding and his group were invited by the yogis to travel with them to the Himalaya. When they reached the foothills of the Himalaya, they came upon a large river "about two thousand feet wide, running bank full, and the current was at least ten miles per hour". One of the yogis – by the name of Jast – told Spaulding that they planned to cross the river where they were, rather than seek a bridge. Jast and his eleven fellow yogis then simply stepped onto the water – fully dressed – and walked calmly to the other side, "not sinking below the soles of their sandals". The western researchers crossed the river later by more conventional means and caught up with the yogis.

Jast said to Spaulding, "Do you think that the men you saw walk across the stream yesterday to save themselves the inconvenience of this trip are in any way special creations any more than you are? No. They are not created in any way different from you. They do not have one atom more power than you were created with. They have, by the right use of their thought forces, developed their God-given power. The thing you have seen accomplished while you have been with us, you, yourselves, can accomplish just as fully and freely. The things you have seen are accomplished in accord with definite law and every human being can use the law if he will."[23]

This very relevant comment by Jast reinforces what Jesus had told the disciples, that "[you too] can do the things I do", and it also reinforces the fact that miracles such as walking on water, are none other than the implementation of natural law.

Shamans past and present
SHAMANS ARE THOSE WHO HAVE PRACTISED VARIOUS METHODS OF TRANscendence in consciousness to access the spirit world and become a medium between the spirit world and our material one. It is a very ancient practice, as it has been reported throughout recorded history. The most ancient extant culture is that of Australian Aboriginals, who occupied the great southern island continent at least 40,000 years ago. "The *medicine-men* were

everywhere credited with the power of flying through the air – perhaps 'being conveyed' would be a better term."[24] They practise two forms of flying, according to R.M. Berndt[25]. One is flying "bird-like through the air." The other is running through the air, a couple of feet above the ground, a practice said to be "in common use" in various tribes. One Aboriginal told Berndt, "You can see his feet moving above that ground, but he travels faster than anyone can run – he never gets tired or out of breath". This running levitation appears to be a similar technique to that just described for Milarepa and also developed by the Kaihōgyō monks and Shugendō practitioners, both of the Buddhist following in early Japan.

Other accounts of running levitation have also been recorded through the centuries. Christina "the Astonishing" (Admirable) (1150–1220) was a Flemish nun who demonstrated this talent. "She was so light in running, that she outran the swiftest dogs", wrote author Augustin Calmet.[26]

Another authority on Aboriginal culture, A.P. Elkin, also comments: "Medicine-men are believed to be able to travel at a very fast pace…[They] run at a surprising pace for any distance, faster than anyone can run, and without getting tired or out of breath. They apparently run less than a metre above the ground. Indeed, it has been said that the air has been made soft and solid, and that it moves along, carrying them with it. The explanation given by other Aborigines is that "these clever men can make their spirits take them along very quickly".[27]

Accounts also prevail of Native Americans also being able to run through the air. A French missionary, Father Papetard, working among the Native Americans in Oregon in the late 1800s, reported to a French medical doctor that he "had seen, more than once, wizards lifted two or three feet above the earth and walking on the top of the tufts of grass".[28] This was alleged to have been witnessed by other missionaries in the area.

Most of the more contemporary accounts of shamanistic practice and associated extraordinary ability come from Africa and also Haiti. One so-called "sorcerer" – Nana Owaka – from Toga in Africa, demonstrated his ability to levitate for a German documentary film crew in the mid-1970s[29]. The film crew were adamant that no deception was involved, and Owaka was initially reluctant to be filmed. A quick perusal on YouTube of a trailer for the documentary, called *Journey into the Beyond* has me hesitant about recommending this film for viewing. I certainly cannot attest to the credibility of most of the stories in the documentary (ghosts and psychic surgery etc), but Owaka's levitation at the very end of the documentary appears to be authentic.

Contemporary accounts
THE INDIAN GURU PARAMAHANSA YOGANANDA, WAS THE AUTHOR OF THE popular book *Autobiography of a Yogi* (published in 1946 and still a "must-read"). He reported several incidences of yogic flying in his fascinating life account.

Paramahansa was encouraged by both his own guru, Swami Sri Yukteswar and later by the Christ-like Indian saint Mahavatar Babaji, to bring the wisdom of yogic science from the east to the west, which he did – to North America from 1920 to 1952. Babaji had earlier told Sri Yukteswar: "India has much to learn from the West in material development; in return, India can teach the universal methods by which the West will be able to base its religious beliefs on the unshakable foundations of yogic science".[30]

In my opinion, Paramahansa Yogananda and Maharishi Mahesh Yogi have been the two notable heavyweights in their honourable and successful conversion of the sceptical west to the secular wisdom of Vedic (or yogic) science in the past 90 years. Both taught the concept of unity underlying all of diversity and also the concept of a universal consciousness. They delivered this important message in their own way with the appropriate pitch for their time. Paramahansa's pitch was more at the feeling and devotional level, but he also used reasoning and science. Maharishi's pitch, during the second half of the last century to this time, has more been at the scientific level (with the benefit of considerable progress in science), but he certainly did not exclude the feeling and devotional aspects in what he taught.

It is because of the sincerity, eloquence and intelligence that accompanies Paramahansa's writings, that I am inclined to accept the authenticity of his reports of flying or levitation.

Yogananda spoke of one yogi who lived close to him in his younger years[31] – Bhaduri Mahasaya – who could sustain a levitated state. His ability was excitedly reported to Yogananda by a friend who observed the yogi "remain in the air, several feet above the ground, last night at a group meeting". Yogananda knew the yogi and had himself observed the impressive demonstration of various Pranyamas[32] by the yogi, after which "he remained motionless in a high state of super-consciousness. The aura of peace after the storm was vivid beyond forgetting," Paramhansa wrote. This aura of peace undoubtedly reflected a high level of brain-wave coherence, which we now know is particularly demonstrable in yogic flying and is also associated with a positive radiating influence to those around the meditator.

Bhadura Mahasaya was also a very private man, loath to be on show to the curious public. "My rule of seclusion is not for my own comfort, but for that of others. Worldly people do not like the candor which shatters their delusions," he said. "Saints are not only rare but disconcerting. Even in scripture, they are often found embarrassing!"

Paramahansa wrote of other examples of levitation and other *Siddhis* demonstrated by those he met through his life. In reading his book *Autobiography of a Yogi*, I could not help but reflect on the dramatic contrast between the world in which he grew up and mine. I've lived a happy and full life, but the materialistic emphasis attached to the value systems of my society is far removed from the very spiritual emphasis of Yogananda's upbringing and his local community. I have a feeling though, that this imbalance will correct itself. Maybe we're already in the process!

AKASHAGIRI (OR MASAHARU NARUSE) IS A JAPANESE YOGI CURRENTLY sharing his time between teaching in Tokyo and an ashram at the root of the Ganges River in the Himalayan Mountains. He is acknowledged as one of the highest practitioners of Kundalini yoga and is also a master in the art of levitation. Apparently he had his mind set on reaching Nirvana[33] as early as the age of 12, at which time he began the practice of yoga. Since the 1970s he visited numerous masters of yoga throughout India, and although he learned some things from these masters, most of the skills he has developed (levitation, pranayama for suspending the heartbeat, etc.) has been gained through self-learning. He has never written anything unless he experienced it himself. In 2001 he joined Maha Kumbha Mela[34] in Allahabad. In the same year, he had been conferred the title of Yogi Raj ("the King of Yoga") from the All India Tantric Society. Like most yogis with abilities in the *Siddhis*, he remains shy of the public. There are a few photos of him in levitation[35] (fig 1), but – as we all know – photographs or video these days are far from proof of anything. There is also a video clip of him speaking about yoga and death that can be viewed on YouTube. He has written a book titled *Levitation by method of Yoga*, that is apparently an enjoyable read even for those who are quite content to keep their feet firmly on the ground.

When asked about the secret of his levitation technique Akashagiri said: "It is to use instantaneously prana or vital energy permeating the universe. Place one's conscious on the destination point for floating. Accordingly as the amount of consciousness increases, existential reversal takes place and the physical self becomes evacuated. Then, the physical body gets attracted toward the consciousness which has been already shifted to the destination. One can thus levitate".

A perusal of YouTube clips on the subject of human levitation confirms that the vast majority of 'levitators' are professional magicians or pranksters. One YouTube documentary that caught my attention, however, was a demonstration of levitation by a Buddhist monk in Nepal after a brief interview by magician Dan White[36]. I'm inclined to think the monk's levitation is authentic.

I HAD MY OWN SPECIAL EXPERIENCE AROUND 1986–87. BACK THEN, I LIVED alone in a townhouse very near Manly on the north side of Sydney Harbour. Every morning and evening, before and after my work as a dentist in Sydney's central business district, I would visit the TM Centre (then located in Manly) to practise the TM-Sidhi program with other meditators. As I have already discussed, the experience of transcendence is for many of us more profound when meditating in a group and the group practice of the technique has a beneficial radiance effect to the surrounding community.

This particular time, I was by myself for an early morning session of meditation. I completed the yogic flying part of the program, which involved then – as it does now – the hopping stage of flying. After flying, we routinely lie down to rest. It was while I was resting, with my eyes closed, that I experienced something wonderful and profound. I felt a tingling sensation throughout my whole body. It's hard for me now to describe the exact nature of this sensation, as I can't compare it to anything I've experienced before or since. All of a sudden – and I still had my eyes closed during all of this – I felt my whole body go very light and then I could not feel the mattress at all. I was still experiencing this strange and very pleasant tingling sensation. I felt like I was floating and lifting slightly, maybe only a couple of inches off the mattress, but I was so absorbed with the extraordinary internal sensations, that I never opened my eyes to confirm whether I had levitated or not.

This was a unique experience for me not since repeated. The floating experience lasted perhaps no more than 10 seconds. There was no-one else in the room to confirm if I had levitated, but even if there were companions with me, they would probably have had their eyes closed too, and not seen it. This first-hand experience – coupled with the science underlying human levitation and the ample historical reportage – supports my absolute belief in our ability to levitate.

It seems that the period of my life I have just referred to – my early 30s – was a period of rapid growth in consciousness for me. I learned the TM-Sidhi program in 1985, aged 31, and it had an initial beneficial impact on my spiritual and practical life. Since those few dynamic years after learning the technique, life has settled back into a steady and less dramatic pace, but I know I am still making progress. I consider the opportunity I have to write this book is a particularly special gift from God – a 'calling' if you wish – for which I am ever grateful.

Akashagiri in sustained levitation. Naruse says: "The timing of this photo was just when I sat on 'a very thin air film (layer)' and my waist just started sinking onto it. You may feel how comfortable I am on this air film. This photo left nothing to be desired in regards to levitation. I am sure that it is going to be the last photo of my levitation." Date of photo: April 26, 1990. (www.naruse-yoga.com). Photo courtesy of Naruse Yoga Group, Tokyo.

Levitation categories
BASED ON THE CASES WE HAVE EXPLORED AND USING DENNETT'S CLASSIFIcations as a guide, we can categorise levitation or flying as such:
1. Ecstatic (or rapturous) levitation – as evidenced by hundreds of well-documented reports in the Catholic tradition but also by other faiths. In these cases, there was no apparent technique learned for levitation, but rather the ability came about spontaneously through an experience of divine union with God. Levitation during such rapturous states appears to be most often unplanned and uncontrollable. The

official explanation traditionally given in Europe has been that God was responsible for the manifestations.

2. Yogic (or meditative) levitation – as experienced by yogis, ascetics and shamans. Levitation as it is seen mostly in today's world or reported in current times mostly from the East appears to be a "fostered talent, intentionally cultivated, controlled, and developed through specific techniques involving breath-control, meditation, fasting, chastity, mantras or other methods".[37] Rather than God being ascribed to as the sole source of this power, it is generally seen as an inherent ability to all individuals, internally generated by the development of the individual's consciousness.

3. Spontaneous levitation – as demonstrated by young children who have had no prior obvious indoctrination with religious concepts and who have had no education in levitation or meditative techniques. Preston Dennett relates several accounts of flying ability as told by adults when they were children, typically younger than 10.[38] A few of these accounts involved flying up or down staircases without their feet touching the stairs. These examples of innocent, spontaneous levitation further support the idea that levitation is an innate, natural ability belonging to all of us, but largely untapped for cultural or religious reasons.

4. Running levitation – as demonstrated by Milarepa, the shamans of earlier Australian and North American indigenous populations, some children in more spontaneous demonstrations of this ability[39], and some Christian saints[40].

5. Mediumistic levitation – as allegedly demonstrated by psychic mediums, but this category also includes those cases of alleged possession by exterior forces or spirits. I am open-minded about 'possession' and 'communicating with spirits' etc, but it is not a subject that holds my attention or interest. One medium of note, however, was Daniel Douglas Home[41] (1833–1886), who could levitate and move around in the air at will. He was apparently subjected to careful observation by respected scientists of the time.

ALL THE ABOVE CATEGORIES[42] – I BELIEVE – HAVE A COMMON explanation that lies with the ability of humans to operate consciously (or unconsciously) at the level of the proposed unified field of all the laws of nature. At this level of 'all possibilities' of space-time, humans can tweak the expression of space-time geometry in favour of a repulsive – rather than attractive – gravitational result. Ecstatic levitation, resulting from devotional commitment, is ultimately the same as yogic levitation. Whether one attains God Consciousness – a state of unity of one's sense of being with God – through devotional love, or through constant experience of transcendental consciousness via meditation or other means, the result is the same. Experience of this unified field is the experience of unity and therefore the experience of the unmanifest nature of God. Regarding the more innocent demonstration of levitation by children, they too have actualised that innate ability that appears to be present in all of us, and for some reason or other, they have no apparent obstacles in working at the level of the unified field of their own consciousness, the same unified field at the base of all our consciousness.

Given the hundreds of historical reports of humans flying, levitating or running above the ground – reports that have come from many different cultures, religions and eras – I think it is unlikely that all accounts are mere figments of the imagination, or stories created to uphold some belief system. I have no doubt that there are at least a few people – and possibly tens or even hundreds – living in the world today who can levitate in a sustained manner or fly at will to a destination. It is understandable that they would wish to keep such ability private.

A demonstration of sustained yogic levitation would provide further convincing evidence that consciousness is intimately connected with a unified field underlying and giving rise to the material world so familiar to our senses. This knowledge alone in a sceptical world would go a long way to improving all aspects of life for people on this Earth, for it provides the ultimate paradigm for the self-development and self-actualisation interest we see today and for which motivational speakers are so well paid. Regardless of the level so far attained in the performance of this particular *Siddhi*, the special coherence in brainwave activity accompanying yogic flying – demonstrable even in our early 'hopping' stage of flying – is in itself an important reflection of the radiating coherence observed with the Maharishi Effect. This makes yogic flying a legitimate goal for all of us.

Different stages of flying
THE GREAT INDIAN SAGE MAHARISHI PATANJALI[43] WAS RESPONSIBLE FOR the ancient Vedic literature referred to as the *Yoga Sutras of Patanjali*. The sutras used by the practitioners of the TM-Sidhi program, including the flying sutra, have their source in Patanjali's *Yoga Sutras*.

Patanajali described three stages or developments in the ability to hover or fly:

Stage 1: The hopping stage
This is the initial L-plate[44] stage in the development of flying ability. Ostensibly, it is no different to an athlete or normal healthy person hopping about while cross-legged, using leg and lower torso muscles for propulsion, but meditators – operating from the level of transcendental consciousness – make their lifts with far less effort and expenditure of energy. They also have a distinct and rather unusual measurement of coherence in EEG recordings of brainwave activity.

Even though this hopping stage of flying (performed typically on foam-rubber mattresses) is perhaps a bit of a let down to a non-meditating observer, the associated marked coherence of brainwave activity – already seen to a large extent in transcendental consciousness – becomes particularly accentuated at the instance of lift-off. So, while it might not look like it, something very special is going on. The experience for the flyers is typically blissful. Furthermore, this brain-wave coherence within the brains of each of the flyers is in itself a reflection of the enhanced positive radiating influence the yogic flyers have on society around them. This is why the inclusion of yogic flying is so important for the social effectiveness of the large groups practising the TM-Sidhi program.

Stage 2: Hovering
This is the stage of sustained levitation, where – clearly – repulsive gravity is employed to allow the individual to hover or float above the ground. It is quite likely that there are some people in the world today who have reached this stage. Practitioners of Maharishi's TM-Sidhi program might be close. Some of the TM-Sidhi yogic flyers have been seen to take longer than one would normally expect to land during their hops.

Would this stage of yogic flying be associated with an even more enhanced expression of brain-wave coherence? We don't know as yet. My guess is that this stage of sustained hovering probably is associated with a more accentuated expression of coherence in the brain. Of course, we would then expect this development of flying ability to further enhance the effectiveness of the Maharishi Effect.

Stage 3: Flying
This ability is clearly rare in today's world, although I suspect a few living today may have reached this level. The Islamic Saint Rabi'a al-Adawiyya al-Qaysiyya had evidently reached this stage and so too had the Christian Saint Joseph of Cupertino and the Buddhist Saint Milarepa. This is the stage where the body flies through the air at will and it is obviously

an ideal form of transport! Some amongst Australia's and America's early native population also are reported to have achieved this level of flying.

THERE JUST MIGHT BE AS MANY HUMANS LEVITATING NOW AS THERE EVER was, although I suspect there might have been periods of human history when it was more common. Earlier in this book I made an attempt to explain why the rishis of thousands of years ago seem to have enjoyed deeper insights into nature's elementary functioning than humans do these days. I mentioned that earlier periods of human history had less emphasis on technological development with fewer distractions that invariably come with technology. More emphasis was also placed on spiritual development rather than material progress in different parts of the world and at different times of human history. Also, with the explosion in human population, much of it sadly struggling with poverty, exploitation and war, there is a collective global and national stress that might adversely influence individual attempts to reach higher levels of consciousness. You see – we're all interconnected!

Despite all the above, there are today examples of great progress in spiritual growth and the concomitant physical powers that can develop with that growth in consciousness. Flying is still possible for each and every one of us. The social phenomenon known as the Maharishi Effect seems to me to be the best answer for a more coherent, friendlier and peaceful world. The prime mechanism of that Maharishi Effect appears to be the yogic flying performed during transcendental consciousness by practitioners of Maharishi's TM-Sidhi program, as maximum measured changes in societal coherence tend to occur at the time large groups practise yogic flying.

It is quite apparent to me now – having practised the TM-Sidhi technique of meditation for nearly 30 years – that achieving a state of levitation (stage two) is probably going to take some time, even allowing for my one-time only experience of hovering back in the mid-1980s. It may or may not happen again in my lifetime, but that does not really concern me. All that really matters to me personally is that I grow in inner happiness, contentment and universal unconditional love.

With the huge gatherings of Maharishi Vedic pandits in India at this present time as part of Maharishi's efforts to gather the $\sqrt{1\%}$ of the world's population for yogic flying, we can hope for an improvement in the present condition of humanity worldwide. This would result from a reduction in collective stress and an associated acceleration of growth in consciousness everywhere. Gradually, it is then hoped that the yogic flyers will achieve stage two and stage three in their evolution of flying ability. It all becomes a positively reinforcing cycle with the result – a better world in which to live.

When that time comes, when the TM-Sidhi practitioners achieve sustained levitation, I doubt the phenomenon will be hidden from public view. With science to back the phenomenon, and the sheer numbers to demonstrate it, only good can come from providing this most dramatic evidence that our consciousness – our very notion of self – is rooted in the proposed unified field of all the laws of nature. Such reinforced knowledge can only help the world.

With regard to those humans with already developed *Siddhis*, such as levitation or flying, it would be natural that they do not wish to upset the "delusions" of the majority and the predominant materialistic, sense-dependant world view. It would not be surprising for these remarkably accomplished individuals to remain private, sharing their knowledge and wisdom only with those who seek them out.

The ability to levitate or fly would be a personal landmark in one's evolution of consciousness, but should not be seen as a final goal in itself. It is possible that the development of such a physical ability could distract the ego and interfere with the ultimate goal of growth in consciousness – the full realisation of one's unity with the rest of humanity, the Universe and God. On the other hand, with careful guidance in knowledge and wisdom, the development of *Siddhis* can be a nice way to assist our fulfilment and enjoyment of life. In the case of flying or levitating, we now know that the group practice of such ability has a powerful beneficial effect that radiates to all of society.

NOTES

1. Preston Dennett summarises and provides references to hundreds of reported cases of levitation and flying in his book *Human Levitation – A True History and How-To Guide*, Schiffer Publishing Ltd, USA.
2. Conscious influence of the laws of nature is predicated on the principle that quantum objects are sensitive to measurement or attention.
3. Now known as the Maharishi University of Management (MUM).
4. Indeed Einstein's famous equation of General Relativity (describing gravity), included the so-called "gravitational constant" (Λ) to counter the expansion of the universe his original equation predicted. He was convinced the universe was static, neither expanding nor contracting. This gravitational constant (Λ) is the dark energy causing the universe to expand.

$$G_{\mu\nu} = (8\pi G/c^4)\, T_{\mu\nu} + g_{\mu\nu}\, \Lambda$$

5. John, 14:12, *The Amplified Bible*, Zondervan Publishing House, Michigan.
6. John Hagelin, PhD; *Foundations of Physics and Consciousness* (course), Maharishi University of Management, Iowa, USA.
7. With a small expected error of about the square root ($\sqrt{\ }$) of 10^{24}, being 10^{12}, which would be barely perceptible.
8. In respect to James Maxwell's efforts in the late 19th century to stress that the Second Law of Thermodynamics (affecting the behaviour of gases) was indeed a statistical law and not an absolute law of physics.
9. In the Chapter One, we saw how the ocean was our source in an evolutionary sense, but that I proposed we had an attraction to the sea for other reasons that reflected similar qualities deep within our own nature. Now we can see that the unified field (Ātmā) can be also seen as our source, and since its qualities reflect those of the ocean, this can be seen as another form of symmetry in nature.
10. www.sufimaster.org
11. "Ruk'u" – to humble oneself.
12. Deepa Kodikal, *A Journey within the Self – A Saga of Spiritual Experiences*, Viva Books, Ch 48, page 191.
13. Maharishi Mahesh Yogi, *Achievements: 1977, Third Year of the Age of Enlightenment* (Seelisberg, Switzerland: MERU Press, 1977), 25.
14. http://www.newadvent.org/cathen/08520b.htm
15. Craig Pearson, PhD, *The Complete Book of Yogic Flying*, Appendix 2, "Floating and Flying Through History", page 547.
16. V. Sackville-West, *The Eagle and the Dove: A Study in Contrasts – St. Teresa of Avila, St. Therese of Lisieux* (London: Michael Joseph, 1969), 186-187
17. Craig Pearson, *The Complete Book of Yogic Flying*, p 548
18. Milarepa, 122–123; Charles & Jordan, 59-60; sub-referenced from Preston Dennett, *Human Levitation – A True History and How-To Guide*, Schiffer Publishing Ltd.
19. *Magic and Mystery in Tibet*, Alexandra David-Néel.
20. "Black Magic" is likely to have been a term used by those ignorant of the true nature of the spiritual practices and discipline that enabled extraordinary powers.
21. Matthew 14: 31; New Testament, *The Amplified Bible*, Zondervan Publishing House, Grand Rapids, Michigan
22. Preston Dennett, *Human Levitation – A True History and How-To Guide*, Schiffer Publishing Ltd., USA, Ch. 23.
23. Spaulding, Baird T. *Life and Teaching of the Masters of the Far East*: Volume 1, 1924, 52-55, Marina Del Rey: CA: DeVorss Publications. Referenced by Preston Dennett, *Human Levitation – A True History and How-To Guide*, Schiffer Publishing Ltd., USA.
24. A.W Howitt, *Native Tribes of South-East Australia*, (London, Macmillan, 1904), p 388.

25 R.M.Berndt, *Wuradjeri Magic and 'Clever Men'*, Oceania 17 (Sydney: Australian National Research Council, 1946-1947), 355-358.
26 Referenced by Preston Dennett, *Human Levitation – A True History and How-To Guide*, Schiffer Publishing Ltd., USA.
27 A.P.Elkin, *Aboriginal Men of High Degree*, (New York: St. Martin's Press, 1945, 1977), 55. Reference by Craig Pearson, *The Complete Book of Yogic Flying*, 550.
28 Leroy, 10-11, quoting Dr.Antoine Imbert-Gourbeyre, *Les stigmatisées* (Paris, Palmé: 1873), Vol. 2, 246 Reference by Craig Pearson, *The Complete Book of Yogic Flying*, 551.
29 Preston Dennett, *Human Levitation – A True History and How-To Guide*, p87
30 Paramahansa Yogananda, *Autobiography of a Yogi*, Ch 36.
31 Paramahansa Yogananda, *Autobiography of a Yogi*, Ch. 7, 'The Levitating Saint'
32 *Prāṇāyāma* refers practically to various breathing exercises practiced in yoga. It is a Sanskrit word meaning "extension of the *prāṇa* or breath" or, "extension of the life force". The word is composed of two Sanskrit words, *Prana* (life force or vital energy, particularly the breath), and ayāma (to extend or draw out).
33 Nirvana – spiritual enlightenment; the disappearance of suffering, desire and the sense of small self.
34 A mass Hindu pilgrimage held every third year at one of four places in India by rotation: Haridwar, Allahabad (Prayaga), Nashik and Ujjain. It is considered the largest peaceful gathering in the world with over 100 million people visiting during the Maha Kumbh Mela in 2013.
35 http://wondersofyog.blogspot.com.au/2010/09/yogiraj-akashagiri-levitating-saint.html
36 A replay of one episode of a TV documentary series called *Supernatural*.
37 Preston Dennett, *Human Levitation – A True History and How-To Guide*, 11-12, Schiffer Publishing Ltd.
38 Preston Dennett, *Human Levitation – A True History and How-To Guide*, Ch 29.
39 Preston Dennett, *Human Levitation*, Ch 29.
40 For example the Franciscan nun Saint Marie-Francoise des Cing Plaies (1715-1791), as referenced by Preston Dennett, *Human Levitation*, p 91.
41 Preston Dennett, *Human Levitation*, Ch 14.
42 Preston Dennett lists other categories in his book, like "mediumistic" levitation – usually attributed to outside spiritual forces or entities.
43 Author of the *Yoga Sutras of Patanjali* and thought to be born around the second or third century CE (Common Era, or Anno Domini – AD). Sutras are aphorisms used while in transcendental consciousness.
44 In Australia, learning drivers must exhibit a large "L" (a "Learner's plate") on the car they are driving under supervision.

PARANORMAL EXPERIENCES IN EXTREME ENVIRONMENTS

"Perhaps the time has come for the next generation of explorers to shift their focus from the physical poles of the past towards spiritual goals."

– Sir Walter Herbert – 2001

Explorers and adventurers in extreme environments feel 'alive' to an extent not often felt in routine life. The qualities of life are identical to the qualities of pure or transcendental consciousness. This state of transcendental consciousness allows for experiences that may be referred to as 'psychic' or 'paranormal', such as precognition, mental telepathy and episodes of unity consciousness.

A GRUESOME SCENE WAS THRUST – UNINVITED – ONTO THE SCREEN OF MY awareness. A dramatic mental picture of three of us lying dead on the road after a horrible car accident arose from somewhere deep in the recesses of my mind. Like a rude child demanding my attention while I was busily engaged in tasks, this picture just wouldn't let me go.

In the late 1980s I was making regular five-hour car trips north from Sydney to document a shipwreck called the *S.S. Catterthun*, lying in just less than 60m of water[1]. In those days, we were breathing compressed air for dives as deep as 70m, and in doing so, were at times pushing the envelope of what was considered safe. This was one of those challenging diving projects from which we all emerged intact, although not without a few mishaps.

During the five or six years documenting the wreck, the biggest threat to our lives was not really the diving, but the driving. Invariably, we would leave after work on a Friday evening, and arrive at our destination in Seal Rocks at close to midnight. On this particular Sunday afternoon, having completed a successful weekend of diving on the wreck, we had just packed our gear into the car and boat when I had this disturbing vision while stepping into my friend's 4WD, ready to commence our long drive back to Sydney. I was travelling with two friends – Neil (driving) and Michael – and the boat we were towing was heavily laden with scuba tanks, cameras and other dive equipment.

I castigated myself for thinking in such a 'negative' manner but, as much as I tried to dismiss the unwelcome mental picture, a very real heaviness and bleakness hung over me. This was clearly more than a random thought. The vision affected me at some deep level and that foreboding feeling wouldn't budge. But, fearing ridicule, I didn't mention the disturbing vision to my friends.

Seal Rocks on the NSW coast. We launched our boat from this beach when diving on the wreck of the Catterthun, which lies 5km offshore in a line from this point of view through the middle of the gap between the rocky island outcrop and the vegetated headland.

More than an hour of travel had passed. I was sitting in the front passenger seat and Michael sat in the back. We were driving some 80km/hour (50 miles/hour) along a straight road when I saw a car stationed at an intersection on the left[2]. There was nothing obstructing his or our view of each other and we naturally presumed the driver would give us the right of way along our stretch of road before making his right turn. Much to our surprise, the car shot out in front of us just as we were almost at the intersection. We were fractions of a second away from colliding heavily into this car. Neil had no choice but to turn our vehicle hard left into this driver's road to avoid collision. We ended up on the far side of the cross-street with our car, boat and us unscathed.

We collected ourselves, exchanged a few words and then the heavy impending feeling I was carrying the whole way just evaporated!

WHAT WENT ON HERE? IT COULD BE ARGUED THAT MY PREMONITION didn't come true. We did survive after-all. Therefore, it wasn't a realised premonition. I can't profess to have a clear explanation of my experience. Neale Donald Walsch outlines a few possibilities in his *Conversations with God* books, anyone of which might apply in my case. The scenario I tend to favour is that my future self was returning to warn my current self of the impending danger. That "rude child" demanding my attention might have been none other than myself an hour or so 'older'. As we're all connected, I cannot dismiss the distinct possibility that my friends were also 'warned' at some level and thus alert to the impending danger.

This premonition was too real an experience to dismiss as mere coincidence or an overly active imagination. It illustrates to me that consciousness is intimately linked with a level of existence that transcends space and time. That realm contains all possibilities, including everything that has happened in the past and all possibilities in the future. Everything that has happened and will or (I suspect) might happen in the future is all in that realm now! Somehow, my awareness accessed this realm and gained a warning of what was imminent. Somehow too, without verbal communication with my friends, this traumatic interruption to our present lives was averted. As I mentioned, they too might have perceived the warning at some level.

Such an explanation is feasible within the unified field model of consciousness. This experience was time transcendence, and the only level of reality where time does not exist is the unified field, the existence of which is supported by modern superstring theory. Time and space (intimately linked) are relative concepts, as Einstein proved 100 years ago.

Einstein was not afraid to apply his exceptional insights of nature's functioning to everyday life. In a condolence letter to the family of his lifelong friend and fellow scientific confidant Michele Besso, after learning of Besso's death in March, 1955, Einstein remarked, "Now he has departed from this strange world a little ahead of me. That means nothing. People like us, who believe in physics, know that the distinction between past, present and future is only a stubbornly persistent illusion".[3]

PRECOGNITIONS, PREMONITIONS, CLAIRVOYANCE AND ASTROLOGICAL predictions make no rational sense, and hence are impatiently dismissed by sensible, practical people. That's strange, because accomplished, successful businessmen often admit to relying heavily on 'intuition', and precognition is really just a form of intuition. The word 'intuition' comes from the Latin *intueri* ("to look within") and the *Oxford English Dictionary* defines it as "immediate apprehension of the mind without reasoning". If, as Einstein was alluding, the past, present and future are all part of the ever-present 'now', and if our consciousness is intimately linked with a unified field, then it would seem plausible that we could intuit the future.

It's perhaps not surprising that many examples of precognition or premonition we hear about come from extreme adventurers or those who venture into extreme environments. In potentially life-threatening situations, a good intuitive ability could even be life-saving. Also, the very sense of "aliveness" often felt by those outside their comfort zone puts them in touch with the essence of life we have spoken about earlier – freedom, unboundedness, timelessness and connectedness.

In many cases, feelings of unease or even clear premonitions are not heeded or acted upon. In my research on the history of the *Catterthun*, I read that a young girl was weeping bitterly at the departure wharf in Sydney in 1895. She was convinced her aunt – a Mrs Mathias – would perish during the sea voyage ahead. "Auntie, Auntie, don't go. You'll be drowned and I'll never see you any-more!" she was heard wailing. Within hours, the young girl's presentiment came true. Her aunt drowned, along with 54 others, in one of the worst shipping disasters in Australian waters.

Medical doctor Jim Duff and fellow mountain climber Nick Estcourt were part of a British expedition to climb K2, the world's second highest mountain and considered by many to be the world's most challenging. Meeting at Heathrow Airport in 1978[4] at the commencement of their trip, Duff recalled: "Nick was as pale as a ghost. He looked really gripped. I asked him if he was okay and he said, 'Jim, I've got this terrible feeling that I won't be coming back from this trip'".

Estcourt and Duff shared a tent at K2 Base Camp. In the morning, Estcourt recounted a strange dream he had had during the night. He had been buried in an avalanche under deep snow, but found himself looking down on the scene from above watching their companion Doug Scott poking among the ice looking for him.

A couple of weeks later, Estcourt, Scott and a Hunza porter, Quamajan, had left Base Camp to begin ferrying loads to Camp 2, in support of the lead climbers. During what was perfect weather, Dr Duff was relaxing in the sunshine when he heard the booming noise of a huge avalanche. Duff saw that it was heading towards Camp 2. He also knew – forewarned by Estcourt and perhaps aided with his own intuition – that Estcourt was trapped in the avalanche. He "just knew".

Apparently, Estcourt had insisted on trading places with Quamajan during a rest period on their ascent. Scott was in the lead, with Estcourt now second and halfway across a trail, and Quamajan following in the rear. A dangerous and massive wind-slab avalanche overwhelmed Estcourt and tore the rope connection between him and the others. Scott cartwheeled backwards and landed hard on the slope. Quamajan also survived, suffering rope burns to his hands. Estcourt was nowhere to be seen.

Next day, at dawn, they all returned to the glacier where the avalanche debris collected. Jim Duff remarked: "Doug [Scott] unclipped from the rope and started stomping around in the avalanche debris, searching for traces of Nick. I was worried about him being out there, unroped. I was sitting on my haunches, calling to him to come back, when suddenly I thought – this is Nick's dream. It's exactly what he described to me." Nick Estcourt died in the avalanche.

Occasionally the mind can disengage from sensory overload. This can happen to soldiers in battle, and is most likely what occurred to Sergeant Mike Strank in the ferocious fighting at Iwo Jima Island in WWII. Strank, a much admired leader and highly regarded soldier, described as a "Marine's Marine" by his comrades, "seemed to drift into a private place. He broke his own silence after a moment with a cryptic remark to L.B.[Holly]: 'You know, Holly, that's going to be one hell of an experience.' L.B. waited for him to continue, before finally asking: 'What are you talking about?' Mike did not reply; he only pointed to a dead Marine sprawled a few feet from the group.

"He was telling me he would die," Holly reflected many years later. "And sure enough, two minutes later, Mike was dead."[5] Strank was killed instantly when a shell landed nearby. He had made a comment to another colleague some days earlier, hinting of his premonition.

How is it that my premonition appeared to be a warning, the predicament from which we somehow extricated ourselves, whereas the premonitions of Nick Estcourt, Sergeant Mike Strank and the young girl at the Sydney departure wharf in 1895 were realised? I do not have an answer, but it certainly makes me think about all the possibilities.

Premonitions and clairvoyance are not necessarily always doom and gloom. It's possible many of you have, or know someone who has, predictive ability, and most of the time it's about some future aspect of our lives, even trivial events.

IF TIME TRANSCENDENCE ALLOWS PREMONITIONS OR PRECOGNITIONS, space transcendence and the conceptual model of one unified ocean of consciousness underlying our individual consciousness allows for mental telepathy. There are many reported instances of mental telepathy. The story I related in chapter five of the whale shark seeking help from three fishermen off the east coast of NSW may represent a form of mental telepathy.

One interesting example I found online involved a social worker by the name of Alba, and a 19-year-old boy Andrea who had contracted polio and a cerebral infection that left him paralysed and unable to talk.[6] It was discovered that, by placing a pen in Andrea's hand and with someone placing their hand onto his, he could write. After a while, there were occasions when Alba felt that Andrea was pushing the pen and she wasn't doing anything. Then Andrea was able to pick up on the thoughts of Alba and answer her with writing, even though she hadn't articulated her thoughts or written them down. This initially frightened Alba, who "let go of his hand and ran out of the classroom". After a week, Alba sat next to

Andrea again, and Andrea explained (with "co-writing") that, because he was unable to talk, as a boy, he learned to communicate telepathically to his parents at night if, for example, he needed to be changed. Soon Andrea had taught Alba how to communicate with him without the need of a pen. They were even able to do this over great distances.

Andrea explained to Alba that such communication was only possible if she allowed it. "When I was relaxed and not scared, my mind worked as a receiver. However, when I doubted if the whole thing could work, I would close my channel of communication and capacity to 'hear him'. In other words, I had to believe in it to have it happen."

Telepathic communication is very common between mothers and their babies. Mothers will sometimes find themselves lactating when their baby is ready for a feed, even when the child is out of earshot. That communicative connection between parent and offspring often survives into the child's adult years. Consider the oft-heard incidents when a young soldier is seriously hurt and the mother senses something wrong on the other side of the world.

I received a very clear and succinct telepathic message around the year 2002. This was not a two-way conversation, but an unspoken comment directed to me as clearly as if the person was standing next to me in conversation. I had just begun my evening meditation and I don't recall having dived particularly deep into transcendental consciousness. "It's time you finished your book; it's time you finished your book", came the strong thought message. It was Maharishi Mahesh Yogi delivering this message in his typical manner of saying something twice for emphasis.[7] The message was as clear as if he had articulated the comment to me with his vocal cords and I had received the message via my ears, only neither was the case. I had never met Maharishi in person and could not think of any way he could have known about my book-writing intentions.

This communication from Maharishi was one of a number of 'encouragements' I have received in regard to this book, in wakeful, dreaming and transcendental states of my consciousness. I'm glad I hadn't sent any message back to Maharishi hinting at a particular time I would complete the work as he might have been disappointed to know that it would be more than 14 years before the book would be published.

There are many shades or degrees of telepathy that most of us experience at least on some occasions in our lifetimes. What of those situations when you are thinking about someone or just about to call a friend on the phone, and that person calls you? Most of us aren't practised in complex communication through thought exchange, but many of us have a 'feeling' for the thoughts or emotions of others that we know – and sometimes even those we don't know personally. Feelings of love, compassion or even anger or disappointment can be conveyed through the ether, as it were. Telepathy is an ability we're probably born with, but most of us let it atrophy through lack of use and with the inevitable indoctrination as we're growing up that such abilities are "irrational". As the social worker Alba said, we have to believe in it to have it happen.

THERE'S ANOTHER 'PARANORMAL' ABILITY THAT MANY EXPLORERS, extreme sports persons and adventurers experience, and that's a feeling of connectedness or oneness with the world around them. I've already hinted at this experience with my own diving explorations. Surfers and deep free divers also speak of this feeling of connectedness and unity.

Tanya Streeter is a British-born world champion free diver. The sport of spearfishing typically involves breath-hold or free diving, but free divers also compete for ocean depth records or to just see how long they can hold their breath underwater (10 mins 22 secs is the current world record[8]).

The pursuit of depth records while holding your breath can definitely be described as an extreme sport. Although now retired from competition free diving, Tanya still holds the woman's world record depth of 160m (525 feet) on a single breath of air – deeper than I have ever been with all the mixed gas diving technology I have embraced over the years. It is clear, when I read her description of her relationship with the ocean, that Tanya has a 'connection' with the ocean that is as deep as the fathoms she has plumbed.

Tanya talks about certain fears she has, although they're not really about diving. "But as soon as I get into the water, those feelings evaporate. I hear myself saying that this is the place I can do anything I want to, where I've never failed."[9] Her description of her feelings echo what I too have already expressed. To "do anything I want to" suggests that quality of freedom and all-possibilities, both with respect to my own ocean diving experiences and in meditation.

Tanya describes herself as a "pragmatic" person, not too disposed to analysing or interpreting these ocean diving experiences.[10] Whatever her motivation was to push her body to the extreme in such a hazardous sport, her connection with the ocean is profound enough that she considers herself an ambassador for the ocean and is a strident worker in ocean environmental issues.

Maurice Herzog (1919–2012) was a French mountaineer who led the expedition that first climbed a peak over 8000m, Annapurna, in 1950[11].

(8000 metres is considered the 'death zone' by mountain climbers, because there is simply no chance of acclimatising to the low partial pressure of oxygen at this height[12].) Herzog's book *Annapurna* details the careful extent to which his team planned their assault of this challenging Himalayan peak. Despite their combined experience and professionalism, or perhaps because of it, only two of them – the author and Louis Lachenal – made it to the top. But the price these two paid was considerable. Neither Herzog nor his partner were breathing from oxygen cylinders, so their bodies and brains would have begun degenerating within hours at the high altitude. Add the extreme cold, and it's not surprising that poor decision-making and declining co-ordination would prevail.

Both Herzog and Lachenal suffered frostbite to their feet and hands before they reached the top. On the beginning of their long descent, Herzog dropped his gloves and was not able to recover them. So began – literally and figuratively – a downhill spiral in their predicament. Both just made it out alive, thanks to the alertness and competence of their team mates, sherpas and expedition doctor. Both men suffered enormously on their return, with complications of gangrene and the eventual loss of fingers and toes.

Was it all worth it? My guess is that Lachenal would say 'no', in hindsight, but Herzog seemed to indicate that it *was* worth it. For Herzog, his experiences included references to those qualities of life and pure consciousness to which we have already alluded. In regard to freedom, he said "playing on the frontiers of life and death, we had found the freedom for which we were blindly groping and which was as necessary to us as bread".[13] On reaching the summit of Annapurna, despite his physical suffering, he experienced 'pure happiness'. "I was stirred to the depths of my being. Never had I felt happiness like this – so intense and yet so pure."[14] It was at a time when the author was close to death – during the long descent – that he felt an unexpected and almost contradictory connectedness with the world around him and immortality. "I looked death straight in the face, besought it with all my strength. Then abruptly I had a vision of the life of men. Those who are leaving it for ever are never alone. Resting against the mountain, which was watching over me, I discovered horizons I had never seen... There is a supernatural power in those close to death. Strange intuitions identify one with the whole world."[15]

> "Someone smarter than myself made me realise that there is nothing bigger than myself. My soul is not contained within the limits of my

body. My body is contained within the limitlessness of my soul – one unified field – one unified field of nothing dancing for no particular reason except maybe to comfort and entertain itself." [16]

– Jim Carrey – actor and comedian.

I REVELLED IN A TV DOCUMENTARY CALLED *COSMOS – A PERSONAL VOYAGE*, narrated and co-written by astrophysicist Dr Carl Sagan in 1978 and 1979, broadcast around the world and on Australian TV around 1980. In my opinion, it still rates as one of the best documentaries of all time. Dr Sagan was a disciplined scientist who adhered very strongly to scientific method. His later book *The Demon-Haunted World – Science as a Candle in the Dark* [17] sought to promote rationality and scepticism in a world that he saw increasingly distancing itself from science. I accept that Dr Sagan would probably look at my book with not only scepticism, but criticism. He was critical of Transcendental Meditation and some of the claims of the organisation behind it.

Sagan's remarkable knowledge about modern science and the history of scientific pursuit was very evident to whoever watched his documentary. But he stood out in another way too – he portrayed an uplifting sense of awe and wonder for our universe and the human species that continues to find its way in one very small corner of that universe.

In the introduction to this book I referred to memories that revisit through the passage of one's life. I have never forgotten these words spoken by Sagan in the first episode of *Cosmos*, and this was a time before I learned to meditate or have any interest in something as esoteric as the nature of consciousness: "Some part of our being knows this [the cosmos] is where we come from. We long to return…The cosmos is also within us. We are made of star stuff. We are a way for the cosmos to know itself".

What incredibly profound words! "We are made of star stuff" and "We are a way for the cosmos to know itself". They "pull strings" at some deeper level of our awareness, which in turn urges us to look for deeper implications in the wording – perhaps that "secret sense of mission" that explorers would rather keep to themselves.

Introducing the DVD set published years later on the *Cosmos* series, co-writer and wife of Carl Sagan, Ann Druyan – a self-described agnostic – pushed the spiritual innuendo even further: "Most of all, we hope to touch you with the soaring spiritual high that comes from grasping science's central revelation – our oneness with the cosmos." [18]

Sagan would counter any implied ambiguity by saying that the "star stuff" to which he was referring is no more than our body's chemical elements created in the solar furnaces stretched across our galaxy, billions of years ago. It is true this particular knowledge alone is wondrous enough, but is the star stuff of which we are made limited to chemical elements alone? Are we connected to the cosmos by more than the shared chemical elements listed in the Periodic Table? Did the cosmos have to wait billions of years for it to know itself through us (or intelligent beings elsewhere in the Universe), or has it always known itself? I wonder if we know deep down more than our discriminating minds will allow us to consciously admit – and that 'knowingness' resonates joyfully at some level within us, when hearing words like those uttered by Sagan and Druyan.

DR EDGAR 'ED' MITCHELL, SC.D, HAD AN EPIPHANY THAT SUGGESTED TO him a more intimate connection with the cosmos than one of mere chemistry. Mitchell – a scientist in the fields of aeronautics and astronautics – was the lunar module pilot of *Apollo 14* and formerly a captain in the United States Navy. He was the sixth person to walk on the moon and spent nine hours walking on the lunar surface. He's therefore one of those fortunate few who have seen the Earth from a distance, and thus gained what has been dubbed an 'overview'[19] perspective of life on our planet. He commented on that "sense of interconnectedness with the celestial bodies surrounding our spacecraft".[20] He also remarked: "That's a powerful experience, to see Earth rise over the surface [of the Moon]. And I suddenly realized that the molecules in my body and the molecules in the spacecraft and my partners had been prototyped, maybe even manufactured, in some ancient generation of stars. But instead of being an intellectual experience, it was a personal feeling...And that was accompanied by a sense of joy and ecstasy, which caused me to say, 'What is this?' It was only after I came back that I did the research and found that the term in ancient Sanskrit was *Samadhi*."[21]

Mitchell's spiritual perspective resulting from his experiences in space was so profound that he founded the Institute of Noetic Sciences in the Sonoma Valley in the USA, an institute that conducts research into meditation, consciousness and human potential. Mitchell's transcendent experiences were not too dissimilar to those of Dr Fritzof Capra. When Capra witnessed the energetic dancing of the primordial particles that comprise all of material existence, it set him also on a path of study and exploration of the relationship between the findings of modern science and the subjective discoveries found in Eastern mystical wisdom[22].

Both Carl Sagan and Edgar Mitchell knew at an intellectual level the mechanics of what happens when large stars end their long lives (or phases of their long lives) with violent explosions. Such unimaginable energies fused hydrogen and helium into the chemical elements that ultimately become the building blocks of our bodies. Carl Sagan felt reverence and awe, simply with this intellectual knowledge, and asserted that such knowledge – patiently derived by observation and experiment – was sufficient to bring about "that soaring feeling, that sense of elation and humility combined, [which] is surely spiritual." I have no argument with him on that. The intellectual grasping of profound knowledge can also enliven those deeper levels of consciousness. Sagan went on to define 'spiritual' in the context of the Latin derivation of 'Spirit' (L: spirare) which means "to breathe". Sagan wrote, "What we breathe is air, which is certainly matter, however thin. Despite usage to the contrary, there is no necessary implication in the word 'spiritual' that we are talking of anything other than matter (including the matter of which the brain is made), or anything outside the realm of science."

Sagan also wrote: "The notion that science and spirituality are somehow mutually exclusive does a disservice to both".[23]

I believe he is saying, "yes – we can have ecstatic and uplifting experiences in life that we can call 'spiritual', although there is no evidence that 'spiritual' experiences are anything apart from activity in the brain, and furthermore our accumulated knowledge on the working of nature – gained through carefully controlled observation and experiment – should be all we rely on to inform ourselves about reality. Furthermore, such 'objective' knowledge in itself is sufficient to raise our spirits and affect us in a manner which could be called 'spiritual'".

I agree with Sagan that science and spirituality should not be mutually exclusive. This whole book is making that very same statement. It's just that Dr Sagan has – in my opinion – tightened considerably the parameters that define where knowledge can legitimately come from and also how we define 'spiritual experience'.

What happened to astronaut Mitchell (with his ecstatic experience of interconnectedness at a cosmic level) and physicist Capra (with his own blissful experience of the motion of fundamental particles) went beyond mere intellectual comprehension. They will surely tell you that they actually experienced this knowledge at a fundamental level. It wasn't information resulting only from their intellectual understanding of this reality – information dependent on the operation of the senses. Their 'realisation' came from somewhere deep within themselves – a level of their self which not only knows of its interconnectedness with the rest of the Universe, but knows that – in its essence – it *is* the rest of the Universe. In other words, the ecstatic experience accompanying this self-realisation represents a convergence of our perception of the material world with that very notion of our self. What is realised is that everything and everyone outside of us are identical to that which we define as our self – our essence, our consciousness. We are all one, not just in the sense of sharing similar chemistry, but in the ultimate sense that everything in the universe is an expression of one ocean of consciousness, one ocean of Self.

Why then is there ecstasy or bliss associated with these 'spiritual' experiences? The experience of pure consciousness (Ā*tm*ā) is blissful because bliss is the nature of that state of being. There could also be a joyful, even celebratory, identification of our discriminating intellect with that level we have just referred to as pure consciousness, when our intellect recognises unity amidst diversity. It *recognises* – or *remembers* – the true meaning of the term "Uni-verse": unity in diversity.

In Mitchell's case, his intellect knew of the commonality and connection between his own body (and everything immediately around him) with the distant cosmos. This connection he knew intellectually as shared chemistry. The effect this had on his consciousness was to trigger a memory in his intellect about an even more profound connection with the cosmos, one of unity. It was a realisation that ultimately, he IS the cosmos! This memory of his true nature was not clearly understood by his intellect straight away, but was expressed as a rare feeling of ecstasy. His research later allowed him to recognise this as an experience known in Sanskrit as *Samadhi*.

MAHARISHI MAHESH YOGI WROTE IN HIS COMMENTARY ON THE *Bhagavad-Gita*[24] that the mind naturally reaches towards increasing states of bliss and joy once we direct our mind in that direction. That is, once we commence the dive into transcendental consciousness in meditation, the mind very naturally seeks more bliss and the whole process of meditation therefore is a very natural process with absolutely no effort required. We just have to initiate the dive. "What a seeker of Truth has to do is only to learn how to take a correct angle for the dive within. This will quite naturally result in Self-consciousness."[25] Maharishi also referred a number of times in his commentary to the natural desire for the mind to seek greater happiness. "It is the nature of the mind to go to a field of greater happiness. When, during meditation, the mind begins to experience the finer states of the object of attention, it begins to experience increasing charm at every step.

There is then no chance for it to go anywhere except in the direction which leads to the Transcendent."[26]

Maharishi's comment about the mind's natural inclination during meditation suggests that any move in the direction of unification – either intellectually (science discovering the progressive unity inherent in diverse nature) or experientially (individual consciousness identifying with the one ocean of universal consciousness) – can trigger happiness, joy or bliss. We saw how Ed Mitchell's intellectual grasping of connectedness between us and the stars triggered an ecstatic realisation of unity. Look at love itself: love unifies or seeks to unify that which is separate. As psychologist Dr Erich Fromm says: "In love the paradox occurs that two beings become one and yet remain two".[27] The genuine love of one for another can trigger universal love – a love of everyone and everything – a truly blissful and happy state!

Everything Sagan said was true, but he was being very conservative and careful with his assertions, as scientists tend to be. I believe he was most likely open-minded enough to accept the possibility of a more profound connection and unity with the universe. That may have been the "secret sense of mission" he hinted at but didn't express with any conviction.

Again, the unified field model of consciousness can explain this experience of interconnectedness and unity. Ultimately, the uplifting experience of 'connectedness' or 'unity' is consciousness simply knowing itself. If your and my consciousness is a unified field that gives rise to everything else, and a quality of this unified field (pure consciousness) is independent, self-sufficient bliss, then it is not surprising that ecstatic experiences of unity and connectedness are often reported.

With this comprehension of interconnectedness and commonality comes also a longing and loving desire to protect the diversity we share in this world, to appreciate that which is different, knowing that in essence we are all One.

NOTES

1. The wreck of the SS *Catterthun*, located 5km out from picturesque Seal Rocks, sank in 1895. The diving project was sponsored by the Australian Geographic Society and the story was published in *Australian Geographic* in July–Sept, 1992, Issue No. 27.
2. We drive on the left side of the road in Australia.
3. *Science and the Search for God: Disturbing the Universe* (1979) by Freeman Dyson, Ch. 17
4. Coffey, Maria, *Explorers of the Infinite*, Ch. 6, p 135; Jeremy P. Tarcher/Penguin, NY.
5. Bradley, James with Powers, Ron; *Flags of Our Fathers*, Pimlico, p 354
6. www.intervoiceonline.org Alba's Story, May 12, 2011. "Inter Voice" is an International Hearing Voices Network.
7. Maharishi, at the time, was living in Vlodrop, the Netherlands.
8. Held by German diver Tom Sietas, without breathing oxygen beforehand. More than 22 minutes breathing O2 first (http://newsfeed.time.com/2012/06/05/german-diver-sets-breath-holding-record-22-minutes-22-seconds/)
9. Coffey, Maria, *Explorers of the Infinite*, Ch 5, p 122; Jeremy P. Tarcher/Penguin, NY
10. Personal communication, June, 2016.
11. Annapurna, one of the Himalayan mountains in north-central Nepal, at 8,091 m (26,545 ft), is considered to be one of the most difficult mountains to climb, and for three years after the French team's successful effort in 1950, remained the highest summit climbed. In 1953 Hillary and Tenzing climbed Mt Everest at 8,848 m (29,028 ft), the highest point on Earth.
12. About 0.07 bar O2. At sea level, we breathe about 0.21 bar of oxygen. Un-acclimatised people would normally become unconscious at about 0.14 bar.
13. Herzog, Maurice, *Annapurna,* Chapter 20, p 428.
14. Herzog, Maurice, *Annapurna*, Chapter 13, p 276.
15. Referenced by Coffey, Maria, *Explorers of the Infinite*, Ch 7, P178

Herzog, Maurice, *Annapurna*, Published June 1st 1997 by Lyons Press (first published 1951).

16. Carrey, Jim, addressing the 2014 MUM Graduation Ceremony in Fairfield, Iowa, USA, concerned about achieving anything bigger than himself.
17. Sagan, Carl; *The Demon-Haunted World*; 1996; Headline Book Publishing
18. Druyan, Ann – CEO Cosmos Studios, Inc (Carlsagan.com site – Cosmos Studios)
19. A term coined by author Frank White to describe the cognitive shift in awareness of astronauts who have seen the whole Earth from space; White, Frank, *The Overview Effect — Space Exploration and Human Evolution* (Houghton-Mifflin, 1987).
20. Coffey, Maria, *Explorers of the Infinite*, Ch. 2, p 39; Jeremy P. Tarcher/Penguin, NY
21. www.ultraculture.org with Vimeo narrations by these astronauts.
22. See Ch 11, p….
23. Sagan, Carl, *The Demon-Haunted World,* Ch 2, p 32.
24. *Maharishi Mahesh Yogi on the Bhagavad-Gita*, A New Translation and Commentary, Chapters 1-6; Penguin Books
25. P 145, commentary on Ch 2, Vs 51
26. P 436, commentary on Ch 6, Vs 26
27. Erich Fromm, *The Art of Loving* (1956), p 24; George Allen & Unwin. ISBN 0 04 157007 3.

Chapter Sixteen

DIVING INTO THE OCEAN OF SELF

"The person should look for peace within and not depend on it in any other place. For when a person is quiet within, the self cannot be found.[1] There are no waves in the depths of the ocean, it is still and unbroken."

– The Buddha, Sutta Nipata

Transcendental consciousness (TC) is that state of consciousness we have all attained to varying degrees during or between our more familiar waking, sleeping and dreaming cycles. It is a recognised physiological state of consciousness with its own distinct, measurable parameters. There are various ways of achieving TC and many benefits.

So far, I have been developing the concept that our notion of self is one universal ocean of consciousness. The unique waves of consciousness expressed from this one ocean represent your and my seemingly separate consciousness operating in the body through individual nervous systems. It's all the one ocean – all the one Self – underlying our notion of individual self.

When we 'transcend' in consciousness – that is, gain that state we call "transcendental consciousness" – we become divers in consciousness, exploring the deeper foundational levels of our own nature and experiencing the one and only unfathomable ocean of consciousness common to all. Our sense of small self is lost in the ocean of big Self.

Transcendental consciousness is not merely a philosophical concept but a state of consciousness – along with waking, dreaming and sleeping states – recognised by scientists. Transcendental consciousness has its own measurable physiological parameters and commonly experienced qualities.

When we 'transcend', what we experience is generally familiar. Physiologists with an interest in this subject tell us that all of us transcend during those transition stages between waking, sleeping and dreaming. They know this by the distinct EEG (electro-encephalogram) readings that accompany such transitions in our consciousness states. Before we describe some of the EEG and other physiological characteristics that define this state of consciousness, let's look at the various methods or circumstances that allow us to transcend.

Methods of transcending

When someone steps out of their comfort zone or familiar environment it is possible to spontaneously transcend in consciousness. I have already compared the experiences I have when diving into the ocean with my experiences in meditation. The activity of diving – either on scuba or free diving – may be considered one technique that allows transcendence, but the degree to which we experience transcendence, if at all, depends much on the comfort level of the diver and is not always consistent. Ocean diving allows the possibility of transcendence because of the significant change or diminution of sensory input into our nervous system and also possibly for other reasons – our evolutionary connection to the ocean and even metaphorical perceptions.

Float tanks[2] were popular during the late 1970s and 1980s. Their effect is similar to the diving experience already described, in that the subject floats in a virtually weightless environment (the water is salinised to increase the buoyancy), and is enclosed in a dark environment with no sound, or only soft relaxing music. The water temperature is also brought to body temperature to minimise the sensation of being in water. Such sensory deprivation, just like ocean diving, allowed the mind to become more self-referral instead of distracted with outside objects and phenomena.

In his book *Transcendence*[3], psychiatrist Dr Norman Rosenthal mentions a state of consciousness that is commonly called "the Watch". In the modern world, with bright artificial house lighting and the distraction of television and computers, we are now lucky if we get one block of sleep lasting eight or nine hours. With extended periods of living in caves, cabins or tents where there is no artificial light or only the dim, warm lighting from a fire or gas/oil lamp, people will often settle into two separate periods of sleep with a wakeful, but relaxed, altered consciousness between, lasting about two hours on average, occurring after midnight – "the Watch". This state of consciousness is – like that achieved in meditation – a state of restful alertness. It is not sleep and it is not dreaming.

Rosenthal refers to the experiences of author Jeff Warren, who wanted to experience firsthand this apparently natural and once-common state of consciousness. He headed off to a cabin in northern Canada during the winter of 2004, and found that after nine long nights, his sleep did indeed break into two periods with a period of altered consciousness in between. Here is his written comment on the Watch: "I awoke and couldn't tell whether or not I was still dreaming. My limbs were heavy, my head sunk deep into the pillow and my whole body was buzzing…The heaviness in my body didn't go away – it continued on and on, a marvellous languor that lasted for over two hours and finally drew me back down into one last early-morning dream."[4]

It is most likely that this state of consciousness, presumably a natural part of the sleep cycle in the right conditions, is a state of transcendence with a similar EEG signature to that seen in meditation.

Athletes are said to be 'in the zone' when they are performing almost automatically at their best with little or no apparent effort – as if they were silently witnessing and enjoying their own athletic performance. Being in the zone – also referred to as the 'runner's high' or being 'locked in' – is a form of transcendence, during which the athlete gains a state of awareness that sees himself or herself as separate or disengaged from the exertion of the activity. It is considered that state where "the most dynamic activity coexists with mental composure, peace and calm".[5] The athlete is the 'doer' but identifies with a deeper aspect of their own self that is uninvolved with the activity. Remember the words of Lord Krishna to Arjuna on the battlefield in the *Baghavad Gita*: "Though I am its author, know Me to be the non-doer, immutable".[6]

It can be a blissful and highly efficient state for an athlete to gain. English medical student Roger Bannister was the first human to break the four-minute mile in 1954. Bannister said, "We seemed to be going so slowly…I was relaxing so much that my mind seemed almost detached from my body. There was no strain. There was no pain. Only a great unity of movement and aim. The world seemed to stand still or not even exist".[7]

Another mature-age man who did not consider himself an athlete, reported excitedly on a program he has been following prescribed by author Douillard: "I ran 17 miles. I felt absolutely fantastic the whole way. I felt as good when I stopped as I did when I started. The amazing thing was that I ran a 6-minute-mile pace for the entire 17 miles. It was unbelievable. I was in the Zone. I felt like I was running on air. It was the easiest thing I've ever done."[8] Compare his feeling to the "running on air", or Lung-gom-pa ("wind meditation") in Tibet – and also known as "running levitation".

IN THE 1960S, MANY OF THE ACCEPTED VALUES AND NORMS IN SOCIETY were deeply scrutinised and tested with alternative ways of thinking and behaving. The latter years of the '60s were all about anti-Vietnam War protests, living more simply and spiritual revitalisation, and the expression of all this through music, free love, lots of colour and psychedelic drugs. Thrown into this mix was a fascination with eastern mysticism and philosophy. LSD (lysergic acid diethylamide) was one of the main recreational drugs of choice at the time. Depending on the existing mental state of the individual and his or her immediate environment, the hallucinatory effects of LSD were profound and mostly positive, allowing the user to experience altered states of reality and unity. The drug is considered to be non-addictive and is not known to cause brain damage. However adverse reactions such as paranoia, delusions and psychosis were possible.

The use of psychoactive substances such as LSD or some mushrooms will certainly allow a state of altered consciousness that could be transcendental. However, the wisdom and practicality of using these agents on a regular basis is certainly questionable, just as attempts to achieve transcendence through extreme sport or adventure is impractical and in many cases not life-supporting as a daily routine. Thankfully there is a gentler, easier and more natural process to transcend – one that can be practically integrated into our daily lives in such a way that all aspects of our lives are supported and enhanced, including physical and mental health, efficiency in our work and study, creativity, interaction with others, general contentment and happiness, as well as spiritual growth. Although widely misunderstood, meditation is the all-round best practice for regular transcendence.

Meditation
"You guys need to work smarter, not harder," said an American dental educator and friend of mine to a group of us during one of his courses many years ago. Achieving more by doing less – through more efficient work practice – should be a goal of all professional and business people. This same mentor also told us that "sometimes it's better to not treat at all. We dentists are always 'doers'. We always feel an imperative to do something when managing our patients' problems. Sometimes it's better to not *do* anything." He was referring specifically to the management of jaw-joint (TMJ) and jaw-muscle pain and dysfunction[9]. In many cases, these episodes of facial pain will resolve without treatment. Simply discussing the problem with our patients and reassuring them can allay anxiety and comfort the patient.

The concept of "doing nothing" is alien to most of us. Meditation allows us to experience just *being* instead of *doing*. There is a beautiful tranquillity associated with the experience of being, which happens when our mind removes its attention from outside objects.

I remember a friend of mine – socially engaged and career motivated – telling me that I'd be far better off giving "this meditation stuff" a miss and spending more time in the gym. What was there to be gained by wasting time on such a useless activity as meditation? How could "doing nothing" possibly develop me as an individual?

She wasn't the only one who viewed meditation as a waste of time. A recent study at the University of Virginia published in *Science* (Sciencemag.org), found that 67% of men and 25% of women would sooner endure an unpleasant electric shock rather than be alone in silence for even 15 minutes.[10]

> *"All human evil comes from this: our inability to sit still in a chair for half an hour."*[11]
>
> – Blaise Pascal,

"Lack of knowledge to 'dive' within oneself is the root of all ills and sufferings of human life."[12]

– Maharishi Mahesh Yogi

It turns out – as has been hinted in previous chapters – that "doing nothing" by way of meditation on a regular basis benefits us physiologically, mentally, socially and spiritually. The simple, regular act of going inward and experiencing our Self, brings about a plethora of benefits.

So what is meditation? In English, we sometimes say we will "meditate" on something to indicate that we will give that something directed thought in order to solve a problem or issue. I am using the word to refer to something very different – the practice of emptying the mind of thoughts, allowing it to become aware of its own nature, to become Self-referral. When the mind disengages from the influence of the senses, it experiences its own essential nature, and this experience can be blissful. Because the nature of pure consciousness is "bliss"[13], the mind simply needs a helping start to begin its dive into the depths of awareness and it will naturally be attracted towards that state of ever-increasing bliss.

Techniques
When I free dive in the ocean, I start with a simple kick or two along the surface to gain some forward momentum. Then I bend at the waist to enable the legs to kick vertically out of the water. With the legs out of the water, I have some weight pushing me down. Once I've made this correct angle to start my dive and my fins have reached the water, a few simple additional kicks take me a couple of metres deeper, after which the compression of air cells in my wetsuit makes me more negatively buoyant and I simply let gravity take me deeper. I have no more need to kick and waste valuable energy. I've made the correct start and the rest comes naturally by itself. Maharishi uses diving in an analogy: "The technique of diving lies only in taking a correct angle and then letting go; reaching the bottom and coming up with the pearls follows automatically. What a seeker of Truth has to do is only to learn how to take a correct angle for the dive within".[14]

Meditation is actually so simple that some people don't need techniques and instruction. Gaining transcendence comes naturally to them, or they are perpetually operating under the influence of transcendental consciousness – which is very much to their advantage! Most of us, however, need a technique to disengage our awareness so we can let go of the reins of the wild horses that represent our senses.[15]

There are many techniques of meditation. I have only practised Transcendental Meditation (TM) and can speak only from my personal perspective with that technique. I was attracted to TM because of the wide-ranging scientific literature that supported it. Also – as I have already mentioned – it is not attached to a religion. TM uses a non-sensible word that is called a mantra – basically a vehicle to enable one to dive beneath the surface level of consciousness, that level which represents the "gross field of objective experience".[16] There is no contemplation on a specific deity, person, object or idea, and there is no concentration on anything either. Contemplation or concentration on anything can encourage the mind to remain attached to that idea or thing, preventing or delaying the dive.

Each person learning TM is given a mantra specific to that person, as determined by a trained and certified teacher in TM. Keeping one's mantra to oneself is recommended.

The process of transcending is simple, but also delicate. The natural impulse to put effort into everything we learn warrants the supervision of a teacher, so that we learn to be innocent, easy and natural with our technique.

Other forms of meditation also use mantras, breathing techniques or forms of contemplation or concentration. Most techniques of meditation – if they have stood the test of time – allow one to gain transcendental consciousness. Some techniques have been proven to be faster and more efficient than others.

If you are considering learning a technique for the first time, then I can highly recommend Transcendental Meditation™.[17] TM has its roots in a long line of masters (Vedic seers) going back to Shankara. Maharishi Mahesh Yogi learned the technique from his guru, Swāmī Brahmānanda Saraswatī (1868 –1953), the *Shankaracharya* (head) of the Jyotir Math monastery in India. Maharishi called his guru simply Guru Dev. You'll recognise the Beatle's reference to Guru Dev in their 1970 song *Across the Universe*. "Jai" Guru Deva means "salutation to" Guru Deva. In Sanskrit, the suffix "a" is usually left out when pronouncing many words. So *Veda* is pronounced "Vēd" (as in "Vaid"); *Deva* (Dēva) is pronounced differently as "Dĕv" (as in "bed"). John Lennon and Paul McCartney, when they wrote this composition, most likely chose to leave the suffix in place for musical metre.

Anyone who has read *Autobiography of a Yogi* by Paramahansa Yogananda will be aware of his line of immediate masters, including Mahavatar Babaji, a great Indian saint with Christ-like abilities, who passed down an ancient technique – known as *Kriya Yoga*. The discipline is maintained and promoted by the Prajnana Mission in India and Kriya Yoga International Organizations.

There are undoubtedly other effective forms of meditation. My advice is to select a technique which has been time-tested and passed down through a line of masters of Vedic knowledge. If you are faithful to a particular religious discipline, then you should not see yourself as an apostate or traitor, simply because you adopt a technique that might be popular with an eastern religious tradition. Pick what serves you and disregard the rest. Meditation – the most practical method of transcendence – will allow you to centre yourself and to experience a more universal aspect of your own nature. You will find the daily practice of meditation improves your physical and mental health and supports your spiritual development.

> *"Happiness which has reasons for it is only another form of misery. Bliss is when you're happy for no reason whatsoever, in the mere fact of existence. We should therefore seek happiness not in outside things but in ourselves."*
>
> – Deepak Chopra

What has Transcendental Meditation done for me?
THIS IS A DIFFICULT QUESTION TO ANSWER, BECAUSE I DO NOT HAVE A "control" – another 'me' who didn't meditate – with which to compare my current self. I've now been practising TM since 1981 and an extended form of TM, known as the TM-Sidhis since 1985.

The TM-Sidhis incorporate some of the *Sutras of Patanjali*, including the flying sutra. These sutras – or Vedic aphorisms – allow some lateral exploration while remaining in the transcendent levels of consciousness. If you think of transcendence as a vertical dive into the ocean of Self, then lateral exploration is working at a depth of consciousness by introducing a subtle thought. Introducing sutras while in a state of transcendental consciousness can enhance and develop those particular traits or skills in life. Maharishi Mahesh Yogi selected a particular set of sutras that he believed would be most beneficial for the rapid development of consciousness in typically busy Western cultures.

The inclusion of the yogic flying sutra of Patanjali is particularly interesting, as it has been shown repeatedly in EEG studies to bring about a dramatic increase in brainwave coherence – above and beyond the increase in coherence already seen in transcendental consciousness. It is likely this symmetry demonstrated in brainwave coherence reflects the fact that the meditator's attention has reached that super-symmetric level of consciousness – the proposed unified field underlying all the laws of nature. In order to levitate, we must reach that level that is beyond time and space, in order to manipulate space to allow repulsive gravity. It is surely no coincidence that this coherence in an individual's brainwave activity corresponds with a greater coherence and harmony in society at large when sufficient numbers of yogic flyers gather together and meditate.

My daily practice of TM and the TM-Sidhis over more than three decades has brought a certain security and contentment for me. Most of my meditations are simply quiet periods when my mind can completely detach from the stresses and worries of work or life events. I reach a place where I feel centred and very much at "home". Some of my meditations are full of thoughts, and as a result can feel very shallow. When I have thoughts, and become aware that I have slipped off my mantra, I just quietly bring back my mantra and slip back into transcendence. Sometimes new thoughts arise again, and when I'm aware that I'm not repeating my mantra, I'll reintroduce it.

Often, I must slip deeply into that ocean of consciousness, because I can reach a state where I have no thoughts at all, but am still aware! Awake! But awake in silence with my attention on nothing at all. It is at this level that I can also feel bliss. It's a beautiful silence – a state of "nothingness" – and it feels great to be in that nothingness. It is "pure awareness simply aware of Itself". Any notion of my small self has disappeared. I'm effectively One with the big Self – the unified field. At this level time can pass very quickly. Pure awareness is hard to explain without experiencing it, just as it is hard to explain the taste of a strawberry without actually experiencing it.

> *"If you realize the self in your inmost consciousness, it will appear in its purity. This is the womb of wonder, which is not the realm of those who live only by reason."*
>
> – The Buddha, Lankavatara Sutra.

THERE IS NOTHING PARTICULARLY DRAMATIC ABOUT MOST OF MY meditations. I do them for the benefits they bring me in everyday life. I believe my health benefits from this regular meditation, although I can give no evidentiary proof for this. I work out at the gym as well and remain physically active, so I'm sure all this helps.

I think the calmness I experience in meditation carries over into my life, but I'm not a perfect exemplar of calmness and serenity in all situations. Just ask my golf buddies!

I can recognise negative traits in myself and in others, but I try to look past the flaws in others and see only the positive. I can't change the flaws in others but I can try to do something about my own. By choosing to see only the positive side of others, I can learn to love them as the unique individuals and miracles of life that they are.

This all leads me to conclude that perhaps one benefit I have attained through regular transcendence is an ever growing love for everyone and everything. I've actually had this disposition for many years now. Perhaps, as I experience unity over and over again in meditation, that sense of unity becomes entrenched more and more in my waking consciousness as well.

When we *know* and *feel* the unity behind all people and all things – including our own self – we can then feel more love and attraction to the unique qualities they represent. This growing love and appreciation for the diversity around me has possibly been the greatest gift I could ever ask for in my daily routine of meditation. How sad it is that so many in the world now feel threatened and fearful by the concept of difference – different cultural practice, different appearance, different ways of worshipping God.

Amongst my many thousands of meditations since learning TM in 1981, I could count on one hand the number of times I've had what might be called supernatural, mystical or divine experiences during meditation. Possibly more of these extraordinary experiences have occurred outside of meditation – during my waking, sleeping or dreaming states of consciousness. They were amazing experiences, but are never the goal of my meditations. My point here is to reassure you that meditation – properly undertaken – is a very innocent and healthy practice, and is certainly nothing of which to be frightened. Far from taking you to an alien place, you will find yourself feeling very much 'at home', in a place of familiarity and comfort.

In the earlier chapter on mythology, I mentioned Deepak Chopra's comment that we shouldn't fear the *unknown*; "If there's anything to fear, it's the known". If the 'unknown' is that ocean of Self that we have explored so little, then there is nothing to fear of those depths that uphold and support each and every-one of us. We have conjured our own fear in imagining what might exist down there, and we have – in agreement with each other – made those fears the 'known'.

An Explanation of the Four states of Consciousness

*"This whole creation is ultimately brahman,
And the Self,
This also is brahman.*

This pure Self has four quarters:

*The first is the waking state,
Experience of the reality common to everyone,
The attention faces outwards, enjoying the world in all its variety.*

*The second is experience of subjective worlds, such as in dreaming.
Here the attention dwells within, charmed by the mind's subtler creations.*

*The third is deep sleep,
  the mind rests, with awareness suspended.*

*This state beyond duality
   from which the waves of thinking emerge,
     is enjoyed by the enlightened as an ocean of silence and bliss.*

*The fourth, say the wise, is the pure Self alone.
Dwelling in the heart of all,
   It is the lord of all,
    the seer of all,
    the source and goal of all.
It is not outer awareness,
It is not inner awareness,
Nor is it a suspension of awareness.
It is not knowing,
It is not unknowing,
Nor is it knowingness itself.
It can neither be seen nor understood.
It cannot be given boundaries.
It is ineffable and beyond thought.
It is indefinable,*

It is known only through becoming it.
It is the end of all activity,
   silent and unchanging,
   the supreme good,
   one without a second.
It is the real Self.
It, above all, should be known."

– Mandukya Upanishad

The physiology of meditation
ALTHOUGH MODERN SCIENCE HAS ENABLED US TO DETECT AND MEASURE many benefits of meditation, we may not understand exactly what is going on in our bodies.

I assist in teaching anatomy dissection to medical and dental practitioners at a nearby university. When I remove the brain from its well-slung position in the skull, I do so carefully to sequentially demonstrate all the cranial nerves as they exit the brain and begin their course through various canals or holes in the cranium. I may not hear much expressed verbally, but I can usually sense a 'wow!' when the young doctors hold this amazing organ in their hands. It's still an organ of great mystery, despite the great advances that have been made in understanding how it works.

The brain is about 1.5 kg (3.3 lbs) of homogenous-looking tissue, with the consistency of soft tofu. It may look homogenous, but the brain contains some 86 billion neurons[18] – specialised nerve cells wired together in such a way that there are thought to be some 100 trillion[19] connections between them. To give some sense of scale, our galaxy – the Milky Way – is thought to contain between 200 and 400 billion stars.

Many of us probably visualise nerves conducting electrical signals much like a copper wire conducts a current through it. However, the electrical signals are conducted in a very different way to electricity in a copper wire. Neurons propagate an electrical signal by allowing positively charged sodium ions to pass from outside the cell into the cell across the cell's membrane. When this happens, negatively charged potassium ions pass from inside the cell to the outside. The result is a wave of 'depolarisation' moving down the long extension (called the axon) of the neuron. The axons look like the 'wires' of the brain.

Electrons travelling through a copper wire travel at the speed of light – 300 million metres per second. Remember that electrons, for all intents and purposes don't weigh anything! They behave like waves as well as particles, and are themselves a form of electromagnetic radiation.

What's actually moving in a nerve fibre are sodium ions, which have protons and neutrons, as well as electrons, and are considerably heavier and bigger. Having mass, they can't travel at the speed of light. If an electron is a pea, the sodium ion is the Sun – a big difference! Also, the sodium ion is moving in a very specific manner through a gel-like medium in the cell called the cytoplasm. It's certainly different to electrons moving through metal. The fastest a message will travel through a nerve fibre is 120m/sec – considerably slower than the 300 million metres per second speed of an electron – but fast enough in most situations for an effective reflex response to a harmful stimulus.

The rising and falling of ion flow through the nerve cells is still an electrical phenomenon because there is an exchange and propagation of positive and negative charges along the nerve fibres. The rising and falling of these ions gives off an electromagnetic field that can be detected and measured by sensitive electrodes lightly attached to the scalp. The particular frequency at which this ion exchange occurs in a nerve cell is measured as a particular frequency in an Electroencephalogram (EEG). EEGs record these distinct brainwaves mainly in the outer part of the brain (the cortex), which reflect the speed of firing of nerve cells in particular brain tasks and in different states of consciousness.

Here are the main frequencies found operating in the brain in electroencephalography and their different roles:

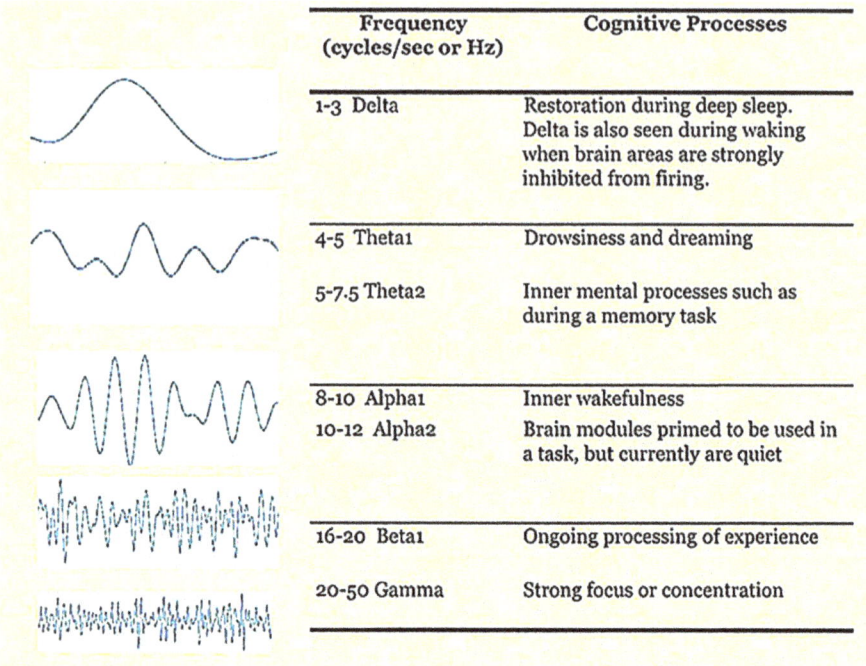

From Brain and Consciousness Course; MUM, Iowa, USA; Keith Wallace and Fred Travis. Courtesy of Dr F. Travis

Right at this moment, your frontal cortex (that part of the brain associated with 'higher' thinking) has a predominant gamma wave activity due to your concentration on this subject. The more focused you are, the higher the frequency of neuronal firing. During normal daily wakeful activity, we would see a predominant beta 1 frequency. When the brain is resting in sleep or dreaming, we see more of the longer wavelengths such as delta or theta 1 frequencies.

In transcendental consciousness, there is a predominant alpha 1 frequency not only in our fore-brain, but in other parts of the brain as well. Most people demonstrate some alpha wave activity in their daily lives, but during transcendental consciousness, this particular frequency becomes very prominent.

Studies by Dr Fred Travis, director for the Centre for Brain, Consciousness, and Cognition at Maharishi University of Management in Fairfield, Iowa, have thrown light on another fascinating aspect of brain function. Travis found that the degree of coherence between different parts of the brain was also more demonstrable with those practising Transcendental Meditation. "Coherence" in this context means that brainwaves of a given frequency are in step with each other – that is, there is a harmony or linking together in the rhythmic expression of waves between different parts of the brain.[20] Clearly, one part of the brain is informing the other what it is doing.

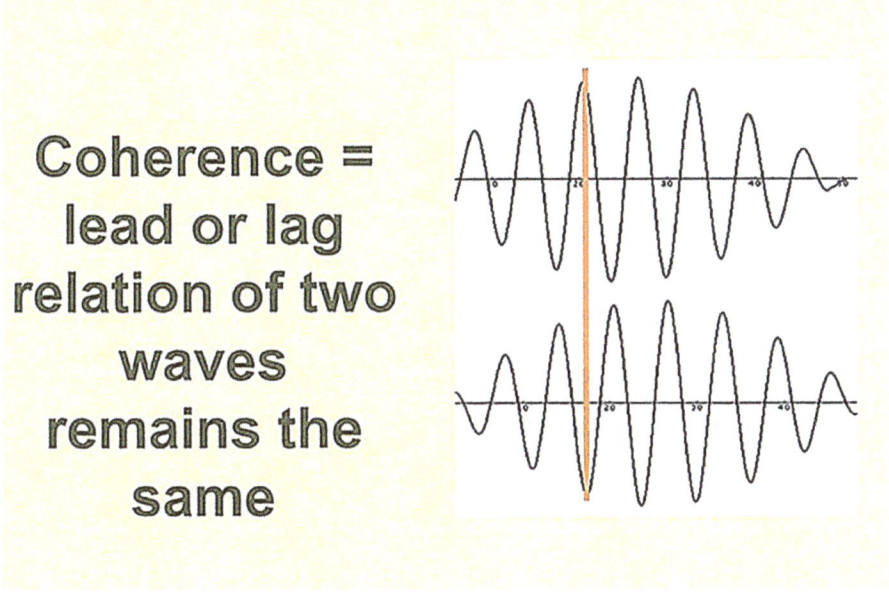

Coherence between different parts of the brain demonstrates a harmonious communication between those parts. The different waves are in step although may not be totally identical with their ups and downs. Keith Wallace and Fred Travis, MUM, Iowa, USA. Courtesy of Dr F. Travis.

Brainwave coherence per se is certainly not unique to transcendence – just the degree to which it is observed. For example, when we close our eyes, alpha wave coherence is typically seen between activity in the visual cortex at the back of the brain and the motor centres ready to command a response on a part (or parts) of the body. This alpha activity represents a restful, but alertful, 'readying' role of the visual cortex and motor centres.

Brainwave coherence – seen at a more global level in the brain during TM – correlates with high levels of intelligence and competence.[21] As Dr Rosenthal says: "To produce a train of thought or execute an action, all cells have to function as a unit, just as soldiers in a battle need to advance in a coordinated way".

Travis's EEG studies also show how transcendence can improve all areas of brain competence. The increased coherence in alpha wave activity was matched to some degree by increased coherence in the lower part of the beta frequency in the prefrontal areas of the brain. Rosenthal points out that: "This important region regulates emotions and impulses, evaluates the relative importance of things, and is crucial for decision making".[22] So, while there is a spread of calmness across the brain, the prefrontal brain region is also organised in a way that improves focus and decision making.

All the above takes place whenever anyone transcends consciousness. Even first-timers initiated into TM demonstrate this pattern of alpha-wave predominance and coherence. The alpha wave activity and coherence quickly disappear until they meditate again. With repeated meditation however, over some years, the EEG readings in the meditator during the waking state of consciousness begin to resemble the pattern seen during transcendence. This permanent influence of transcendental consciousness on normal active life is what Maharishi Mahesh Yogi refers to as "Cosmic Consciousness" – the continual state of transcendent pure awareness maintained during normal activity.[23]

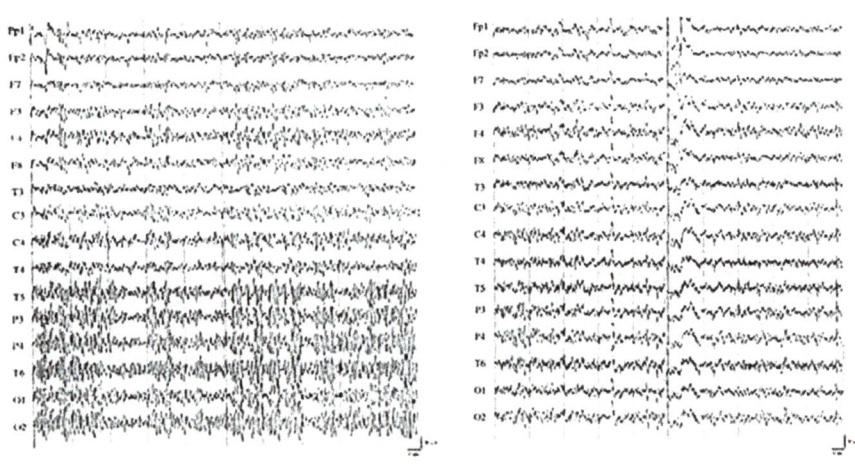

Four Months TM Practice

TM   Eyes Open

Travis, 1991

In the early months after initiation into TM, the increased coherence in brain wave activity seen during meditation is not carried over into daily activity during the waking state of consciousness. Keith Wallace and Fred Travis, MUM, Iowa, USA. Diagram courtesy of Dr F. Travis.

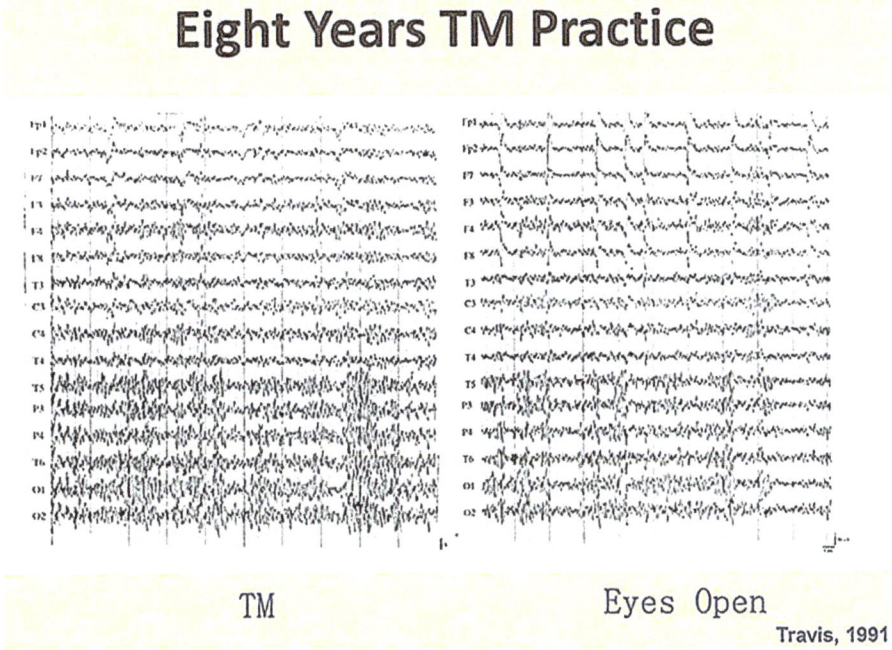

Travis, 1991

After eight years of practice of TM, the high levels of coherence in global brain wave activity are reflected to a large extent into daily activity, that is, when the subject is not meditating and engaged in activity. This is developing Cosmic Consciousness. The increased amplitude (or pitch) of the recorded waves results from constructive interference of neurons oscillating in the alpha range. Keith Wallace and Fred Travis, MUM, Iowa, USA. Diagram courtesy of Dr F. Travis.

Maharishi likened the process to dyeing a cloth: "One analogy will make this clear: we dip a white cloth in a yellow dye and let it remain in the dye to be coloured for a few minutes. Then we take it out and expose it to the sun till the colour begins to fade. We repeat the same process, again putting the cloth into the sunlight till the colour fades. Similarly, we meditate for about half an hour and follow this by coming out into practical life for about ten hours, by which time we begin to feel that we are out of the influence of the morning meditation. We meditate again in the same way and again let the influence fade by coming out into practical life; we keep repeating the process of gaining the state of universal Being in transcendence (Samadhi) during meditation and of coming out to regain individuality in the field of relative existence. This allows more and more infusion of Being into the nature of the mind even when it is engaged in activity through the senses.

When the full infusion of Being has been accomplished, then the state of cosmic consciousness has been gained."[24]

His assertions over many decades that TM carried out regularly will transform the consciousness of the individual, have now been verified with objective scientific study which shows a distinct change in EEG patterns between meditating and simply having eyes closed, and also during the waking state between short-term meditators and long-term meditators.

The alpha brain-wave frequency seems to be a foundational frequency of the brain and is there when the processing functions of the brain settle down, but there is still wakefulness. The alpha wave itself may be our connection to the underlying field of pure consciousness. I mentioned earlier that transcendental consciousness is available at the transition points (junction points) between the other states of consciousness, whether someone meditates or not. Usually, this state of consciousness is brief, however it might account for some of the special "out of the ordinary" experiences we have, particularly at night. This would support Travis's theory that the alpha wave is a foundational frequency. As Maharishi says: "The three relative states of consciousness, exist and run through their continuous, ever-changing alternation on the basis of the fourth state [Transcendental Consciousness] underlying them".

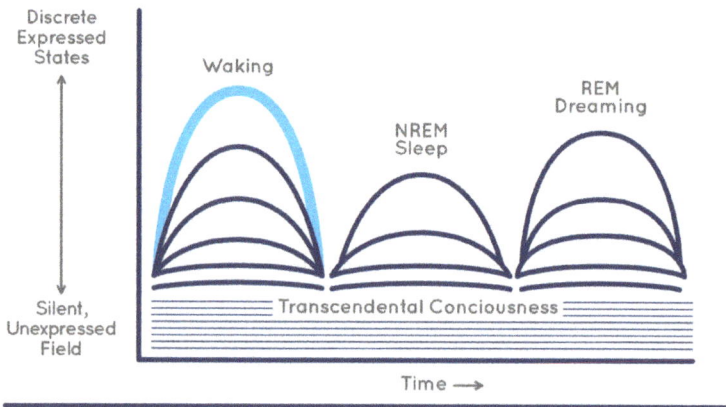

Transcendental Consciousness (TC) is a fundamental state to the other more familiar states of consciousness. Indeed, the Alpha 1 wave seen in EEGs is also likely the fundamental frequency of the brain and our key to TC. This diagram illustrates how we can slip into TC innocently during transitions between sleep, dreaming and awakening. The diagram also resembles the ocean itself – the underlying ocean (in this case transcendental consciousness) supporting waves of familiar states of consciousness. Keith Wallace and Fred Travis, MUM, Iowa, USA.

What happens during yogic flying?
SOME YEARS AGO, MAHARISHI DECIDED TO ALLOW THE WORLD TO WATCH the yogic flyers hop about on their firm mattresses. Being a practitioner of the TM-Sidhis (which includes yogic flying), I had mixed feelings about the wisdom of Maharishi's decision. The hopping about on a mattress must look ridiculous to the uninitiated.

Yogic flying is yet another example of how appearances can deceive when it comes to exercising these 'technologies' of consciousness. Remarkable things are happening inside the brain during this hopping-stage of levitation.

During a two-second interval just before the flyer 'lifts off', brainwave coherence across a wide range of frequencies peak – even more powerfully than during the Transcendental Meditation technique alone. EEG measurements of non-meditators who jump from a sitting position do not show these increases in EEG coherence. Craig Pearson notes: "This suggests that yogic flyers access a much deeper and more powerful level of consciousness and project thought and action from there – a level at which the mind and body, silence and dynamism, are more profoundly coordinated".[25]

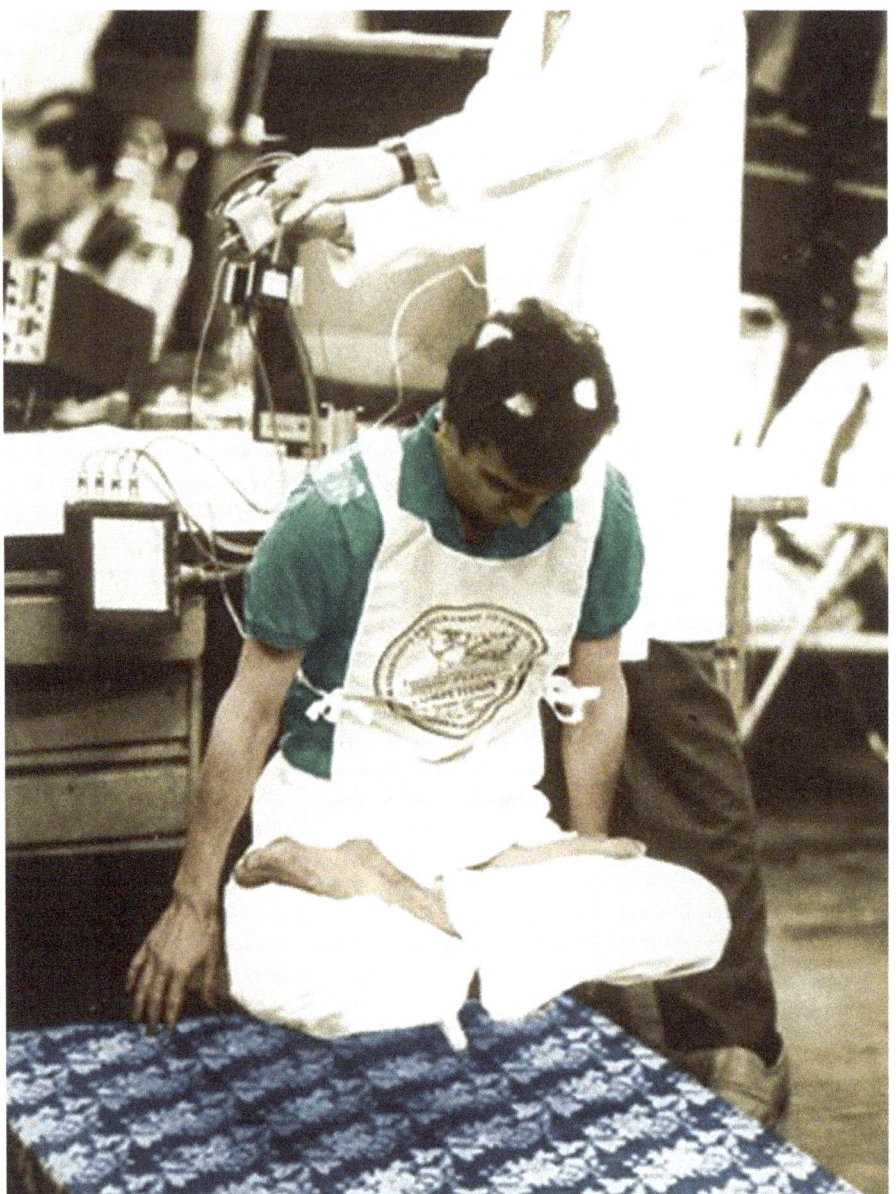

"Scientists measure the changes in brain functioning of a Yogic Flyer. During the two-second interval immediately prior to liftoff, they observe a marked shift towards greater brainwave coherence – indicating the phenomenon of liftoff emerges from an entirely different brain state. Similar measurements of non-meditators who jumped from a sitting position did not show these increases in EEG coherence." Image and description courtesy of Dr Craig Pearson, The Complete Book of Yogic Flying.

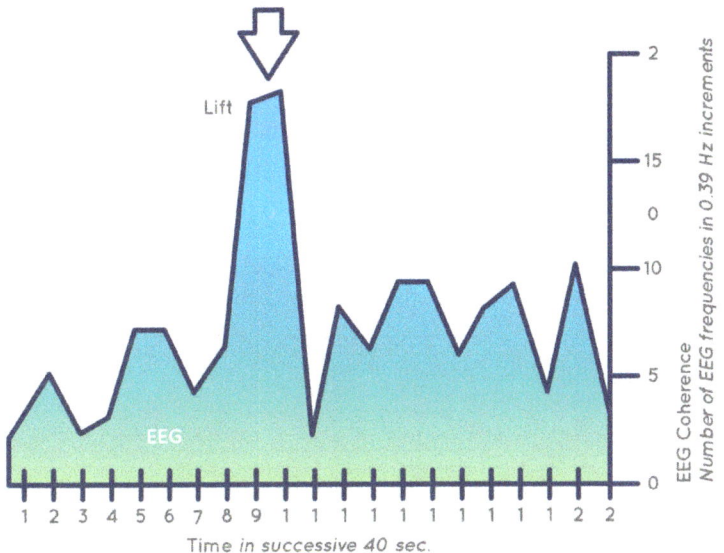

At the point of 'liftoff' in yogic flying, EEG coherence increases dramatically even compared to the already increased level of coherence attained in transcendental consciousness. Illustration based on a diagram courtesy of Dr Craig Pearson.

I have already described the three stages of yogic flying or levitation, as originally outlined by Patanjali: hopping, hovering and flying.[26] So what does it feel like when I hop? For about 30 minutes prior to the experience, I have usually been engrossed in transcendental consciousness – experiencing peace and stillness within. The gentle introduction of the flying sutra initiates – usually instantly, but sometimes with a delay – a desire to hop! I could resist it if I wished, but it's more effortless to just go with it. It's a muscular thing involving the legs and lower torso. Some of the younger flyers spring themselves quite high off the foam rubber. I've never been convinced that is good for our lower backs in the long term, so I decided to moderate that hop. I long for sustained levitation, which will surely be an even more ecstatic way to experience and radiate that coherence – plus better for all our backs! But as I explained in an earlier chapter, the phenomenal activity of levitating or flying is not the ultimate goal of our meditations. That ultimate goal is the full development of our consciousness. The flying sutra aids in that personal evolution and also contributes significantly to societal peace and harmony. That's why we do it.

Other health benefits
TRANSCENDENTAL MEDITATION (TM) HAS HAD MORE SCIENTIFIC scrutiny than any other technique of meditation. This is because there is a carefully administered standardisation and consistency in the teaching of the technique. There is also a large sample base, important in any statistical study, and Maharishi Mahesh Yogi, very early on, was enthusiastic to have TM and its benefits verified by modern science. The result has been the accumulation of more than 350 peer-reviewed research studies on the health and social benefits of the TM technique published in more than 160 scientific journals. These studies have been conducted in many U.S. and international universities and research centres including Harvard, Stanford, Yale and UCLA Medical Schools. For a convenient reference to the many articles, refer to: http://www.tm.org/research-on-meditation.

The regular experience of transcendental consciousness neutralises and even reverses the damaging effects of chronic stress to the individual physiology. The stress response is a necessary reaction of the body in dealing with acute threats to its safety. From an evolutionary perspective however, this response was meant to deal with sudden, short-term threats like an animal attack, immediate environmental hazard or violence from other humans. It was not meant to deal with the prolonged, continuous, unresolved stresses that modern humans finds themselves increasingly exposed to.

Research on Transcendental Meditation has found that it works in reducing the negative effects of chronic stress. TM reduces blood pressure, lowers insulin resistance (useful for preventing diabetes), slows biological ageing and has been found to bring about a 48% reduction in the rates of heart attack, stroke and death. The American Heart Association recently (2013) released a statement saying that decades of research indicate TM lowers blood pressure and may be considered by clinicians as a treatment for high blood pressure.[27]

Research on meditation has also shown a wide range of psychological benefits. For example, a 2012 review of 163 studies that was published by the American Psychological Association concluded that Transcendental Meditation had relatively strong effects in reducing anxiety, negative emotions, trait anxiety and neuroticism while aiding learning, memory and self-realisation. The review concluded that "the effects found in the current analyses show that meditation affects people in important ways".[28]

Does the brain cause consciousness?
NOT TOO MANY DECADES AGO, THE MERE MENTION OF "CONSCIOUSNESS" IN front of a scientific audience would have elicited a similar response to what I noticed in some of my general audiences in earlier years – uncomfortable posturing and bewilderment. The view of most scientists – reliant as they are on objective methods of enquiry – was that consciousness was subjective and therefore not amenable to study.

Along came Francis Crick of the Salk Institute for Biological Studies in La Jolla, California. Krick and fellow British molecular biologist James Watson were the Nobel Prize-winning scientists famous for their discovery of the structure of DNA in 1956. Crick transferred his interest from molecular biology to neuroscience in the late 1970s, and in the 1980s devoted all his energies towards a scientific understanding of consciousness – up to that point – a taboo subject in the field of neuroscience. It was Crick who gave legitimacy to the serious pursuit of consciousness as a subject of scientific study.

Materialists – those who adhere to a reductionist approach in their scientific pursuits – will contend that the brain is the source and generator of conscious awareness, and that with the death of the brain, consciousness ceases to exist. The classical (Newtonian) scientific framework that defines their mode of study, constrains most neuroscientists to a view that consciousness has its genesis inside the brain. One prominent European neuroscientist visiting Australia pretty much summarised the opinion of her profession by saying that "it [consciousness] is all between the ears".[29]

Neuroscientists are understandably buoyed by the considerable advances they are making in their research and understanding about how the brain works. They believe it's just a matter of time before this holy grail of scientific pursuit is discovered.

Some commentators support their reductionist view by relating the accounts of those with severe, otherwise untreatable epilepsy. As a last resort, the corpus callosum – the large bundle of nerve fibres connecting the left and right hemispheres of the brain – is sometimes surgically severed. A patient undergoing this drastic measure might typically give two conflicting answers to a question. It is almost as if there are two competing persons within the same body.[30]

A closer examination of this argument however, suggests to me that this is a case of the brain's conflict in processing information and making appropriate conclusions based on the specialised functions of each side of the brain. As much as it might appear to outside observers that there are "two conscious minds" in the one skull, appearances can deceive.

In addition to neuroscientists, many other scientists soon entered the intellectual and experimental quest for a better understanding of the nature of consciousness. These included psychologists, philosophers, physicists, anaesthesiologists ("anaesthetists" in Australia) and computer scientists.

Australian philosopher David Chalmers is one who helped define the parameters of research. He called the "easy problems" those areas of research that could explain human behaviour or ability through neural mechanisms. An example he gave was: how does the brain integrate information from many different sources and use this information to control behaviour? The 'hard problem' for neuroscientists on the other hand is the question of how physical processes in the brain give rise to subjective experience, or "why does the *feeling* which accompanies awareness of sensory information exist at all?"[31] The explanation for the apparent multiple-personality traits of the split-brain patients just referred to falls into the 'easy problem' category, although Chalmers acknowledges that research into the so-called easy problems is usually very challenging.

Christof Koch, formerly a professor of computation and neural systems at the California Institute of Technology, and – at the time of writing – chief scientific officer at the Allen institute for Brain Science in Seattle, is another respected name in the field of consciousness research. He teamed up with Francis Crick, and together they looked for neural correlates[32] in the brain that could ultimately explain conscious experience. Crick (who passed away in 2004) and Koch were certain that the answer to the quest for the source of consciousness lay in the disciplined field of neuroscience. Koch has expanded his view on the genesis of consciousness in recent years to accommodate what he calls a "version of panpsychism modified for the 21st century"[33]. Panpsychism means that mind (*psyche*) is found everywhere (*pan*). This philosophy is consistent of course with many of the eastern religions and philosophies, but is actually one of the oldest of philosophical doctrines. It certainly is also consistent with the ideas I have been promoting in this book, although 'mind' and 'consciousness' are not identical concepts.[34]

Koch accepts consciousness as "universal" and a "fundamental aspect of reality", and capable – in theory – of being expressed in all living and non-living things. However, the critical criterion according to Koch is that for an entity to be "conscious" it must have an inbuilt information system of sufficient inter-connectivity (integration). The more complex that integrated system is, the more "conscious" the entity can be. Here he acknowledges "integrated information theory" of psychiatrist and neuroscientist Giulio Tononi of the University of Wisconsin.

Another researcher of note is Stuart R. Hameroff, an American anaesthesiologist who teamed up with British physicist Roger Penrose of the University of Oxford. They proposed that consciousness arises from quantum-physical processes taking place in microtubules, small protein structures inside all cells that play a critical role in cell reproduction, acting as the spindles that pull daughter chromosomes apart. There is even some evidence in Hameroff's field of anaesthesiology that these microtubules are affected by the anaesthetics, so possibly playing a role in the loss of consciousness on the operating table.

Hameroff – like Koch – believes that consciousness is "actually fundamental and intrinsic to the universe, that it's built into the universe". He continues: "We need our brain to build this complex picture of consciousness – conscious images, conscious thought and so forth – but the raw precursors of consciousness, the components of consciousness, are what philosophers call *qualia*. I think they are inherent in the universe, much like mass, spin, and charge are fundamental irreducible components[35]. Quantum processes in the brain connect our brain to these fundamental processes intrinsic to the universe."[36] Hameroff has discussed the quantum nature of consciousness with Deepak Chopra, who – as I do – holds the Vedic view that consciousness is everywhere and everything is consciousness. "I wouldn't go that far," says Hameroff. "I would say that protoconsciousness is everywhere – that there's a field, if you will, or the very fine structure of the universe, which is everywhere and which is holographic, repeating at different scales, nonlocally. Consciousness is a fundamental property built into that. It's not everything because there's also mass, spin, or charge, which may not be consciousness.[37] Still, intrinsic to the universe, everywhere you go, are the raw precursors of consciousness."

Hameroff inaugurated the first Toward a Science of Consciousness conference in Tucson, Arizona in 1994, and this has become an annual event with the assistance of David Chalmers. The broader perspective and debate ensuring from these inter-disciplinary meetings will keep the unfolding science of consciousness heading inexorably towards a truly unified theory. After all, that's what happened in the physical sciences.

In 1992 physicist Steven Weinberg mentioned that the goal of physics was to uncover "a theory of everything".[38] Currently, superstring theory might be the theory of everything. Weinberg referred to the 'hard problem' by saying that, if the existence of consciousness cannot be derived from physical laws, a theory of physics is not a true theory of everything. It was on that comment that Chalmers proposed that "conscious experience be considered a fundamental feature, irreducible to anything more basic." Chalmers argued that "if existing fundamental theories cannot encompass it [consciousness], then something new is required".

In his article in *Scientific American*[39], Chalmers complicated this approach towards simplicity and unity by saying: "Thus, a complete theory will have two components: physical laws, telling us about the behaviour of physical systems from the infinitesimal to the cosmological, and what we might call psycho-physical laws, telling us how some of those systems are associated with conscious experience. The two components will constitute a true theory of everything." The problem with this proposal (admittedly made two decades ago) is that we are still dealing with "two components" that cannot by definition constitute a "unified theory". It seems we're still stuck with the Cartesian dichotomy of *res extensa* (material things) and *res cogitans* (thinking things).

CHALMERS' COMMENT, AND FOR THAT MATTER, THE VIEWS OF KOCH AND Hameroff, do not appear to allow a single theory or model of consciousness that also accommodates the physical universe. Why can't we turn around our perspective? Instead of looking for a physical theory that accommodates consciousness, why can't we seek a consciousness theory that accommodates the material and phenomenal world – a "theory of everything" based in consciousness, that *is* consciousness, which in turn accommodates physical laws? Have we not all agreed that consciousness is the most certain, basic aspect of our own existence – *cogito ergo sum*? Have we not also asked, if consciousness is the most basic perceived aspect of our own existence – and we are part of nature – why consciousness isn't the most basic aspect of all of nature?

Chalmers, Koch and Hameroff are respected leaders in the methodical search for a theory of consciousnesss. They all now regard consciousness as a "fundamental", "irreducible" quality found everywhere in nature, but stop short of adopting the Vedic philosophy that consciousness pervades all and is the cause of all things. However, the direction of their research would appear to be converging towards the Vedic view of consciousness, which is basically the unified field model of consciousness we have referred to.

Neuroscientist Russell Hebert is currently undertaking some experiments that might support the brain as a reflector or mediator of pure consciousness and not the generator of consciousness.[40] His work has revealed specific synchronous alpha wave activity (zero-lag phase relationship; see Fig 2) between the front and back of the brain in subjects practising Transcendental Meditation. Communication (coherence) between the front and the back of the brain has been shown to break down dramatically under general anaesthesia, and low levels of "alpha synchronisation likelihood [between front and back of brain] have been associated with mild Alzheimer's dementia". We earlier mentioned that the speed of messages via neurons in the brain is relatively slow compared to electrical signals travelling along a wire. Truly synchronous brainwave activity between distant parts of the brain would therefore more likely represent a quantum-generated phenomenon rather than a neurological (cellular) phenomenon.

I'm sure we'll see an increasing contribution to the field of consciousness research from physicists and mathematicians. No longer do we view consciousness arising from any particular solitary part of the brain. The small pea-sized pineal gland is no longer considered the "seat of the soul" as Rene Descartes asserted centuries ago. While particular parts of the brain have specific roles in sensory perception and delivering commands to other organs and muscles in the body, pure self-awareness (consciousness not focused on any particular content) is considered these days to involve more 'global' communication between different areas of the brain. Indeed, if Hebert's work is any indication of where the study of consciousness is heading, brain research will become more focused on patterns of wave activity between different areas of the brain and their interactions with each other. Hebert's observation of "standing" waves and "travelling" waves of EEG activity in the brain would suggest that the challenges ahead lie more in the domain of physics than biology alone.

It has been proposed that synchronous oscillations or rhythms in thalamocortical loops in the gamma band of frequencies create the conscious state. While the role of the thalamus and its communication with the cerebral cortex in the front of the head is still considered crucial to conscious experience,[41] it seems surprising to me, having acquainted myself with the studies of Fred Travis, Keith Wallace and Russell Hebert demonstrating the likely role of alpha waves as a "foundational" wave in different states of consciousness, that gamma waves – associated with a strong "object" referral orientation of the brain's attention instead of a "self-referral" orientation – would be attributed such importance.

To this day, no plausible theory has been proposed that explains consciousness as an emergent property arising purely from neuronal processes in the brain.

The Vedic perspective

THROUGHOUT THIS BOOK, I HAVE EXPLORED AND DEVELOPED THE hypothesis that consciousness is the suspected unified field of all the laws of nature and is therefore fundamental to our very existence and certainly to our notion of self. If you see merit in this hypothesis, then you will also see the improbability that nature would 're-invent' consciousness as a product of the brain. The more logical way of seeing the brain is an organ of the body that mediates consciousness through our nervous system, rather than being solely responsible for generating consciousness. From the perspective of the unified field model of consciousness, consciousness can be argued to ultimately be the "generator" of the brain, rather than the other way around.

"Maharishi Vedic Science[42] accepts that brain activity is necessary for experience, but locates a field of consciousness that generates and is expressed through the material world."[43] To experience anything, we need to have dichotomy and separation; we need to have hot and cold, rough and smooth, love and hate, red and blue. We have physical senses to discriminate amongst this field of diversity. Thus, to experience, we need a nervous system with the brain as the chief executive officer.

In the following passage from the Katha-Upanishad (Part 111), "mind" is that part of consciousness "engaged in the projected field of manifest diversity",[44] and therefore usually tied up with sensory experience. The "intellect" is actually a finer level of this individual level of consciousness, and is more involved with discrimination, and deciding what to do with sensory input.

Part 111

111

Know the Atman (Self) as The Lord of the chariot, and the body as the chariot. Know also the intellect to be the driver and the mind to be the reins.

1V

The senses are called the horses ; the sense objects are the roads; when the Atman is united with body, senses and mind, then the wise call Him the enjoyer.

V1

But he who is full of discrimination, and whose mind is always controlled, his senses are manageable, like the good horses of a driver.

X1

Beyond the great Atman is the Unmanifested; beyond the Unmanifested is the Purusha (the Cosmic Soul); beyond the Purusha there is nothing. That is the end, that

NOTES

1. Compare with comment from St Rabi'a, that her "being has disappeared for I have become as nothing to my self". Ch 15.
2. Also called isolation tanks or sensory deprivation tanks.
3. Rosenthal, Norman; *Transcendence – Healing and Transformation through Transcendental Meditation*; Jeremy P. Tarcher / Penguin; p 32–35.
4. Rosenthal, Norman; *Transcendence – Healing and Transformation through Transcendental Meditation*; Jeremy P. Tarcher / Penguin; p 34.
5. Douillard, John; *Body, Mind & Sport*; Bantam Books, 1994; p 9-10.
6. *Maharishi Mahesh Yogi on the Bhagavad-Gita; A New Translation and Commentary*, Ch 4, Vs 13
7. Douillard, John; *Body, Mind & Sport*; Bantam Books, 1994; p 4.
8. Douillard, John; *Body, Mind & Sport*; Bantam Books, 1994, p 6.
9. These days, commonly referred to as temporo-mandibular disorder (TMD)
10. Wilson, Timothy et al, University of Virginia, *Science* (Sciencemag.org), Issue 6192, 4 July, 2014.
11. Pascal, Blaise (1623–62), French philosopher, mystic and physicist.
12. Maharishi Mahesh Yogi (2001). *The science of being and the art of living,* New York, Plume/Penguin Putman Inc., p. 50. (Original work published 1963).
13. A state of happiness not reliant on any particular cause.
14. *Maharishi Mahesh Yogi on the Bhagavad-Gita; A New Translation and Commentary*, Chapters 1-6, Penguin Books; Ch 2, p 145.
15. See page quote from *Katha-Upanishad*, page 25 of this chapter.
16. *Maharishi Mahesh Yogi on the Bhagavad-Gita; A New Translation and Commentary*, Chapters 1-6, Penguin Books; Ch 2, p 136.
17. Go to http://www.tm.org/learn-tm to find a qualified instructor near you.
18. Neurons are also sometimes referred to as "neurones".
19. A trillion is 1000 times a billion in the American numerical system to which I refer here.
20. Coherence should be distinguished from synchrony in neurological terms. Coherence refers to stability in the phase relationship between wave activity in one part of the brain with another. Coherence can have a leading or lagging relationship (see diagram). In synchrony, waves in different parts of the brain are up at the same time or down at the same time. There may be differences in wave amplitude (height).
21. Rosenthal, Norman; *Transcendence – Healing and Transformation through Transcendental Meditation*; Jeremy P. Tarcher / Penguin; p 22
22. Rosenthal, Norman; *Transcendence – Healing and Transformation through Transcendental Meditation*; Jeremy P. Tarcher / Penguin; p 23
23. Maharishi has also defined the ongoing evolution of consciousness beyond "cosmic consciousness" as next, "God Consciousness" and finally "Unity Consciousness", See Appendix for a description of these developed states of consciousness.
24. *Maharishi Mahesh Yogi on the Bhagavad-Gita*, Ch 4, p 313
25. Pearson, Craig; *The Complete Book of Yogic Flying*; Maharishi University of Management Press; p 64
26. Chapter 15, *Levitation and Flying*, page..
27. Brook RD et al., 'Beyond Medications and Diet: Alternative Approaches to Lowering Blood Pressure. A Scientific Statement from the American Heart Association', *Hypertension*, 61:00, 2013.
28. Sedlmeier, Peter; Eberth, Juliane; Schwarz, Marcus; Zimmermann, Doreen; Haarig, Frederik; Jaeger, Sonia; Kunze, Sonja; The Psychological Effects of Meditation: A meta-analysis'; *Psychological Bulletin*, Vol 138(6), Nov 2012, 1139-1171.
29. *The Sydney Morning Herald* article circa 2011-2012.
30. Mlodinow, Leonard, *War of the Worldviews*, Deepak Chopra and Leonard Mlodinow, Rider Publications, p191

31 Chalmers, David, *Wikipedia*
32 "Neural correlates of consciousness" refer to the observations that there are specific patterns of brain activity for every observed state of consciousness or direction of one's attention to any object.
33 Koch, Christof, 2014, Jan 1, *Is Consciousness Universal?* Scientific American Mind (www.scientificamerican.com/article/is-consciousness-universal/)
34 See Glossary
35 Mass and spin are in fact particular "flavours" or qualities of vibration of one underlying quantum field, so in a sense are reducible.
36 Hameroff, Stuart, MD, 'What is Consciousness? A Conversation with Stuart Hameroff'. *Noetic Now Journal*; Institute of Noetic Sciences, Issue 13, August 2011. (Interviewed by Marilyn Schlitz, IONS President)
37 Remember that we correlated these properties – the fundamental spin types of the underlying quantum field, with the *mahabutas* described by the subjective experience of early seers exploring the depths of their own consciousness.
38 Weinberg, Steven; *Dreams of a Final Theory – The Scientist's Search for the Ultimate Laws of Nature;* Random House Inc, New York.
39 Chalmers, David J., 'The Puzzle of Conscious Experience'; *Scientific American*, December, 1995
40 Hebert, Russell et al; 'Enhanced EEG alpha time-domain phase synchrony during Transcendental Meditation: Implications for cortical integration theory'; *Signal Processing*; www.ElsevierComputerScience.com
41 Travis, Frederick; 'Core and Matrix Thalamic Nuclei: Parallel Circuits Involved in Content of Experience and General Wakefulness'; *NeuroQuantology,* June 2012, Vol 10, Issue 2.
42 The study of ancient Vedic knowledge integrated with many fields of modern science including physics, mathematics, medicine, agriculture and architecture as instigated by Maharishi Mahesh Yogi.
43 'Main Point' in on-line *Brain and Consciousness* course; Fred Travis and Keith Wallace, MUM, Iowa, USA.
44 Maharishi Mahesh Yogi, *The Science of Being and the Art of Living*, tenth printing, 1984, p 30.

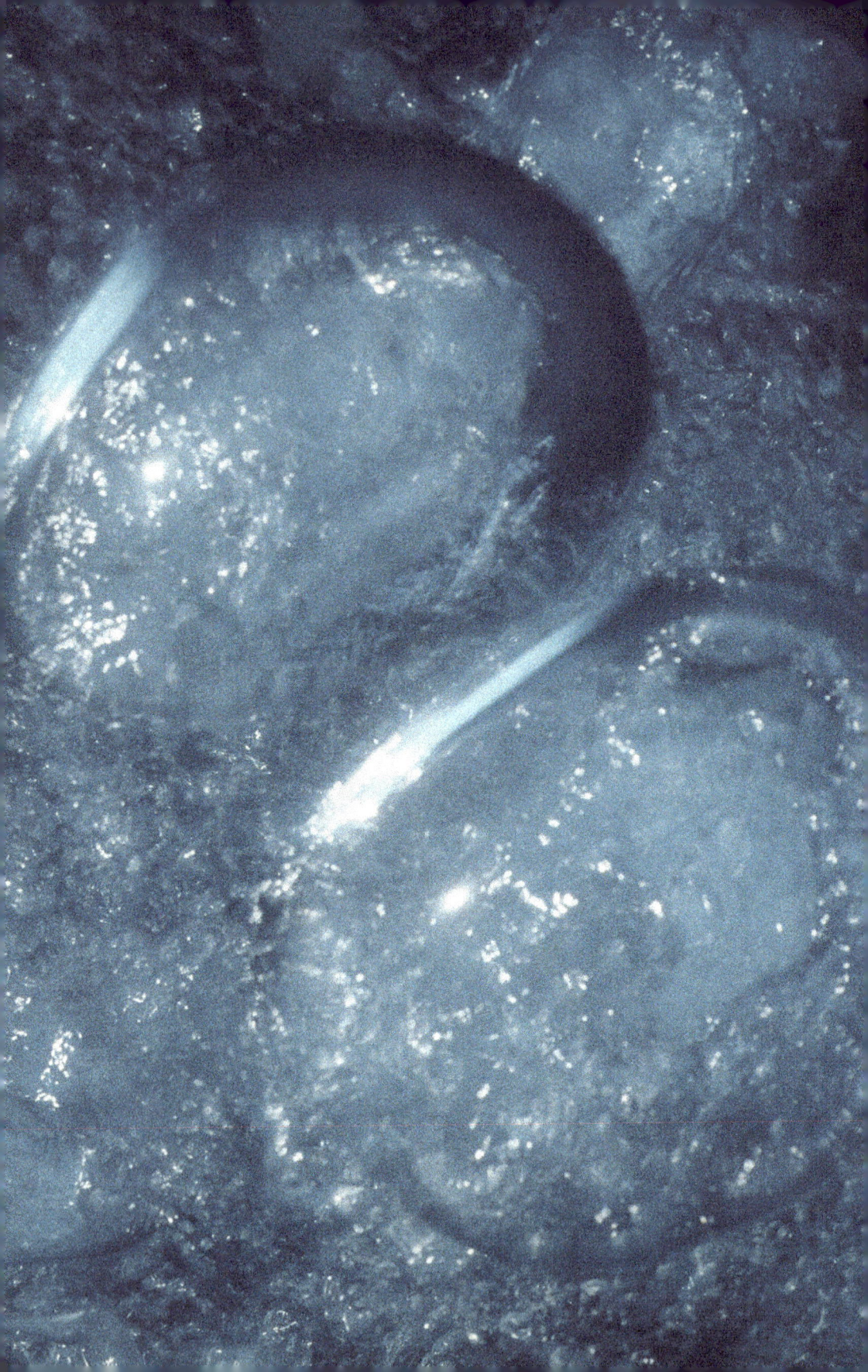

Chapter Seventeen

GOD, LIFE AND LOVE – AN OCEAN OF LIFE

"There is Light within a Person of Light, and it illuminates the entire cosmos."[1]

– Jesus Christ – Gospel of Thomas

Becoming familiar with the Ocean of Self allows us to experience God rather than simply know or believe in God. In experiencing that Ocean of Self within, we soon discover it also as an Ocean of Love. In time, we become full of Life and Love (cosmic consciousness) and realise the Kingdom of God within.

The importance of experience

To gain a deeper core-level understanding of God, life and love, it is important to experience the deeper Self underlying our usual sense-dependent notion of self. Earlier in the chapter on physics, Dr Hagelin stressed that physics may have "walked the Planck" with its reliance on objective observation in further deciphering the subatomic world below the Planck scale. Subjective understanding of this sub-Planck scale realm – the realm of the proposed unified field – by going within and directly experiencing the dynamics of the Self, is likely to be the sensible path for a better understanding of this realm of the superstrings, which lies beyond time, space and causation. The same argument applies to a better understanding of our own nature – that Ocean of Being we have referred to as the big Self or Pure Consciousness. I have proposed that the unified field described by superstring theory and pure consciousness (Ātmā) are one and the same thing.

> "This Self cannot be realized by studying the scriptures,
> nor through the use of reason,
> nor from the words of others
> – no matter what they say.
> By the grace of the Self is the Self known,
> The Self reveals Itself."
>
> – Mundaka Upanishad

It's as if we need to get off one train and board a totally different train to further move along the track towards Self-realisation. The first train, which has taken us through the gross, material world of the relative, has arrived at its terminal. It has served us well. It is now necessary to further explore the most subtle field of existence beyond what our tools can measure or divide – the field of the absolute. That train will be the vehicle that takes us into the inner realms of our own Self to better understand that which lies at the basis of everything else in the universe.

Years ago, while on an adventurous diving trip aboard a charter boat off the east coast of New Zealand's North Island, I had a dream which I think was more than just a dream. In that dream I approached a young man, who looked familiar, sitting on a low brick wall at the main entrance to the St James railway station, near where my dental practice was in Sydney's central business district. He asked me what train he should catch to reach a certain destination (I have forgotten what that destination was – and it was probably not important). I told him what train to catch and which platform he needed. I then asked him: "You're Babaji aren't you?"[2] He did not respond to my question, but instead placed some money into my hands. That was the end of my dream.

I believe the famous Indian saint Mahavatar Babaji had come to me in that dream, not representing the individual known as Babaji, but representing the whole of mankind. That is why he did not respond affirmatively to my question. His asking directions of me to reach a certain destination, was a request for help in the path we should take in our ongoing search for Self-knowledge and spiritual enlightenment. Collectively, we need to board a new train and take a new path in our pursuit of such knowledge. This new train represents a paradigm shift in the method through which we acquire knowledge and understanding. We cannot rely on the physical senses alone in this path towards Self-knowledge. Transcending consciousness through regular meditation is the best vehicle to take this journey.

With a realisation of the Absolute through direct experience, we will gain a better perspective of that which is the Relative – the expressed material and phenomenal world. We will also bring ourselves closer to that core-level understanding – a true visceral comprehension of God, Life and Love. I believe this dream represented further validation and encouragement for the themes I have been presenting in this book.

A special note from the author
From here on in this chapter, I will draw frequently from the writings of Neale Donald Walsch, author of the *Conversations with God* series of books. He is one who writes of his direct communications with God. I am aware that any treatise or academic position that draws heavily from one source is usually treated with suspicion. That certainly applies to my professional life in the field of dentistry. However, in discussion of these topics, the selection of references available is slim.

Although I was a sceptic when I first laid eyes on Neale's books, I was very quickly drawn to the wisdom they contained. How could I be suspicious of his claim to be conversing with God when I too have had such direct communication with God and even conversation, although not to anywhere near the extent of Neale's? Also, in careful and critical reading of the content of these conversations, I have found them to be almost entirely consistent with my own experiences, my understanding of the unified field model of consciousness, and my hope for the existence of a God like the One who speaks to the author in these books.

God

EARLY ONE CHRISTMAS MORNING A FEW YEARS AGO, WHEN WE HAD SOME extended family staying with us, I went to the local fishermen's co-operative retail outlet at the Coffs Harbour Jetty to purchase some prawns (typically called "shrimp" in America) for lunch. As I was leaving, my attention was seized momentarily by an attractive young lady approaching with her family. I was pondering the uniqueness of her beauty – a face unmatched with any of the billions of other humans in this world, a great many of them, of course, just as beautiful in their own way.

Quite spontaneously I struck up my own very natural conversation with God. I said (as a thought message) "Aren't you clever God?" I received an immediate, crystal clear and unmistakable thought message back. "Aren't *you* clever?" was God's response. It wasn't a booming voice from the heavens which only I could hear. It was more unmistakable than that. It was as if someone close to me had replied to my comment in simple conversational language. It was a message directed straight to the very core of my alert being. The need for ears or eyes was bypassed. And yes – for those sceptics who would assert I was just talking to myself – I *was* speaking to my Self, and hearing back from my Self. The big Self is that ocean of consciousness within us all and common to us all. It is the big Self at the basis of our smaller selves. The message had no distance to travel at all! It was sent by the Self and received by the Self. God – or at least my notion of God – is not separate from anyone of us. We are all embodiments of God.

I have not mentioned God much in this book. Most people seem to feel uncomfortable or at least ambivalent when anyone mentions God. I believe this relates to the common depiction of God as a separate ruling entity, and also the purported ownership of 'God's authority' by any number of religious institutions. Also, because we are seeing atrocities committed in the name of 'God', many believe a world without religion would be a better world.

No amount of argument or rational debate can prove the existence or non-existence of God. This is also one of the reasons we generally like to keep the subject of God at a personal level or else confined to inside the walls of churches, temples, mosques or synagogues. So we find ourselves in one of two situations in approaching an understanding of God. One is a concept of God that we learn through faith alone: that is, what we have been told about God through scriptures and the institutions we have entrusted in the interpretation of those scriptures. The other is a concept of God obtained through personal experience and/or identity with God. The two comprehensions are likely to be very different. The second approach to our relationship with God – one of direct experience and even communication – is also likely to be considered improbable or highly doubted, and a practice even discouraged by established religions.

The reader of this book will already suspect that this ocean of consciousness that I have equated with the unified field or superstring field currently explored by modern science *is* God. That would be a correct conclusion, but the unified field is not the be-all and end-all of God. Rather, God is the be-all and end-all of everything. By "everything", I mean the unified field and all that is manifested from the unified field. There is nothing that is not God. There is no separation of anyone or anything from God. There cannot be. If there was, then the God that is everything minus this, that or someone, is by definition a lesser God than an all-inclusive God.

> *"He is the First and the Last; and the Manifest and the Hidden; and He is knower of all things"*[3]
>
> – Hoque, Qur'an

> *"'I am the Alpha and the Omega, the Beginning and the End', says the Lord God, He Who is and Who was and Who is to come, the Almighty."*[4]
>
> – Revelation

I have quoted scripture with the above verses, as there is wisdom and knowledge to guide us in the scriptures of most of the long-established religions.

The following excerpt is a quote from God in Neale Donald Walsch's conversations describing God's nature:

> *"This is the energy of life. This is what you have chosen to call Absolute Love. This is the God and the Goddess, the Alpha and the Omega, the Beginning and the End. It is the All-in-All, the Unmoved Mover, the Prime Source. It is that which you have sought to understand from the beginning of time. The Great Mystery, the Endless Enigma, the*

eternal truth. There is only One of Us, and so, it is 'THAT WHICH YOU ARE'." [5]

What greater gift could the God that I have hoped for, offer us than to make us One of God, an individual expression of God, a manifestation of God?

"You and I are One. We cannot be anything else if I Am what I Am: All That Is." [6]

And yet, still prevalent today, we have the continuation of the Cartesian-Newtonian paradigm that continues to pervade our way of thinking. This mode of thinking sees God as separate from us, ruling His kingdom from some world apart from ours. What we need is a true Unity model of seeing the world, a model that is consistent with the current direction of our disciplined sciences, a model that sees all that is diverse and separate as emanating from one source. Such a model would accommodate the idea of you and me as an expression of God, not a creation in the usual, restricted sense of being made of something else. I believe the unified field model of consciousness accommodates this needed paradigm shift.

"WE NEED A NEW GOD"[7]. THIS WAS ONE OF THE VERY MEMORABLE comments Neale Donald Walsch made to God in one of his books. In Neale's commentary God just happened to agree. "The old one never worked," God said in reply. We – the 'believers' – need to move beyond the idea of God as separate to us, having needs and demands, having conditional love, being of the male gender and for that matter any gender, prepared to punish His subjects with the eternal fires of hell and having preference for some of His subjects over others. To embrace a "new God" is actually of critical importance. Do I need to detail what's happening in the world today?

To be honest, I identify with and agree with many of the comments made by atheists in today's media. Their stances with regard to social and personal issues of the current times are usually less frightening, more inclusive, tolerant, compassionate and freer than what is promoted by many of the religious zealots of the world. The God so often portrayed by the dogmatists is not my God. No wonder the self-proclaimed atheists and agnostics of the world reject the notion of such an entity.

Just as it is now important to look within the self, that is, to rely on the subjective path to knowledge to further explore the nature of the unified field or the ultimate nature of consciousness in our scientific pursuits, so too is it important to develop our individual consciousness to reach that state we have referred to as Cosmic Consciousness, which will then naturally evolve to God Consciousness. We will never understand God through the intellect alone, and that includes the rote learning of scripture. We must experience God as One with our own Self.

You might be aware of the three-in-one (triune) nature of God that has been described as the Holy Trinity. Three aspects of God have been described in the bible.[8] The patriarchal nature of traditional religions accounts for the male orientation of this description of the Trinity. God the 'Father' is the all-knowing aspect of the One God; that aspect of God which 'gives rise to'. This is God the 'Knower'.

God the Son is the experiencing aspect of God; that aspect of God which is 'risen'. To experience anything, one needs dichotomy (duality) expressed through multiplicity and diversity – the physical world. God experiences God-Self through each and every one of us. We are the embodiment of God, the acting out of knowledge. Then there is God the Holy Spirit (or Holy Ghost). This is pure Being. Being represents the "disembodiment of all that the Son has experienced of Itself." Being is the "exquisite is-ness possible only through knowing and experiencing". [9]

God the Son is you and me. It is Jesus Christ too. Jesus, the self-proclaimed "Son of Man"[10] was trying to tell us – I believe – that we too can be as God-realised as He was. In the Gnostic *Gospel of Thomas*[11] Jesus said something which explains just what is meant by "God the Son":

"The kingdom is inside you and outside you at the same time. When you come to know yourself, then you will be known. You will realize then that it's you who are the sons of the living Father. But as long as you do not know yourself, you will live in poverty, and you will be that poverty."[12]

Jesus also said: "When you make the two one, you will become the sons of men".[13] When we can see the unity in diversity, we will adopt a broader sense of self. We will identify ourselves with all the rest of mankind and not see ourselves as separate from broader humanity. That is what I believe Jesus meant in referring to Himself as "the Son of Man". By referring to Himself or any of us as "the Son of Man", Jesus means that the individual identifies with all of mankind and sees himself or herself as a representative of all mankind.[14] Babaji, when he came to me in the dream I related earlier in this chapter, was also identifying himself as the whole of humanity. Likewise, "Son of God" means that the individual identifies with God and sees himself or herself also as a representative of God.

"Without the ocean, the wave does not have the power to be a wave. Without me, you do not have the power to be you. And without you, my power is not made manifest. Your joy is to make me manifest. The joy of humanity is to manifest God."[15]

We are collaborators with God, partaking in the experience of life. We are individual expressions of God – Sons of God – "experiencing ourselves anew in the grandest version of the greatest vision ever we held about who we really are"[16]. That is God's purpose to life and it is also ours. While it is true that we are 'expressions' or 'individual manifestations' of God, it would be a mistake (in more ways than one) to go around saying "I am God!" The wave is indeed part of the ocean, but it is not the whole ocean. The individual wave does not have the fullness of the whole ocean. The individual wave does not include all the other waves within it, whereas the ocean does. But the individual wave can draw as much of the ocean into it as it wishes, or it might decide to absorb itself into the ocean, losing its individual identity – its small self – and assuming the whole ocean, becoming the big Self. It is no longer an "I" but sees itself through all individuals. In identifying Itself through all the I's, it just IS.

When God said to me: "Aren't *you* clever!" in response to my assertion that God was clever for the creation of the world around me, God was emphasising that all of us are equal players in the creation we call "life". Because this was a thought message, there was no mistaking on my part that God was referring to all of us – not just me as an individual – as being co-creators of this world and universe. We have come out of the Oneness to experience ourselves anew in the manner just described, and have assumed bodily form to do so. By the way – as it should be apparent with the early chapters in this book – I have no problem with Darwinian evolutionary theories, which allow life to unfold in the time-space dimensions of life. While still incomplete, modern evolutionary theory is proven science.

The Ocean of Life I referred to in the first chapter as the marine predecessors of all living plants and creatures on this Earth, can now hopefully be appreciated in its broader dimension. The Ocean of Life is an Ocean of Consciousness, is God, is an Ocean of Being, is an Ocean of Self (Your Self), is an Ocean of Spirit, and *is all there is*.

Although the concept of unity seems simple enough to comprehend, we have a hard time truly grasping unity as it applies to the Oneness of All Things. The intellect can grasp the notion of unity, but it cannot fully comprehend its true significance without also experiencing unity.

IN 1987, I WAS A YOUNGER, SINGLE MAN LIVING ON MY OWN IN THE SYDNEY beach suburb of Dee Why. At 3.30 in the morning, I awoke for no apparent reason and remained peacefully still in my bed, more or less on my back. I felt rested and without thoughts when I became aware of a warm, all-loving and comforting presence in the room. Although I didn't see anything, in my mind I interpreted the 'presence' as being just in from the doorway and about where the wall meets the ceiling. I don't think geographic location really mattered. My interpretation of a specific site probably reflected my need to relate to a source for this entity.

I then felt a kind of tingling: an electric sensation or a lively but very pleasant energy move up through my whole body, from my feet to my head. It was as if every cell in my body was joyfully enlivened to this event. Then, a feeling of pure love welled up from within me and poured out towards this beautiful presence. That sending out of love took about three or four seconds. Then, the same intense, pure, unconditional love poured back into me from that entity – for about the same length of time. Then came a simple, but very clear thought message from this divine source – "Your underwater photography is good".

If I heard someone say that to me verbally, I would ask for clarification. Did that person mean "your underwater photography is award-winning stuff and I'm impressed"? Or did that person mean "your pursuit and love of underwater photography is a good activity for you to be undertaking"? As much as my ego might have enjoyed the first interpretation, this was after-all a thought message, and that form of communication is a very unequivocal way of conveying a message. It is a much better form of communication than the use of words alone, which can be misunderstood or misinterpreted. The message was clear – my photography was indeed a worthwhile and commendable activity.

After that message, I looked at the digital clock to check the time and then went back to sleep. When I awoke a couple of hours later, I went about my business of being a dentist for the day. I do recall reflecting occasionally on just what the significance of my underwater photography was. How was I to put it to "good" use? Was my goal to assist the suffering ocean environment in some way? Perhaps. Or was there a means whereby my photography could assist me in exploring those connections between my experiences as a diver in the ocean and broader existential issues that concern (or should concern) humanity – life itself, death, interconnectedness, love and other issues of a spiritual nature?

Over a year or more reflecting on this communication I concluded that my photography could assist both issues – the physical environment and spiritual education. However, I increasingly felt myself being drawn to the interesting comparison of the diving experience with the transcending experiences I had in meditation. By this time, I had been practising

Transcendental Meditation for some six years and the advanced TM-Sidhi program for two.

LET ME REVISIT THE BEAUTIFUL EXPERIENCE I HAD THAT NIGHT IN 1987. First of all, who or what was it that communicated with me? I believe it was God. I'm hoping by now that you can accommodate this assertion given my explanation of God as not separate from you or me, but very much the essence of you or me. I'm open to the possibility that my communication may have been with an individual spirit such as Jesus, a saint or a deceased family member, but whoever communicated with me did not see it important to convey identity as such. The Source was pure and untainted by quality or description.

I felt entirely and completely at home during this special encounter. I easily returned to sleep without feeling that anything was 'abnormal' and went about my usual activities the next day without even reflecting on it that often. That special merging with the pure spirit felt like 'home'. Somewhere in my existence as a soul or whatever conscious entity I have been (and remain) I must have been there before. Maybe I am there now![17] It was as if something deep down in my memory was revived. It was truly 'home' in the deepest and most fundamental way we could imagine. I must have come from there and to there I will surely return. Maybe in the ultimate transcendent, spiritual sense, I have never left!

The thought message "Your underwater photography is good" was not a command or request. It was up to me to decide how I wished to pursue that reinforcement of the worthiness of my love of diving and photography. Over the many years since that divine message, I have found myself enjoying the exploration of our spiritual nature and relating that to my experiences in diving. I discovered that there are wonderful metaphors with the ocean and diving that can help me better acquaint myself with Vedic (yogic) knowledge and share that knowledge and any personal insights with others. I have shared some of these ocean-related experiences with you and my interpretation of them. The experiences I have had while diving on shipwrecks or with ocean animals seem to consolidate some of the theory related to Vedic science (the subjective science of consciousness) and other spiritual writings.

Someone might ask, "why were *you* so privileged to have received word from the Almighty? This could be your vivid imagination working overtime during the dreaming hours of sleep". On the question of privilege, we must remind ourselves that God is not separate from us, but is integral to our very Being, so an intimate and personal encounter with God is within everyone's ability to experience at any time – and even at all times. I am certainly not the only person to have had this special encounter, nor am I in any special 'favour' with God. I know that God sees all of us as special and equally as precious. After all, we are all One with God, part of God, individual expressions of God, God manifest. Would God love any part of God's Self more than another part?

This "selectivity" question reflects the predominant separation paradigm that still pervades our world view and our way of thinking. It was raised in the play *Sacrifice* by Rabindranath Tagore, the Nobel Prize-winning Indian poet. The king's brother Nakshatra mentions that "it is strange that the King should have heard from gods and not the priest". The King, Govinda, replies: "God's words are ever ringing in the world, and he who is willfully deaf cannot hear them".

In Neale Donald Walsch's first book in the *Conversations with God* series, God says: "I talk to everyone. All the time. The question is not to whom do I talk, but who listens?"

It is a matter of attuning our awareness to our true spiritual nature. This attunement could be alive and running at all times, but for some of us – myself included – it is only rarely turned on. Jesus says much the same in his comment: "Behold, I stand at the door and knock; if anyone hears and listens to and heeds My voice and opens the door, I will come in to him and will eat with him, and he will eat with Me".[18]

This divine communication has been a major encouraging influence behind the writing of this book. I believe we can all help each other in spiritual awareness and development. I am certainly no special scholar when it comes to matters spiritual or even philosophical. I have my share of imperfections, shortcomings and idiosyncrasies, and I have made some errors in my interaction with others. I am just one other unique person, sharing my experiences and insights in the hope that they resonate in some way with your own experiences and insights.

Life

LIFE *IS* GOD, AND GOD *IS* LIFE.

We are part of life, and life is the theatre that allows God to experience All that God is through us and all creatures. Life is God manifest, "God made physical"[19] and if we look at the triune nature of God, then Life too can be seen as God the Son, or the experiencing aspect of God.

Rabindranath Tagore wrote beautifully of the spiritual dimension of life, and in this verse, he illustrates this cooperative nature of God and us: "My poet, is it thy delight to see thy creation through my eyes and to stand at the portals of my ears, silently to listen to thine own eternal harmony? Thy world is weaving words in my mind and thy joy is adding music to them. Thou givest thyself to me in love and then feelest thine own entire sweetness in me."[20]

Biologists would normally define life as "a distinctive characteristic of a living organism from a dead organism or non-living thing, as specifically distinguished by the capacity to grow, metabolize, respond (to stimuli), adapt, and reproduce"[21]. In our context, I would prefer to look at life as the whole of manifest existence as we know it – us, fellow living things on this planet and all the non-living background as well. All of life – what we refer to as living and non-living – is conscious. This allows us to see all of life as a dynamic, interrelated web of connections instead of material separate things.

Living organisms can pro-create. This creative ability of living things can also be seen to varying degrees in what we refer to as the non-living things of our universe. We have learnt that the stars in our Universe are busy creators of varied chemical elements, those components that can ultimately become the DNA of life. So too, creation might be occurring in the deep sea thermal vents, here on Earth and possibly other planetary bodies, where just the right conditions of pressure, heat, water (or perhaps another liquid hydrocarbon medium like methane[22]) and component elements can bring about more complex molecules – the building blocks of life. Creation therefore works at many levels in nature. All of it can be rightly seen as life.

Life in this broader context is the contextual arena that allows us – and God – to experience anything. Again, to experience we must have dichotomy expressed through multiplicity and diversity.

"It is the nature of Life to express itself. That is what Life does. It cannot not do this, or it would not be. Now change the word 'life' in the above sentence. Notice that 'life' can also be called 'God', 'That Which Is', 'the Essence', 'the Energy', or whatever else you wish to call it. No matter what word you use, you are still talking about Life. In the process of Self expression, Life quite literally 'expresses' Itself. That is, It pushes itself out from Itself, giving birth to Itself as an aspect OF Itself, that it might Know Itself in its Own Experience."[23] "It is in this way that entire universes are born."[24]

Can you see all of the Trinity inherent again here in Life itself – the three-in-one aspect of God working again through God the Son (Life)? This demonstrates how important it is to comprehend the unity when looking at each of the parts. When Life gives "birth to Itself as an aspect of Itself", we see again God the Father (Life, the expresser) and God the Son

(Life expressed) and the Holy Spirit (that quality of Being – bliss and love) resulting from Life experiencing Itself. Can you also see the creative nature of this three-in-one description of God?

Jesus also emphasised the important relationship between "life" and God when He said: "It is the spirit that gives life; the flesh is useless. The words that I have spoken to you are spirit and life. But among you there are some who do not believe."[25]

Again, poet Rabindranath Tagore, demonstrating his own deep insight into the glory of life, and hinting that life is indeed the arena for God and us to experience ourselves anew as who we truly are, said: "In this playhouse of infinite forms I have had my play and here have I caught sight of Him that is formless".[26]

As Maharishi Mahesh Yogi so poignantly commented in that video-recorded lecture in Iowa: "Life is a Miracle; Life is a Miracle". That we are experiencing diversity and multiplicity so realistically, in the knowledge of our essential Unity, is the true miracle that we call Life.

Death
SOMEONE MIGHT SAY: "LOOK! WHEN SOMEONE DIES, WHAT WE ARE looking at is definitely NOT conscious. There's nothing there! Those EEG readings you talk about are flat! There's simply no consciousness!"

Here is another example of where appearances deceive. Any information we have about that person who has died is after all, second-hand. What we see is a brain no longer functioning. But – as obvious as it is to say this – our usual connection with each other is through speech, body language and other physical forms of communication. How can we know that our deceased friend is no longer conscious? Was his or her 'essence' the body? Based on what we have explored in this book, no – it's not. The unified field model of consciousness allows for consciousness to continue because the proposed unified field lies beyond time and space and is therefore not subject to cause and effect. Consciousness itself can't die. Who and what you are – in essence – can't die. It just *is*, and will always *be*.

"When you understand that life is eternal, you understand that death is your illusion, keeping you very concerned with, and therefore helping you believe that you *are*, your body. Yet you are *not* your body, and so the destruction of your body is of no concern to you."[27]

Lord Krishna explains to the archer Arjuna that our existence, in the real sense, cannot be destroyed by weapons. "Weapons cannot cleave him, nor fire burn him; water cannot wet him, nor wind dry him away."[28] In Maharishi's commentary: "Reality is one, omnipresent, devoid of any duality, without components – that is why It cannot be slain. The body is composed of different parts – that is why it can be slain".

In discussing the nature of consciousness related to physical death, I am now entering an area of which I have scant detail to relate. Some personal experiences I have shared in this book certainly convince me that there is more to our personal existence than that contained in our mortal bodies.

If, when we die, our brains no longer mediate our consciousness, does that mean we lose our individuality and 'personality' after we drop off this mortal coil? Based on what we are told from the main religious traditions, no – we will all maintain most or all of those individual traits that define us, with possibly the exception of physical bodily appearances and traits. Based on my reading of Neale Donald Walsch's excellent publications, I agree that the 'soul' contains, forms and shapes the body and probably retains much information about the body, including memories, after death. The soul also is an expression of universal consciousness (the unified field) and can also be seen as an individual wave of consciousness on the One Ocean of Consciousness. Unlike the physical body, which appears very distinct and separate from other bodies, the soul – again according to my understanding of Neale's books – truly does reflect the qualities of a wave. A wave – while having its own individual qualities – has no boundary that separates it from the ocean. So too, an individual soul is not so separated from other souls. But I don't think we need to see that as being chained to other souls. We will experience more freedom than ever after death – ultimate freedom.

You will hopefully recall my story and interpretation of Rhys's acceptance of death and his adoption of manta rays as his vehicle into a vibrant new life. The manta rays and their ocean playground were symbolic of everything we see as splendid and wondrous about life. Popular author and eminent neurologist Oliver Sachs recently passed away at the age of 82 with metastatic cancer.[29] Just a few months ago, I was reading about his personal preparation for death. He admitted to some fear of dying, but tempered this feeling by writing, "Over the last few days, I have been able to see my life as from a great altitude, as a sort of landscape, and with a deepening sense of the connection of all its parts. This does not mean I am finished with life. On the contrary, I feel intensely alive, and I want and hope in the time that remains to deepen my friendships, to say farewell to those I love, to write more, to travel if I have the strength, to achieve new levels of understanding and insight."[30] These priorities of a dying person are well worth noting. I believe that his feeling "intensely alive" was just a forerunner to his experience at death, which will be the experience of more intense life than ever. In the 'end', *Life is all there is.*

"First, understand that death is not an end, but a beginning; not a horror, but a joy. It is not a closing down, but an opening up.

The happiest moment of your life will be the moment it ends.

That's because it doesn't end, but only goes on in ways so magnificent, so full of peace and wisdom and joy, as to make it difficult to describe and impossible for you to comprehend."[31]

Love
Love is God and God is Love.
"Love is the ultimate reality. It is the only. The all. The feeling of love is your experience of God."[32]

On the 17th November, 2012, I walked down the corridor of the aged-care facility in which my mother[33] resided. Living a few hundred kilometres from each other, I had not seen her for many months. She was walking slowly in my direction and our eyes connected. As we got closer to each other, I felt a magnanimous wave of love welling up inside of me. It was a positively emotional experience. My dear beautiful mother – afflicted with advanced dementia – folded into the embracement of my arms with her head into my chest. The love of a mother for her offspring is unique in this world, and such a love – felt deeply by her son since his earliest memories – was naturally reciprocated as unconditionally as it has always been received.

After a few seconds of this exchange of pure love, my mother – unable to carry out a meaningful or coherent conversation for some time – said to me: "I'm really proud of you. I'm really proud of you". Mothers tend to be proud of their children for whatever small achievement they make, and I had heard this remark before, during her more vital years. Still, I was wondering where this remark had come from and why she said it. She was certainly not privy to anything going on in my life.

Then she said, "You're different to the rest of us. You have a special calling". My mother's cognitive decline had progressed to a level where she was incapable of stringing together many words, and certainly not of this profundity. Where had that comment come from?

It became clear to me that my mother had accessed a part of her consciousness that is all-knowing, and beyond space and time. I know she was referring to the path I was exploring that has culminated in this book, but there was no rational way that I or anyone could explain that knowledge she possessed. I strongly believe that pure love, intensely felt or expressed, can allow us to transcend and access that wider pool of reality – the ocean of Being. Love is that powerful. My mother had dipped into that broader universal ocean of love, the ocean of her own being, a field of all knowledge beyond the need of the brain and unaffected by the health of the brain.

Love is God. When considering the three-in-one (or triune) nature of God, love can be considered as God the Holy Spirit, described as "pure Being" and the essential "Is-ness" resulting from both God knowing and experiencing. Pure Being is bliss, and can be experienced by us all in transcendental consciousness. Pure Being (bliss) becomes pure love through the experience resulting from our engagement in diverse creation. To 'love', there has to be more than one. Love is bliss transferred from one to another.

Love – or the Holy Spirit – is binding. It is the 'glue' that holds the universe together. Love attracts and binds, yet – as Maharishi reminds us – "it binds in freedom. It holds together the bonds of freedom. It knows no discord, disunity is foreign to love, discord is foreign to love, disharmony is foreign to love".[34] It reminds us of our unity while rejoicing in diversity. Love enables us to celebrate our diversity and "different-ness" by drawing us together and connecting us together.

In the *Gospel of Thomas*, Jesus said: "Whoever speaks against the Father will be forgiven, and whoever speaks against the Son will be forgiven. However, whoever speaks against the Holy Spirit will not be forgiven, neither on earth nor in heaven."[35]

We are told that all the canonical and non-canonical gospels were written down for the first time some decades after Christ's death. We can never be sure of the verbatim accuracy both in remembering what Christ said and in the translations. If Jesus did use the word "forgiven", then I find that at odds with my understanding of God as a non-judgemental God who has no cause to forgive or not forgive. But the gist of what Jesus is saying here can be understood. God the Father and God the Son do not care if someone speaks against God or Life or humanity, or simply doesn't believe in God. That person is not condemned. Love however is the Holy Spirit and is also that essence of Life that is all-important for everyone. Love keeps us united and in harmony. Love allows us to experience – in life – who we really are. Without it, we probably wouldn't exist, but we can certainly deny that quality that *is* us, or we can harden our hearts and not let that quality of Love grow and be fully expressed. On the other hand, being full of love and in realisation of its relevance to our existence, we will in time find our own way to realisation of our unity with the Father (God) and the Son (Life and fellow mankind). Without love, or living in denial of that essence that *is* us, there is little chance of us finding our way anywhere – certainly in this life. Without the light of life, we would wither away.

The sower's parable in the *New Testament* comes to mind here: "And he told them many things in parables, saying: 'A sower went out to sow. And as he sowed, some seeds fell along the path, and the birds came and devoured them. Other seeds fell on rocky ground, where they did not have much soil, and immediately they sprang up, since they had no depth of soil, but when the sun rose they were scorched. And since they had no root, they withered away. Other seeds fell among thorns, and the thorns grew up and choked them. Other seeds fell on good soil and produced grain, some a hundredfold, some sixty, some thirty. He who has ears, let him hear.'"[36]

Love – the essence or seed of Life – can wither away if it is not nurtured. Love needs to be implemented and exercised in daily life to bring us happiness and a sense of wholeness and belonging. Ultimately, love will bring us to a realisation of God through our experience of what God is – Love and Life.

Love is – like life itself – mysterious and wondrous in its ways. Why have so many songs been written about love? You will surely remember the 1984 hit "Silly Love Songs" by Paul McCartney. Why would we want to "fill the world" with just another silly love song?

Love is Life, because – as I have already stated – Life is God and Love is God too.

"Love is the sweet expression of life, it is the supreme content of life. Love is the force of life, powerful and sublime. The flower of life blooms in love and radiates love all around it."[37]

Can we see the Holy Trinity inherent in Love itself? Yes – all parts are indeed needed for Love to exist, but in Love we see the wholeness of the different parts bound together in freedom. Love is that state of Being resulting from God the Father (the Source of Life) experiencing Itself through God the Son (expressed Life). God can experience Love through us when we direct Love to each other, and also when we direct Love back to God. And we can experience Love being directed from God to us, even though it is always there. Love flows freely back and forth between the Father and the Son. Love is that unbreakable bond that keeps God the Father and God the Son forever and always One. In reality, we cannot ever break that bond, although we can think and believe we can separate ourselves from God.

Love is God the Father, and Love is God the Son – us. The "separateness" implied in the Trinity dissolves in Love, because the Trinity becomes effectively "Love Loves Love".

"Personal love is concentrated universal love," says Maharishi Mahesh Yogi.[38] But love cannot be confined and held under restraint. Perhaps you have had the experience of intense personal love exploding into universal love – a love of all things, an uncompromising love of Life. In this way, you feel more 'alive' than ever.

"Then, the eyes lift to God, and God raises his arms and extends his heart, and then the reality dawns: the stream of man's love finds the ocean of God's love, and flows into it, and this is the glory of love.

The man and God unite. They unite in the eternal ocean of love."[39]

THE MYSTERIES OF LOVE WILL FOREVER HOLD US FASCINATED, AND MANY more songs will be written about love. The experience of love is always sought, as a creek will seek the river and the river the ocean. Love can take errant turns, and feeling isolated or unconnected, can lead to selfish and harmful actions – a desire to possess another to overcome that sense of aloneness.

If I have sounded in any way critical of organised religion thus far, it is only to point out the self-imposed limitations and errant or incomplete interpretations of profound individuals who have rightly inspired the scriptures. One of the clear messages of Jesus Christ however, and one of the great strengths of the Christian churches evident to this day is the all-important message and practice of love. It is obvious that many, many saints and highly spiritually accomplished individuals in Christian tradition have gained their divine status through the practice of unbridled pure love. Love, allowed to flourish through service to others can allow transcendence in consciousness and is a powerful path to God realisation.

Service to fellow humans is an excellent way to fill our hearts with love and grow in love. But we can do more. As Maharishi says, "And having gained the status of the deep, let us then open our hearts for the ocean of love to flow, and let it flow in fullness". He follows this with, "And how do we improve the depth of our heart? By probing deep into the purity of our being. By exploring the finer regions of the impulse of love that murmurs in the silent chamber of our heart. By diving deep into the stillness of the unbounded, unfathomable ocean of love present within our hearts. By a single technique of self-exploration or by what is commonly known as the Transcendental Meditation technique".[40]

I love Life
WE HAVE JUST DESCRIBED THE THREE-IN-ONE NATURE OF GOD – THE Holy Trinity. With this understanding we can better see ourselves, life and love as One with God, and at the same time as different qualities or expressions of God. When we say to another "I love you", we are uttering

a very powerful statement. It is effectively the three-in-one nature of God at work. "I", "you" and "love" are all qualities of God, and are all parts of the Trinity.

Think about the different combinations in which you can combine the words God, love, life, you, I and me. A broad and comprehensive statement would be: "I Love Life". I've seen these very words displayed on t-shirts. Feel free to swap around any of the component words: "life loves you", "I love love", "love loves love", "I love God", "God loves me", "God loves life", "life loves life".

When you say any of these three words, say the phrase slowly and ponder each word. When you say any one word, think at the same time of the other two words. You just might feel the Oneness of all three words. All are statements of God's nature. All statements express God expressed. All these statements are powerful.

IN THE VERY BEGINNING, PURE CONSCIOUSNESS, ĀTMĀN, BRAHMIN, GOD was all there *is*. Pure consciousness, having nothing else to be aware of, became aware of Itself and was thus Self-referral. Consciousness the knower (*Rishi*) was aware of Itself as the known (*Chhandas*) through a process of knowing (*Devata*) that was also itself – still pure consciousness. This is the triune nature of pure consciousness – consciousness simply knowing Itself. But this three-in-one interaction of the One with Itself escalated, each part swapping roles as "observer", "observed" and "process" of observation. The interaction became more playful and convoluted, and exploded outward into the ever expanding reverberating, vibrational energy of the superstrings – the energy of life and very likely "the Word" spoken of in the Christian scriptures – which ultimately manifested as the space-time arena in which creation as we know it appeared. Life as we know it is the creative result of the interacting dynamics of pure consciousness.

Within that immense "playhouse of infinite forms" we call life, living individual beings of all types evolved on this planet Earth. We as human beings evolved within the last two million years and developed that deep sense of enquiry. We've pondered for millennia the nature of our existence: 'where did we come from?', 'is there a God?', 'is there meaning to all of this?', 'can I get away with simply looking after myself and my own needs?', 'what happens when I die?' We collectively became a "way for the Universe to know itself"[41] and for God to experience God-Self in countless more ways, ever closer to Self–realisation, the creation ever closer to knowing itself as the Creator.

The *Samhita* (or "Wholeness") that is *Rishi, Devata* and *Chhandas* can be compared somewhat with the Triune nature of God, but there have actually been an unfathomable number of *Rishi, Devata, Chhandas* combinations and permutations to be finally expressed as molecules, chemicals and as human organisms. As such, we can swap around the role of *Rishi, Devata and Chhandas* to each of God, Life and Love or God the Father, God the Son and God the Holy Ghost, because each can become the "knower" of the other or the knower of Itself.

The powerful statement "I Love Life" is also a creative one because it mirrors the very expressive, creative energy of Life, of God and of Love. "I love you" can be creative too! It can be pro-creative. We all know that!

Why don't you repeat "I love Life" silently (or loudly if you wish) often, with reflection on each word? Any effect might not be obvious, but I'm sure it will have some positive effect.

If you're into life and love, but profess to be agnostic or atheist, you may be closer to God-realisation than you think. It may be that the God you eventually discover for yourself, is very different to that concept of God you currently (don't) adhere to. It doesn't matter whether you believe in God or not. God certainly doesn't care, or feel upset or unloved; nor does God judge you negatively for it. Far better than mere belief or faith, is the *realisation* of God. We realise God through both experience and understanding. Therefore, carry on in love, and let love grow in the ways we've just discussed – through loving service to others and through regular meditation. When we experience that essence within, we will also realise that same essence underlying all things without. This is the knowledge and realisation that allows us ultimate self-empowerment. This is the Perfect conclusion to our search – to see Ourselves as individual representatives of a Perfect God, experiencing who we really are in a Perfect Life, sustained by an ocean of Perfect Love. That Ocean of Love beckons us to become divers and bathe in its depths, to play within it, to refresh and rejuvenate ourselves in it, to be at One with it and to know it as none other than our Self.

> *"Love, like a flame, cannot fail to give out light."*
> – The Sufi Message of Hazrat Inayat Khan: The Art of Personality.

NOTES

1. *Gospel of Thomas*, Logion 24
2. I had been reading *Autobiography of a Yogi* by Paramahansa Yogananda on board the dive boat at the time. The author had told the story of Babaji in his book, which included a photograph of the saint.
3. *Hoque*, Qur'an 57:3
4. *Revelation 1:8*
5. Walsch, Neale Donald; *Conversations with God – Bk 3*, p 180-181
6. Walsch, Neale Donald; *Conversations with God – Bk 3*, p 57
7. Walsch, Neale Donald; *Tomorrow's God*, Ch 1, p 3.
8. **Matthew 28:19** "Go ye therefore, and teach all nations, baptizing them in the name of the Father, and of the Son, and of the Holy Ghost".
9. Walsch, Neale Donald, *Conversations with God – Bk 1*, p 30.
10. Matthew 26: 63
11. Considered as the most important surviving non-canonical gospel, discovered in 1945 near Nag Hammadi, Egypt. Many of the churches dismiss the significance of the gospel, arguing for example that one or two of the sayings seems contrary to Christ's teachings. The author would agree with that criticism, but there are also many sayings that complement the unified field model of consciousness and themes developed in this book.
12. The Gnostic *Gospel of Thomas*, 62
13. The Gnostic *Gospel of Thomas*, 172
14. The 'Son of Man' was also a messianic title, referred to in Daniel 7:13-14. "..and behold, on the clouds of the heavens came One like a Son of man,…". I see this reference as consistent with one who identifies with and acts on behalf of all mankind.
15. Walsch, Neale Donald, *Home With God*, p72.
16. Walsch, Neale Donald, *Friendship with God – An Uncommon Dialogue*, p174
17. If we accept that time is a relative phenomenon, then in the absolute spiritual existence, we are there now!
18. Revelation: 3.20
19. Walsch, Neale Donald. *Home With God*, p 72
20. Tagore, Rabindranath (1861–1941) , *The Gitanjali or `song offerings*', (Tagore won the Nobel prize for literature in 1913).
21. http://www.biology-online.org/dictionary/Life
22. Moskvitch, Katia; 'Is There Life in Titan's Methane Sea?' *Cosmos – The Science of Everything*, Issue 61, Feb-March, 2015, Ps 60-69
23. Walsch, Neale Donald, *Home With God*, p 252.
24. Walsch, Neale Donald, *Home With God*, p 212.
25. John 6:63-64
26. Rabindranath Tagore (Nobel Laurate Indian Poet)
27. Walsch, Neale Donald; *Conversations with God*, Bk 3, p143
28. Bhagavad Gita, Ch 2, Vs 23; *Maharishi Mahesh Yogi on the Bhagavad Gita, A New Translation and Commentary*, Chs 1-6; Penguin Books
29. Oliver Sachs: 9 July 1933 – 30 August 2015
30. *The Sydney Morning Herald*, February 23, 2015; Sachs was a professor of neurology at the New York University School of Medicine.
31. Walsch, Neale Donald; *Conversations with God*, Book 2, p69.
32. Walsch, Neale Donald; *Conversations with God*, Book 1, p 56
33. Doreen Jane Spencer, 1930–2016
34. Maharishi Mahesh Yogi, *Love and God*, p 21
35. *The Gospel of Thomas*, Logion (saying) 44
36. Matthew 13:3–9

37	Maharishi Mahesh Yogi, *Love and God*, p 13; published 1973 by Age of Enlightenment Press; obtainable through MUM Press. http://www.mumpress.com/books/maharishi/a10.html
38	Maharishi Mahesh Yogi, *Love and God*, p19
39	Maharishi Mahesh Yogi, *Love and God*, p18
40	Maharishi Mahesh Yogi, *Love and God*, p21
41	Sagan, Carl, *Cosmos*, TV documentary series.

Postscript

As much as any time in history, it seems people are placing a lot of emphasis on difference – different culture, different beliefs, different appearance or different religion. Currently, we're seeing rising nationalism, which is inherently okay – except when it comes with weakening internationalism. Only by realizing our essential unity, can we embrace and even celebrate our differences.

We are all one, and one with everything else in this universe, but most of us live unconscious of this unity. We are all individual expressions or manifestations of one field of consciousness. In this book the ocean has been used as a metaphor to develop this understanding. Yours and my individual consciousness is likened to individual waves of consciousness on one universal "ocean" of consciousness. Since we identify our notion of "self" with our consciousness, then that big Self which we relate to as our "essence," is the same essence (the Ocean of Self) that everyone else relates to. With a realisation of our "one-ness" - our essential unity - we can then rejoice in our differences rather than live in fear of our differences.

With a true realisation of our shared "Self", we will naturally have no wish or desire to hurt another, because we would not want another to hurt us. In hurting another, we hurt ourselves. How can we not, if we are all ONE?

This notion of **Unity** is perhaps the most important message in this book, but there is another practical message: the concept of **empowerment**.

The Ocean of Consciousness (or Ocean of Self) that gives rise to our individual consciousness has been argued to be the hypothesised "unified field" or "superstring field" currently being explored by modern science. Modern science tells us that the superstring field is also likely the basis - indeed the source - of everything else, material and phenomenal, in the Universe. Therefore, our individual consciousness, being an expression of one wave of consciousness from the underlying ocean of consciousness (the proposed unified field) is capable of working at the level of the unified field and creating anything. Thus, so-called miracles are possible for each and every one of us.

This empowerment theme is an important one for humanity to register. It's important and has a practical implication because there is a proven method by which humans can create waves of peace and harmony in the societal milieu, bringing about a significant reduction in violence and aggression. The 'technology' of consciousness I am talking about is the "The Maharishi Effect". The phenomenon is not magic or 'hocus-pocus' but the implementation of knowledge and observation based on a renewed paradigm of understanding consciousness – a paradigm that views consciousness as a field phenomenon rather than the product of neuronal activity alone.

All efforts towards conflict resolution within communities or internationally have so far been very limited in their effectiveness. It seems the world is becoming less friendly and co-operative, despite our technological advances. We desperately need to step back from our problems and see if there are solutions that lie "outside the box" – a box which has trapped us within our own self-imposed boundaries. The Maharishi Effect has its premise in the identification of consciousness with the proposed unified field. By working at the level of this unified field, we are not only working "outside the box", but are working outside of *all* geometry. Our solutions to the big problems in the world today can be found in that field that transcends all concepts of space and time – the field of pure universal consciousness known as Ātmā.

The Maharishi Effect has been proven again and again with rigidly structured studies. Independent examiners and reviewers can find no fault with the study methodologies. The big stumbling block in the acceptance of the technology has been the widespread inability to comprehend that human consciousness could have its basis in the hypothesized unified field. These scientists remain stuck inside their own proverbial "box" of perceptual constraints that hold them to a view of the world that is inconsistent with the directions of modern science.

In the face of all other efforts that have failed, what do we stand to lose in trying a proven – if unconventional - approach to conflict resolution? So what if we don't fully understand it? Isn't it sufficient that we accept that it is still a scientific approach that has been shown to work, even if we are humble enough to admit that we don't fully understand the science?

While I appreciate and respect those who feel uncomfortable with change and are happy to sit with what they perceive as the predominant, 'normal' view of things, I feel there are times when we should question tradition and rituals – as comforting they might be – and bravely step beyond the constraints of the past. If necessary, let's try dancing on thin ice to see where it takes us. If someone falls in, we can help that person out. Let's dare to tread beyond the edge of the known world to see where it takes us. There's nothing to fear of the "unknown".

If you're a politician or successful business person who really wants to make a difference and leave a legacy, give some thought to how you might tread carefully outside that box that so confines us to insufficient answers to complex social problems. There are ways we can "test the waters". The global initiative to have 16,000 Vedic pandits in one place exercising the state of transcendental consciousness and yogic flying, needs financial support to house so many people. Such support can be made by going to www.vedicpandits.org

For the sceptic out there who is willing to step outside the proverbial box but wants some sort of incremental feedback and reassurance, then the ideal would be to still have a couple of hundred yogic flyers in each city. While the studies have already been done proving the effectiveness of the Maharishi Effect, you could initiate or support a smaller group in your community and engage the toughest scientific scrutiny possible with the help of an appropriate university or academic organisation to measure the benefits. The cost-benefit ratio of such a social program should prove to be highly favourable. Again the vedicpandits.org site provides contact information if you are in a position to initiate such a project.

Finally, the themes developed in this book admittedly reflect 'eastern' philosophy which for many could be seen as fundamentally at odds with 'western' thinking and religious tradition. I have attempted to break down this divide, as I believe it is an artificial one. When I examine the essential messages of Christ or the messages delivered by prophets of the other major religions, I can only see a positive correlation between the fundamental messages of Vedic science and the major religions. It is my sincerest hope that the solid knowledge of Vedic or yogic science will increasingly be incorporated into the religions of the world today.

THE SEVEN STATES OF CONSCIOUSNESS

Maharishi Mahesh Yogi pointed out that "knowledge is structured in consciousness", and therefore the way we see ourselves, others and the world around us, is determined by the state of consciousness we have attained. As we develop 'higher' states of consciousness beyond the familiar waking, sleeping and dreaming states, our physiological functioning will change too. Our nervous systems will change and adapt to enable more refined experience. It is not a matter of simply adopting new attitudes or moods based on reading or understanding alone. It is also likely that the full development of a higher state of consciousness (eg. Cosmic Consciousness) is not necessary before one gains some experience (or occasional experiences) of even higher states (eg. God Consciousness).

Waking Consciousness
THE FAMILIAR ALERT STATE OF CONSCIOUSNESS RECEPTIVE TO AND dependant on sensory experience and in constant flux depending on our mood, health and emotions at the time.

Sleeping Consciousness
THE PHYSICAL AND MENTAL STATE OF REST DURING WHICH WE BECOME inactive and unaware of our surroundings. Most physiological functions slow down (body temperature, blood pressure, breathing), yet the brain – despite our total or largely unconscious state – remains active – as active, according to some studies, as during waking.

Dreaming Consciousness
OCCURS AT VARIOUS STAGES DURING SLEEP, USUALLY DURING REM (RAPID eye movement) sleep, which comprises about 25% of our sleep time. The dream state is an "illusory, unpredictable world where familiar laws of nature release their hold and anything can happen – improbable shifts in time and place, unfamiliar combinations of people and events." During dreaming sleep, the brain inhibits signals to the muscles so we cannot act out our dreams. Sleep and dreaming are critical for our physiological and emotional health. Neurons are regenerated, new synaptic connections are made in our cerebral cortex processing memories or integrating what we learned in the day.

Transcendental Consciousness – the fourth state of consciousness
IN THIS STATE, "ATTENTION HAS SETTLED INWARD, BEYOND PERCEPTIONS, thoughts and feelings."[1] Consciousness has detached itself from sensory experience and is therefore left to be aware of its own inherent nature – consciousness simply aware of itself – unbounded and pure. This is the 'ocean of consciousness' or 'ocean of Self' we have dived into, and in the

process, the small 'self' (the wave of consciousness at the surface) has been lost, as the awareness is only of the big 'Self' (the ocean of consciousness beneath).

Cosmic Consciousness – the fifth state of consciousness
With regular experience of Transcendental Consciousness (TC), even waking, sleeping and dreaming states of consciousness become infused with the qualities of TC, which result in heightened wakefulness and alertness and better physiological functioning at all times – lower heart and breath rate and faster recovery from stress. EEG studies demonstrate an increase in brain wave coherence in individuals who meditate regularly over a long time. This reflects an overall improvement in all aspects of brain function.

God Consciousness – the sixth state of consciousness
With "unbounded awareness established on the level of the conscious mind" (TC), the perception becomes more and more refined to the extent that it is capable of "cognition of the finest relative [value] on the surface of the gross relative". This "finest relative" value is that level where the unified field becomes vibrant, where the 'unmanifest' first becomes 'manifest'. "It is not 'God's consciousness', but direct experience of the full range of God's creation."[2] It is at this level of consciousness that one might have "not only love and devotion to God but of direct, personal experience of God and of all things in the light of God."

Unity Consciousness
Up until this point, all of the expressed universe is still seen as separate entities co-existing, even though – in God Consciousness – the finest level of material existence is felt and appreciated. As we grow in God Consciousness, we become increasingly aware of the absolute level of life, Ātmā, pure consciousness, the infinite, in everything. Since this level of life is also the level that defines our own sense of self – the big "Self", everything in creation is perceived as an expression of our own Self. Amidst all multiplicity and variety – one can directly perceive the unity. One can see at all times, not just the seemingly distinct multiple waves of life forms but the whole ocean of Life that underlies, supports and is the essence of this variety of gross forms. The small 'self' has truly been lost to the big "Self" at all times and in all situations. As Maharishi says, "The knowledge has bridged the gulf between the knower and the object of knowing. The object is being verified in its total reality when the infinite value of the object, which hitherto was underlying, has come up to be appreciated at the surface."[3]

Within this state of consciousness, with everything perceived as resulting from the dynamics of our own Self, we gain command of all the laws of nature – the ability to do anything with mere intention.

NOTES

1 Pearson, Craig, PhD, "The Supreme Awakening – experiences of enlightenment throughout time – and how you can cultivate them", Maharishi University of Management Press, p 41
2 Pearson, Craig, PhD, "The Complete Book of Yogic Flying", Maharishi University of Management Press, p 80
3 Maharishi Mahesh Yogi, "Seven States of Consciousness", *Science of Creative Intelligence*, Lesson 23

Glossary

Ātmā: the unbounded and eternal field of pure consciousness (ocean of consciousness), pure intelligence, that is the essential Being, or Self, of everyone. It is also the unified field or superstring field explored by modern science. In the terminology of religion, it is identical to the light of God, or Being of God that is the essence of both individual and cosmic life.[1]

Avatar(a): Incarnation of a Hindu deity in human or animal form, for example one of the incarnations of Vishnu, such as Rama and Krishna.

Bhagavad Gita: A narrative framework of a dialogue between Pandava prince Arjuna and his guide and charioteer Lord Krishna. A scriptural epic in Sanskrit that is part of the Hindu epic *Mahabharata* (chapters 25-42 of the sixth book of *Mahabharata*). The *Gita* uses the imminent war between the Pandavas and Kauravas as a comparison to the 'battlefield' of life experience.

Brahman: the supreme Entity, God, the entirety, the Almighty, together with its manifestation or expansion into all diversity of creation. Ātmā on the other hand is the 'unseen' or 'unmanifest' aspect of Brahman.

Consciousness: the state of being aware, whether that awareness is of its own nature or what is going on around it. Seven states of consciousness have been defined by Vedic science scholar Maharishi Mahesh Yogi – waking consciousness, sleeping consciousness, dreaming consciousness, transcendental consciousness, cosmic consciousness, God consciousness and unity consciousness.

Ego: The sense of individuality or 'my-ness', and also 'am-ness' (which is closer to 'Is-ness' – totality of existence, Ātmā). Related to Jiiv (the small self), but the ego can remind itself of and assume its larger existence as Ātmā (the totality of the ocean rather than just the wave).

Intellect: ("buddhi" in Sanskrit), the discriminating aspect of ourselves that decides what to do with absorbed sensory experience. According to Maharishi Vedic Science, the 'intellect' fits in between the very subtle 'feeling' level of expressed consciousness (the level at which intuition arises) and 'mind' which thinks and creates action on the basis of what the intellect has decided. More subtle than the 'feeling' level of consciousness is that sense of 'myness' and then 'amness' (both levels of individual sense of self, and includes the individual aspect of the 'soul') and the most subtle level is "Isness" (Ātmā, the big Self, ultimate reality, Brahman and the essential aspect of the 'soul').

Karma: literally just 'action', but typically understood to represent destiny or fate resulting from action performed in this or a previous life.

Jiiva: an individual, an entity, the small 'self'. That which relates to 'myness' and 'amness'.

Life: (as defined in our more comprehensive context) all of manifest existence, seen ultimately as a dynamic inter-related web of relationships. Life results from the dynamic vibrational 'sounds' that come about from pure essential consciousness knowing and interacting with itself. These 'sounds' provide the particular code that represents the behaviour of the superstrings at the basis of all material and phenomenal aspects of nature ("the Constitution of the Universe").

Mantra: a generally non-sensible word used as a vehicle to allow transcendence in meditation.

Math: hermitage – a building or shelter where an individual or group of people live in spiritual practise.

Maya: The spell of illusion or delusion

Mind: ("Manas" in Sanskrit), the individual capacity to experience, absorb and store sensory experience. Is not identical to "consciousness" because consciousness is essential awareness and is independent of sensory experience; that is, consciousness can be aware of its own nature. The 'mind' can be considered consciousness in action, and thinks and creates action on the basis of what the intellect has decided.

Namaskara: Salutation

Pragyaparadh(a): mistaken intellect (or mistaken intelligence); disturbed buddhi (intellect), dhriti (patience) and smriti (memory, sense of direction). The individual's ego identifies itself with the small self and forgets its connection with the big Self (Ātmā). In Ayurveda (the ancient Indian health care system that focuses health management at the level of consciousness), Pragyaparadh aggravates all the doshas (the essential constitutional makeup of every individual).

Prakritis: Sanskrit for 'nature' and in the healthcare system of Ayurveda refers to the essential body type or 'blueprint' that influences the innate tendencies in your physiology and psyche (mind). Also correspond to the 'superfields' (gravity, gauge and matter superfields) in quantum physics. Vata Prakriti (comprising the Akasha and Vayu tanmatras) corresponds with the 'gravity' superfield. Pitta Prakriti (comprising the Tejas and Apas Tanmatras) corresponds with the gauge superfield, and Kapha Prakriti (comprising the Apas and Prithivi Tanmatras) corresponds with the matter superfield. Ayurveda uses the term 'doshas' when referring to the present balance or imbalance of the prakritis in an individual.

Prana: The Sanskrit word for 'life force', 'life energy' or 'vital principle' and is the 'cosmic energy' that permeates the universe on all levels (including the inanimate). Could be considered to be the 'light of God' that permeates everything and enables life. Can also be considered to be Ātmā or the unified field explored by modern science.

Pranayama: control of breath. "Prana" is Breath or vital energy in the body. On subtle levels prana represents the energy responsible for life or life force, and "ayama" means control. Pranayama typically refers to special breathing exercises in Yoga.

Samadhi: deep meditation; directing the senses inwards, thereby centring the mind on the Self

Self: (with big 'S') the ocean of consciousness underlying and giving rise to individual consciousness ('self' with small 's'). Equivalent to 'ocean of being', ocean of spirit, Ātmā, the unmanifest or "hidden" aspect of God, the proposed unified field or superstring field in modern physics.

Siddhi: a supernatural power or faculty acquired through yogic or spiritual advancement. In Maharishi Vedic Science, the spelling "Sidhi" was adopted for simplicity and for specificity in regard to TM-Sidhi as an advanced technique of Transcendental Meditation.

Soul: the non-physical aspect of an individual that continues to exist after the death of the body. The soul has traditionally been understood (in post Biblical Hebrew times at least) as (a) the inner, essential, divine part of man, and (b) that which leaves the body at the time of death and continues its life elsewhere. Maharishi's Vedic Science teaches that (a) – the inner, essential nature of man – is Ātmā (the one universal ocean of consciousness) and (b) – the individual aspect of one's identity that leaves the body after death – is jiiv (the small self). These are two distinct entities, or at least two distinct aspects of the one reality. The 'soul' should not be seen as hiding somewhere within the body, but instead as an unconfined but individual field (or 'wave') of intelligence that contains the body (rather than the other way around) and supports the existence of the body. The 'soul' therefore can be seen as a purer aspect of the individual self that still maintains its sense of individuality but is also innately aware of its connection to other souls and indeed all of creation.

Surya Namaskara: sun (Surya) salutation

Sutra: In Sanskrit, means "string" or "thread". Usually refers to an aphorism, and in the TM-Sidhi program is gently introduced after a period of transcendental consciousness to enhance that quality through all aspects of the self.

Yoga: Unity, connection

Veda: the sacred books of knowledge in India. Can also be considered as meaning "life" in its broadest sense as all manifest existence and knowledge of life.

Upanishads: ancient philosophical treatises which form the theoretical basis for the Hindu religion. Also known as Vedanta ("the end of the Veda"). Considered by Hindus to contain revealed truths ("Sruti") concerning the nature of ultimate reality ("Brahman").

NOTES

1. Finkelstein, Evan I., *Universal Principles of Life Expressed in Maharishi Vedic Science and in the Scriptures and writings of Judaism, Christianity, and Islam.* A dissertation submitted to the Graduate School of Maharishi University of Management in partial fulfilment of the requirements for the degree of Doctor of Philosophy, June, 2005

Acknowledgements

The book *Ocean of Self* has been a concept of mine for some 25 years. I started writing chapters as far back as then, but the book just didn't "come together" until recent years. There are many people who have positively influenced me or assisted me in one form or another in the long fulfilment of this goal.

To my wife and life-partner Becca, who has made it possible for me to engross myself in this great life adventure of ocean exploration, I dedicate this book and thank her – and love her - from the bottom of my heart. Becca has shared the same passion for diving and underwater photography, and excelled in both. How could I have possibly indulged myself in these wild adventures without a partner who shared the same passion? What we have witnessed together in our diving adventures has enriched us in so many ways. University-qualified in computer science and mathematics, her critiquing of my manuscript before I sent it to the editor was very much appreciated. In addition, her IT skills enabled us to bring the finished manuscript and illustrations to an eBook design template and then the final uploading to the major eBook platforms.

In my work with Australian Geographic over a number of years, I came to admire the writing skills of journalists Liz Ginis and Ken Eastwood. Both extended valuable support and encouragement in the writing of this book. It was Ken Eastwood – Associate Editor at Australian Geographic for more than a decade – who took on the task of editing my manuscript. I am privileged to have had the editing services of such an accomplished professional. I also thank the Australian Geographic editorial staff for their generous permission for me to reproduce some of their artist illustrations in my book.

The front cover of any book provides the vital first impression. It sets the theme of the book and hopefully invites readers to investigate the contents. The graphic artist who designed the first eBook cover and many of the internal diagrams was Clare Das Neves. I am grateful for Clare's creative abilities and skill. Evan Shapiro of *Green Avenue Design* (*Cilento Publishing*) designed the current expanded cover for printed books. Evan is also responsible for the printed book layout and has guided me towards the online self-publishing service *IngramSpark* for 'print-on-demand' paper books. Not only is Evan a skilled book designer, he's published his own fiction book. I have truly appreciated his generous advice and support with the whole exercise of eBook and physical book publishing.

Jennifer Althaus (nee Douglas) www.jenniferalthaus.com has been my publicist and publication adviser since my uploading of the eBook version of *Ocean of Self* in 2017. Jennifer is also an author, and her experience with the publishing industry has helped me avoid the pitfalls befalling many aspiring authors. Jennifer connected me with Evan Shapiro.

Dr Johan Svenson from the Maharishi University of Management (MUM) in Iowa, USA, reviewed my physics and Vedic science chapters, and gently nudged me into line in a number of areas. With a degree in mathematics and a background of formal study in physics, Johan put on his "sceptical scientist" hat and made sure I wasn't making unfounded or over-reaching conclusions with the theories, discoveries and assumptions of the broader physics community. As the University's Assistant Professor of Maharishi Vedic Science, he also critiqued my chapters in Vedic science. The chapters on modern science and Vedic science were difficult – yet crucial - chapters for me to write, and I thank Johan for guiding me with his impressive knowledge, obvious intelligence and wisdom.

Internationally renowned Harvard-trained physicist Dr John Hagelin has inspired me over many years with his profound knowledge, insights and skill at communication. Dr Hagelin played a critical role in the development of a highly regarded grand unified field theory that featured in a cover story of *Discover* magazine. He has conducted pioneering research at CERN (European Centre for Particle Physics) and SLAC (Stanford Linear Accelerator Center), and been bestowed the prestigious Kilby Award, which recognises scientists who have made "major contributions to society through their applied research in the fields of science and technology." Professor Hagelin heads the physics department at Maharishi University of Management (MUM), is director of the Institute of Science, Technology and Public Policy at the university, and is now President of MUM. Professor Hagelin has worked closely with Maharishi Mahesh Yogi for many years, both scholars exploring the connections of the ancient body of subjective knowledge of ultimate reality (Vedic science) with the similar discoveries and theories of modern science. Dr Hagelin's published articles, video-recorded lectures and on-line courses have given me the chance to grasp the exciting discoveries and correlations of both sources of knowledge – subjective and the objective. I am honoured to have had his encouragement and generous support towards my efforts in the production of this book, and thank him for the use of some of his illustrations and graphs.

This book explores the concept of one universal ocean of consciousness underlying our individual waves of consciousness. There are many ways of 'diving' into this ocean of consciousness, and a good technique of meditation is the best, most efficient way to make this 'dive'. I can only relate to the technique known as Transcendental Meditation, because that's the only technique I have ever used. This book however does not aim to be parochial. I'm not 'pushing' one technique, one organisation or any particular philosophy. There are "many roads to Rome" as the saying goes. If the reader decides to introduce the practice of meditation into their daily lives, then it is up to the reader to decide which techniques best suits them.

Maharishi Mahesh Yogi was known to most people as the 'giggling guru' who at one time introduced the Beatles to the practice and philosophy of Transcendental Meditation. The profound knowledge, wisdom and skills he has given the busy western world remain largely unrecognised. Cleverly, he collaborated with many scientists and academics to integrate the discoveries recorded in the Vedic literature with those of modern science. This scientific approach validated the decision of many – myself included - to incorporate the regular practice of meditation into their busy lives. I firmly believe that one day, the world will see Maharishi in a more appreciative light. I thank Maharishi for the gift of the practical technique of Transcendental Meditation (which I started in 1981) and the advanced TM-Sidhi program (which I learned in 1985). Both have been embedded into my daily routine. I also thank him for his considerable knowledge that has helped me understand what is going on in transcendental consciousness. As Maharishi himself has emphasised – complete knowledge is based on both understanding and experiencing. One without the other is less fulfilling and less consolidating.

I thank Dr Frederick ('Fred') Travis, Director of the Center for Brain, Consciousness and Cognition at MUM, for his generosity in allowing me to use some of his illustrative material in my brief coverage of the neuro-physiology of meditation. He also sent me some valuable articles to assist my understanding and communication of the physiology of consciousness in this book. Dr Craig Pearson, also of MUM, has written two extraordinary books (referred to in this book) which illustrate his grasp of the profound knowledge of both modern science and Vedic science and his ability to effectively communicate this knowledge. Dr Pearson has generously allowed me to reproduce some of his illustrations.

My good friend since early teenage years – now Professor Garry Hoban from the Faculty of Social Science, School of Education, University of Wollongong – read and critiqued my earlier draft manuscript on modern science. I am grateful for his contribution and our continuing precious friendship over most of our lives.

Diving into the ocean of consciousness on an almost continual basis are those who chose the path of the 'recluse', as opposed to the majority like myself who balance regular transcendence with the busy life of a 'householder'. My friend Andrew Lawson Kerr has remained with the Maharishi Purusha program for decades now, and I can only imagine the depths he has explored and the realms he has experienced in his carefully structured meditation routines in the Himalayas. Although Andrew lives in a far-away land living a very different life to me, we have remained in contact, exchanging thoughts, ideas and support. I thank Andrew for sharing with me his wisdom and knowledge, especially in my research towards this book.

Medical practitioner Dr Tim Carr and I graduated at the University of Sydney – he in medicine and I in dentistry. Tim was only a year or two ahead of me at the same secondary-school in one of the north-west suburbs of Sydney, so we've also known each other for a long time. It was Tim whom I approached around 1980 to find out more about this Transcendental Meditation 'thing'. I have him to thank for embarking on that ongoing path of exploration. Tim – an idealistic doctor who wanted to promote health rather than just treat disease – adopted the adjunct path of Maharishi Ayurveda and – while still practising conventional medicine - has become one of Australia's leading exponents of the ancient practice of Ayurveda. I thank Tim for his friendship, advice and encouragement offered in the many years of this book's production. I have also benefited from my Ayurvedic consultations with Dr Carr over many years.

I am fortunate to have some fellow diving friends who live but a short distance from me and are also excellent photographers. Gary Bell runs Oceanwide Images – a nature stock image library - with his wife Meri. Brett Vercoe works with the Solitary Islands Marine Parks Authority and also runs a library of both video and stills images above and under the sea – Liquid Focus. Both have generously contributed some excellent images to this book for which I am very grateful. I am also grateful for the contribution of images from respected photographers Russell Ord (surf and wave imagery) and Darren Jew.

Jim Tsinganos is a professional illustrator whom I commissioned to illustrate St Rabi'a, a revered saint in Islam who could levitate at will. St Rabi'a offered words of wisdom relevant to the philosophy of this book. I thank Jim for his artistic talent and creative rendition of St Rabi'a's remarkable story.

Jesse Andrewartha is a talented Australian computer -generated imagery (CGI) producer – and fellow underwater explorer - working in the USA. How fortunate am I that Jesse could find the time in his already busy schedule - servicing clients with much bigger budgets - to provide the graphic imagery for my 'flip-book' pictorial concept in chapter 12? Thank you Jesse.

Noel and Eve Jarratt experienced the heart-wrenching loss of their 12 year-old son Rhys in 2002. With their permission and support, I have related the beautiful story of Rhys and his relationship with manta rays in the last two weeks of his life. I had the privilege of meeting Rhys personally the day before he died. In this tragedy, I relate what I perceived as a positive – even uplifting – aspect to Rhys's approach to death in those final days. I thank Noel, Eve and Rhys's brother Ric for their support. I know that manta rays are now viewed by the Jarratt family in a very special and revered way.

Dr Deepak Chopra has achieved global household fame with the publication of numerous books on Vedic science and its relevance to physical and mental health and spirituality. Qualified as a specialist endocrinologist in the field of medicine, Deepak is gifted with not only a remarkable grasp of Vedic science, but a rare ability to communicate by word or in speech this profound but little understood body of knowledge. I've had the privilege of meeting Deepak personally twice - in the mid to later 1980s - when he visited Sydney for talks and presentations. His knowledge – communicated so effectively via the written word, audio-book or lecture – has provided me a wonderful resource in the formulation of my own understanding of consciousness and its relevance to health and our spiritual development.

Another scientist who has greatly influenced my own philosophy is physicist Dr Fritzof Capra. Most of us see physicists as mathematical geniuses entrenched in their lonely world of incomprehensible blackboard equations and equally perplexing ideas of how the world works. Fritzof is one of those rare scientists with the ability to see a broader, more comprehensive picture of reality which includes our own consciousness. Like Deepak Chopra, he too has the ability to effectively communicate difficult concepts. The depth of his knowledge, whether it be contemporary science or eastern philosophy, is impressive. Dr Capra's books have had a big influence towards my own efforts to communicate the nature of consciousness. I had the unexpected pleasure of meeting Fritzof – on the ski slopes of Aspen, Colorado, USA, where he conducted a book signing of his then-recently-released book, *The Turning Point*, in 1983.

In more recent times, author Neale Donald Walsch came on the scene with his *Conversations with God* series of books. I recall dismissing these books when I first saw them on the shelves of retail book shops. Someone made a comment to me however that encouraged me to purchase his first book. I've bought every subsequent book since! They are simply amazing on one level, but encouraging on another level – because we soon learn that Neale is no more special in God's eyes than you or me, and that we can all have a conversation with God. The knowledge I've procured from Neale's books has helped me interpret and better understand my own special experiences, and I've also found that this knowledge collaborates with Vedic (yogic) science – and in particular Vedic science as interpreted and taught by Maharishi Mahesh Yogi (*Maharishi Vedic Science*). If you have not yet read the book, please don't allow the mention of "God" to raise alarm bells with your feelings. Please read the book first. I have a lot more to say about God and life in general towards the latter part of this book.

I must acknowledge some generous dispensers of knowledge and techniques via the internet. Until relatively recently, prospective new authors had to trudge along the almost impossible path of getting their work recognised and then published by a well-established publishing company. Most of the big publishers will only look at submissions recommended by allied literary agents. Even getting literary agents to look at new manuscripts is a daunting task for many beginning authors. For many of us, self-publishing is the 'way-to-go' in this new age, but even that can seem an overwhelming undertaking. Joel Friedlander of *The Book Designer* (https://www.thebookdesigner.com) is one of those contributors to the internet from which I have learned much regarding the technicalities of self-publishing. The computer conversion program, *Calibre* (https://calibre-ebook.com), was used to convert my Word documents (laid out in an eBook design template available through *The Book Designer*) into the specific eBook file formats.

And now sounding like a TV program - I declare that the views and philosophy expressed in this book are mine alone and do not necessarily represent the views and philosophy of those I have here acknowledged.

Finally – because at some level they probably also exerted an influence in my writing of this book – I thank my gym buddies – Kevin, Neil and Lardi – for their very helpful advice, which I did 'take into consideration'.

Mark N. Spencer
Boambee, NSW, Australia
December 2016

The author, Dr Mark Spencer
Photo by Gary Bell, Oceanwideimages.com

www.ingramcontent.com/pod-product-compliance
Lightning Source LLC
Chambersburg PA
CBHW051542010526
44118CB00022B/2551